George Hill

Selections from Pope, Dryden, and Various Other British Catholic

Poets

Who Preceded the Nineteenth Century

George Hill

Selections from Pope, Dryden, and Various Other British Catholic Poets
Who Preceded the Nineteenth Century

ISBN/EAN: 9783337064105

Printed in Europe, USA, Canada, Australia, Japan

Cover: Foto ©Thomas Meinert / pixelio.de

More available books at **www.hansebooks.com**

SELECTIONS

FROM

POPE, DRYDEN,

AND VARIOUS OTHER

BRITISH CATHOLIC POETS,

WHO PRECEDED THE NINETEENTH CENTURY: WITH
BIOGRAPHICAL AND LITERARY NOTICES OF THOSE
AND OTHER BRITISH CATHOLIC POETS OF THEIR
CLASS, COMPRISING A BRIEF HISTORY OF
BRITISH CATHOLIC POETRY FROM AN
EARLY PERIOD.

DESIGNED NOT ONLY FOR GENERAL USE, BUT ALSO AS A TEXT-
BOOK OR READER, AND A PRIZE-BOOK, FOR THE HIGHER
CLASSES IN CATHOLIC EDUCATIONAL INSTITUTIONS.

By GEORGE HILL,
Author of "The Ruins of Athens, Titania's Banquet, and other
Poems."

Examined and Approved by Competent Catholic Authority.

NEW YORK
THE TROW & SMITH BOOK MANUFACTURING CO.,
46, 48, 50 GREENE STREET.
1868.

Entered, according to Act of Congress, in the year 1867, by
JOHN F. TROW & CO.
In the Clerk's Office of the District Court of the United States for the Southern District of New York.

CONTENTS.

	PAGE.
Preliminary Remarks.	11
CÆDMON.	13
Extract of a Version of one of His Satan's Speeches.	13
ST. ALDHELM.	14
ALFRED.	14
ST. BEDE.	15
ST. BONIFACE.	15
ALCUIN.	15
Extract of his Address to his Cell.	15
CŒNA.	15
LEOBGITHA.	15
THAN, P. DE.	16
NANTEUIL, S. DE.	16
THOROLD.	16
GAIMAR, G.	17
DAVID.	17
WACE, W.	17
BENOIT.	17
GUERNES.	18
LANGTON, S.	18
LAYAMON.	18
ORME.	18
ROBERT OF GLOUCESTER.	18
LANGTOFT, P.	19
MANNYNG, R.	19
In Praise of Good Women.	19

Contents.

	PAGE
METRICAL ROMANCES.	20
From "The Squire of Low Degree."	21
DAVIE, A.	23
Extract of a Description of a Battle.	23
BASTON, R.	23
ROLLE, R.	24
What is in Heaven.	24
LAWRENCE, M.	25
PLOUGHMAN, P.	25
GOWER, J.	25
From the Episode of Rosiphele.	26
CHAUCER, G.	27
The Nun.	32
The Oxford Student.	33
His Description of Himself.	34
Custance is Banished, etc.	35
From a Prayer to the Blessed Virgin.	36
BARBOUR, J.	37
Apostrophe to Freedom.	37
From a Description of the Battle of Bannockburn.	38
WYNTOUN, ANDREW OF.	39
JAMES I. OF SCOTLAND.	39
From "The King's Quhair."	40
JOHN THE CHAPLAIN.	41
OCCLEVE, T.	41
LYDGATE, J.	41
Christ describes His Sufferings.	42
A Pleasant Retreat.	44
CHESTER, T.	45
CAMPEDEN, H. DE.	45
HENRY THE MINSTREL.	45
The Death of Wallace.	45
BERNERS, J.	47
From the Epilogue.	47
WILLIAM OF NASSYNGTON.	48

Contents.

	PAGE.
HARDING, J.	48
SCOGAN, J.	48
NORTON, J.	48
RIPLEY, G.	48
KAY, J.	49
HENRYSOUN, R.	49
"Blessed be Simple Life," etc.	49
DUNBAR, W.	50
A Vernal Morning.	50
From "Meditation written in Winter."	51
"The Merle and the Nightingale."	51
"No Treasure Without Gladness."	52
DOUGLAS, G.	53
From a Description of May.	54
WADE, L.	55
BURGH, B.	55
CAXTON, W.	55
FABIAN, R.	55
BRADSHAW, H.	55
Feast Described.	56
HAWES, S.	56
Giant Described.	56
SKELTON, J.	56
MORE, SIR T.	60
Fortune Described.	60
HEYWOOD, J.	61
BELLENDEN, J.	61
Virtue Speaks.	62
MARY, QUEEN OF SCOTS.	62
"Alas! What Am I," etc.	63
JAMES V.	63
HEYWOOD, J.	63
SOUTHWELL, R.	64
From "Content and Rich."	68
"The Image of Death."	69

	PAGE.
From "St. Peter's Complaint."	70
"Mary Magdalen's Complaint.".	71
"Love's Servile Lot."	71
"Times Go By Turns."	71
"New Prince, New Pomp."	73
"At Home in Heaven."	73
"Stanzas on the Death of Mary, Queen of Scots."	74
"Life's Death, Love's Life."	74
"Fortune's Reach."	75
"Of the Blessed Sacrament," etc.	75
"The Death of Our Lady.".	75
Prayer.	76
Detached Passages.	76
LODGE, T.	77
A Solitary Life Commended.	77
Human Miseries.	78
Advice to Sons.	78
From "Diana's Epitaph."	79
SHAKSPEARE.	80
MASSINGER, P.	82
CONSTABLE, H.	82
Love's Troubles.	83
SHIRLEY, J.	83
The Garden.	84
Death's Final Conquest.	84
DIGBY, JOHN.	86
DIGBY, SIR K.	87
"Fame, Honor, Beauty," etc.	89
DAVENANT, SIR W.	89
Rhodalind Described.	92
Birtha Described.	93
Praise, Prayer, and Penitence.	93
Temples of Prayer, etc.	94
Picture of the Ascension.	96

Contents.

	PAGE.
Scripture and its Abuse.	96
Books.	97
Truth.	97
Secret Love Discovered.	97
From "The Christian's Reply to the Philosopher."	97
Epitaph on Mrs. Cross.	98
Song.	98
HABINGTON, W.	99
Castara.	100
Upon Beauty.	100
From "Cupio Dissolvi."	101
"Non Nobis Domine."	102
"Nox Nocti Indicat Scientiam."	102
The Pomp Without the Spirit of Devotion.	103
From "Of True Delight."	103
"To a Tomb."	104
"Laudate Dominum."	104
COCKAIN, SIR A.	105
To Plautia.	105
CRASHAW, R.	106
From "Hymn to the Name of Jesus."	107
"Translation of 'Dies Iræ.'"	108
"On a Prayer-Book."	109
"On the Glorious Assumption of the Blessed Virgin."	109
Christ's Victory.	110
From "A song."	111
Temperance, or the Cheap Physician.	111
From "To the Morning."	112
St. Theresa.	113
From "On Hope."	113
On Nanus.	114
From "Description of a Religious House."	114
From "Epitaph on Mr. Ashton."	115

Flowers.	115
Power of Love.	115
The Author's Motto.	116
SHERBURNE, SIR E.	116
Mary Weeping For Jesus Lost.	117
The Message.	117
Good Friday.	117
"And They Laid Him in a Manger."	119
A Sylvan Scene.	119
A Maid in Love With a Youth Blind of One Eye.	119
From Antipater Sidonius.	120
Cassimir.	120
Cupid Dislodged.	120
The Fountain.	121
Magdalen.	121
DRYDEN, J.	122
From "The Hind and the Panther."	127
"Religio Laici."	105
"Absalom and Achitophel."	156
"Mac Flecknoe."	162
"The Medal."	165
"Eleonora."	166
"Ode to the Memory of Miss A. Killigrew."	171
"Epitaph on Miss M. Frampton."	174
"Epitaph on Mrs. Paston."	175
On Milton.	175
From "Alexander's Feast," etc.	176
"A Song for St. Cecilia's Day."	180
"Threnodia Augustalis."	181
Verses to the Duchess of York.	182
"Epistle to Sir Godfrey Kneller."	183
"Epistle to the Duchess of York."	185
"Epistle to Mr. Congreve."	186
A Paraphrase of Chaucer's Character of a Good Priest.	186

Contents.

	PAGE.
Translation of the Te Deum.	188
"Veni Creator Spiritus" Paraphrased.	190
Hymn for St. John's Eve, etc.	191
Cleopatra's Voyage.	192
Attachment to Life.	192
Omens Presaging the Downfall of Egypt.	192
Detached Passages.	193
DRYDEN'S SONS.	198
WYCHERLEY, W.	199
WARD, T.	200
Defacement and Spoliation of Churches.	200
GARTH, S.	201
From "The Dispensary."	202
"Epilogue to Addison's Cato."	204
Ancient and Modern Manners.	204
Choice of a Wife.	205
To the Poetaster at Saddler's Hall.	205
Detached Passages.	205
POPE, A.	206
From "Windsor Forest."	210
"The Temple of Fame."	213
The Messiah.	218
From "The Essay on Criticism."	221
"The Rape of the Lock."	227
Eloisa to Abelard.	236
"Epistle to Robert, Earl of Oxford."	242
" " Mr. Jervas, the Painter."	243
" " Miss Blount."	244
To Mr. J. Moore, etc.	245
"Elegy on an Unfortunate Lady."	246
Epitaph on Mrs. Corbet.	248
From "On Two Lovers Killed by Lightning."	248
Epitaph on Mr. Fenton.	249
" on Mr. Gay.	249
From "Moral Essays," Epistle I.	249

	PAGE.
From "Moral Essays," Epistle II.	254
" " " III	259
" " " IV.	264
"Epistle to Mr. Addison."	266
The Essay on Man.	267
"Prologue to the Satires," An Epistle to Dr. Arbuthnot.	284
"Epilogue to the Satires."	293
"The Dunciad."	295
"Imitations of Horace."	296
"Prologue to Addison's Cato."	299
Translation of the Emperor Adrian's Address to his Soul.	301
The Universal Prayer.	301
From Ode on St. Cecilia's Day.	303
The dying Christian to his Soul.	303
Ode on Solitude.	304
On a Lady Singing to her Lute.	305
On a Certain Lady at Court.	305
To Miss M. B. on her Birth-Day.	306
On his Grotto.	306
On a Celebrated Opera-Singer.	307
The Balance of Europe.	307
From the French.	307
The Garden of Alcinous.	307
The Companions of Ulysses transformed by Circè.	308
The Parting of Hector and Andromaché.	309
The Battle of the Gods.	313
Night-Scene, etc., from the Iliad.	314
Ulysses recognized by his Old Dog Argus.	314
Detached Passages.	315
HAMILTON, W.	318
Self-Love.	318
Impiety.	319

SELECTIONS

FROM

POPE, DRYDEN, AND VARIOUS OTHER BRITISH CATHOLIC POETS WHO PRECEDED THE NINETEENTH CENTURY: WITH BIOGRAPHICAL AND LITERARY NOTICES, ETC.

THE biographical notices, and many of the critical and other incidental remarks, contained in the following pages, have been compiled from various foreign works,* and are generally presented in the words of their authors.

A primary object with the compiler has been, to include much of the best poetry of Pope and Dryden, and, also, numerous select specimens of that of various British Catholic poets who preceded them, and yet flourished subsequently to the reign of MARY. From poems by those of a previous period, as being, to most

---

* Warton's Hist. E. Poets: Ellis's Specimens E. E. Poets: Campbell's Specimens B. Poets: Johnson's Lives E. Poets: Biograph. Britan.: Wood's Athen. Oxon.: Turner's Hist. Anglo-Sax.: Chambers's Cyc. E. Lit.: Knight's E. Cyc.: Chalmers's Biog. Dic.: Rose's Biog. Dic.: Aldine Ed. var. poets: Separate memoirs: etc.

readers, of inferior interest, the specimens are comparatively few and brief. In the notices, however, of the poets of that period, will be seen how greatly British literature is indebted to them for its gradual increase and improvement. In their various, as well as numerous productions, they have left an ample repository of not only words, but, also, sentiments, images, characters, and incidents, to which the most eminent even of their successors, perhaps, have added much less than is commonly supposed. It will, also, be seen that a considerable number of those early writers are said, and that others of them are believed, to have been of the religious order, a class who, both regular and secular, may be thought to have, until a period comparatively late, neglected the cultivation of letters beyond what the performance of their professional duties strictly required.

The catalogue of Catholic poets is, possibly, much reduced, in consequence of our not knowing what, if any, religious creed some of the British poets who wrote subsequently to what, in this work, is termed "The English Catholic period," professed, or, perhaps, even appeared to entertain; so deficient, in that respect, are the accounts of them. In the present compilation, however, certain inferior poets, supposed to have been Catholic, are not noticed.

In some of the earlier Selections, the original spelling, for the convenience of readers not familiar with it, is partly modernized. The later and larger portion of the Selections commences with those from Southwell.

PART I.

POETS OF THE ENGLISH CATHOLIC PERIOD.*

THE first Anglo-Saxon writer of note, who composed in his own language, and of whom there are any remains, was CÆDMON, a monk of Whitby, who died about 680. He was the author of many poems on the *Bible histories*, and on miscellaneous subjects. His account of The Fall of Man, somewhat resembles Milton's in "Paradise Lost." † The following is an extract of a version of one of his *Satan's speeches*.‡

"This narrow place is most unlike
that other that we formerly knew,
high in heaven's kingdom,
which my master bestowed upon me,

---

* A period here supposed to extend from the time of the first introduction of Catholicity into Great Britain to that (in 1534) when, in England, the Papal jurisdiction was by law abolished.

† The Scriptural paraphrase, in the remains ascribed to him, is presumed by Hickes to be of a date later than his. On this subject, however, and Milton's possible acquaintance with those remains, see Turner's Hist. Anglo-Sax.

‡ Thorpe's Cædmon.

though we it, for the All-powerful,
may not possess.
We must cede our realm ;
yet hath he not done rightly,
that he hath struck us down
to the fiery abyss
of the hot hell,
bereft us of heaven's kingdom,
hath decreed
to people it
with mankind.
That is to me of sorrow the greatest,
that Adam,
who was wrought of earth,
shall possess
my strong seat.
Oh! had I the power of my hands!
But around me lie
iron bonds ;
I am powerless.
Here is a vast fire
above and underneath ;
the flame abateth not.
My feet are bound,
my hands manacled."

ST. ALDHELM, who died in 709, appears to have excelled all his native predecessors, not only as a composer, but, also, as a singer and reciter of poetry. Of his Anglo-Saxon poems there seem to be no remains.

ALFRED, who reigned and flourished in the ninth century, was the author of one of the best Anglo-Saxon

Poets of the Catholic Period. 15

lyric or miscellaneous poems now extant, a version of the poetry of Boëthius.

During the seventh and eighth centuries poems in Latin were composed by some of the Anglo-Saxon ecclesiastics, as ST. ALDHELM, ST. BEDE, ST. BONIFACE, ALCUIN,* and CÆNA. We have even a relic by LEOBGITHA,† an Anglo-Saxon lady. Of the remains of these poems the most pleasing specimen, perhaps, is Alcuin's address to his cell, on his quitting it for the world, an extract of which is subjoined.

O mea cella mihi habitatio dulcis amata,
    Semper in æternum, O mea cella, vale!
Undique te cingit ramis resonantibus arbos,
    Silvula florigeris semper onusta cornis.
Flumina te cingunt florentibus undique ripis,
    Retia piscator qua sua tendit ovans.
Pomiferis redolent ramis tua claustra per hortos,
    Lilia cum rosulis candida mixta rubris.
Omne genus volucrum matutinas personat odas,
    Atque creatorem laudat in ore Deum.

---

* This eminent scholar and writer was nobly born, and became a monk at York. Subsequently he found a special patron in Charlemagne, who not only appointed him to institute a school in his own palace and assisted in person at his lessons, but sent him as ambassador to King Offa, consulted him in affairs of state, and usually called him his master. He, at length, permitted him to retire to the monastery of Tours, where he died in 804.

† So called by Turner. She seems to have been the Abbess ST. LIOBA, noticed by Butler, who, he says, "understood Latin, and made some verses in that language."

Poets of the Catholic Period.

[*Translation.*]*

"O my loved cell, sweet dwelling of my soul,
Must I forever say, 'Dear spot, farewell!'
Round thee their shades the sounding branches spread,
A little wood with flowering honors gay;
The blooming meadows wave their healthful herbs,
Which hands experienced cull to serve mankind.
By thee, mid flowery banks, the waters glide,
Where the glad fishermen their nets extend;
Thy gardens shine with apple-bending boughs,
Where the white lilies mingle with the rose;
Their morning hymns the feathered tribes resound,
And warble sweet their great Creator's praise."

Of the Anglo-Saxon poetry of the English Catholic period, there are various remains by uncertain authors.

POETS STYLED, "THE NORMAN POETS OF ENGLAND," WHO, THOUGH THEY WROTE IN FRENCH VERSE, AND WERE NOT ALL NATIVES OF THAT COUNTRY, APPEAR TO HAVE RESIDED THERE.

Under this head may be mentioned, as conspicuous, PHILIPPE DE THAN, author of treatises on subjects of popular science, entitled, *Le Bestiare*, and *Liber de Creaturis*, a work replete with erudition; SAMSON DE NANTEUIL, who translated the *Proverbs of Solomon;* THOROLD, to whom is ascribed the fine romance of

---

* In Turner's Hist. Anglo-Sax.

Poets of the Catholic Period. 17

Roland; GEOFFROI GAIMAR, who, in verses remarkable for their facility and elegance, composed a *History of the Anglo-Saxon Kings;** and DAVID, a troveur of eminence, whose works are lost. A writer, however, of much greater celebrity, was their successor, named MAISTRE WACE, a native of Jersey. In 1155, he composed a poem, entitled, *Le Brut d'Angleterre* (Brutus of England), the chief hero of which is an imaginary son of Æneas of Troy, who is represented as having founded the State of Britain. The poem itself is a version of a history of Britain, which Geoffrey of Monmouth had previously translated into Latin prose. The following works are, also, ascribed to Wace: *History of the two irruptions of the Normans into Neustria and England; Life of William Long-sword; Romance of Richard; History of the Dukes of Normandy; Compendium of the History of the Dukes of Normandy; Life of St. Nicholas; Roman du Chevalier au Lion;*† *Roman du Rou; and History of the origin of the Feast of the Conception.* The number and excellency of his compositions induced Henry II. to bestow on him a canonry.

Contemporary with Wace was BENOIT, to whom Henry II. confided the task of writing a *History of the Dukes of Normandy:* He is supposed, also, to have written a *History of the wars of Troy.* The first of these poems contains about 23,000 verses, and the last, about 20,000. He is much commended for the accuracy of his facts, and his various and lively pictures of contemporary manners.

* Apparently only part of a larger work, comprehending the whole history of England.
† Also ascribed to Chrestien de Troyes.

18   Poets of the Catholic Period.

GUERNES, an ecclesiastic of Picardy, was the author of a metrical *Life of St. Thomas a' Becket*, completed in 1177, which he says that he had, more than once, *publicly* read at his tomb in England.

STEPHEN LANGTON, the celebrated Cardinal and Archbishop, is said to have composed a *Canticle on the Passion*, in 123 stanzas, in which the historical details are produced in a manner as interesting as the subject.

These poets appear to have flourished in the twelfth century.

THE RHYMING CHRONICLERS.

LAYAMON, a priest of Ernleye, the author of a metrical translation of *Wace's Brut*, composed, perhaps, about 1180, may be regarded as the earliest writer of this class.

Next to Layamon's may be noticed a work called *Ormulum*, a paraphrase, in verse, of the *Gospel histories*, by one ORME, or ORMIN.

ROBERT OF GLOUCESTER, a monk of the abbey of Gloucester, called "The British Ennius," wrote a *History of England*, which he appears to have completed about 1280. It contains more than 13,000 rhymed couplets. The orations with which he diversifies his narrative, are generally appropriate and dramatic, and not only prove his good sense, but exhibit no unfavorable specimen of his eloquence.

Poets of the Catholic Period.

PETER LANGTOFT, of the monastery of Bridlington, was the author of an entire *History of England*, down to the reign of Edward I., which, therefore, could not have been completed before 1272. Though a native of England, he composed it in *French* verse.

ROBERT MANNYNG, a canon of the monastery of Brunne (thence called ROBERT DE BRUNNE), was a native of Yorkshire. He was received into his order in 1288. In 1303, he began, if not completed, under the name of *A Handling of Sins*,* a metrical paraphrase of a French treatise on *The Decalogue* and *The Seven deadly Sins*. His second work is a metrical *Chronicle of England*, partly translated from *Wace's Brut*, and partly from the chronicle, before mentioned, of Langtoft. He, also, translated into English verse the treatise of St. Bonaventure, *De cœna et passione Domini et pœnis S. Mariæ Virginis*. Warton conjectures that he composed a version of *Chateau d'Amour*,† and Hearne ascribes to him the metrical romance of *Richard Cœur de Lion*. He was, for the time, an elegant writer, possessing a great command of rhymes.

[*In praise of good women. Spelling reduced.*]

[From "The Handling of Sins."]

Nothing is to man so dear
As woman's love in good mannér.
A good woman is man's-bliss,
Where her love right and steadfast is.

---
* Designed to be *sung to the harp*, at *public* entertainments.
† A figurative title of The Blessed Virgin.

There is no solace under heaven,
Of all that a man may neven,[1]
That should a man so much glew[2]
As a good woman that loveth true.
Ne dearer is none in God's hurd,[3]
Than a chaste woman with lovely wurd.

METRICAL ROMANCES.

The era of the earlier English Metrical Romances is supposed to have been the reign of Edward II. (1307-27.)* *Sir Guy, The Squire of Low Degree, The King of Tars, Sir Degore, Ipomedon, King Robert of Sicily,* and *La Mort Arthur,* are the names of some of them. Others, possibly of a later date, are entitled, *Sir Thopas, Sir Isenbras, Gawan and Gologras,* and *Sir Bevis.* Their authors, a single instance excepted, appear to be uncertain. This class of poems probably were all of a serious, and, more or less, of a religiously chivalric character.

"It is reasonable to suppose," says Warton, "that many of our ancient tales in verse, containing fictitious narratives, were written, although not invented, in religious houses. The romantic history of *Guy, Earl of Warwick,* is expressly said to have been written by WALTER OF EXETER, a Franciscan friar, about 1292.

* One only can be assigned with certainty to the 13th century, unless THOMAS THE RHYMER, who died shortly before 1299, was the author of *Sir Tristrem.*

[1] Know.   [2] Delight.   [3] Family.

Poets of the Catholic Period. 21

We may fairly conclude that the monks often wrote for the Minstrels," whom they "were fond of admitting to their festivals." These "Minstrels" were an order of men in the middle ages, who subsisted by the arts of poetry and music, and sang to the harp verses composed by themselves, or others. The Welsh monasteries in general were the great repositories of the poetry of the British bards.

The following specimen from *The Squire of Low Degree* is curious, as noticing some of the diversions of the fair sex in those ages, and partially indicating the state of the arts.

[*Spelling partly changed.*]

To-morrow ye shall on hunting fare,
And ride, my daughter, in a chare:[1]
It shall be covered with *velvet* red,
And clothes of fine gold all about your head,
With damask, white, and azure-blue,
Well diapered with lilies new.

* * * * *

Homeward thus shall ye ride,
On *hawking* by the river's side.
When you come home your men among,
Ye shall have revel, dances and song;
Little children, great and small,
Shall sing as doth the nightingale.

Then shall ye go to your even-song [2]
With *tenours* and *trebles* among;
Your censérs shall be of gold,

[1] Chariot. [2] Vespers.

Indent with azure, many a fold.
Your choir nor *organ*-song shall want,
With *counter*-note and descant.

Then shall ye go to your suppére
And sit in tents in green arbére.
An hundred knights, truly told,
Shall *play with bowls* in alleys cold,
Your disease to drive away.
To see the fishes in pools play,
To a *draw*-bridge then shall ye,
The one half of *stone*, the other of *tree*.
A barge shall meet you full right,
With twenty-four oars full bright,
With trumpets and with clarion,
The fresh water to row up and down.

Then shall ye, daughter, ask the wine,
With spices that be good and fine,
Gentil[1] pots with ginger green,
With dates und dainties you between.*
Forty torches brenyng[2] bright,
At your bridges to bring you light,
Into your chamber they shall you bring
With much mirth and more liking.

When you are laid in bed so soft,
A cage of gold shall hang aloft,
With long pepper fair burníng,
And clovès that be sweet smellíng,

[1] Beautiful?   [2] Burning.
* You between them.

Poets of the Catholic Period. 23

Frankincense and olibanum,
That when ye sleep the taste may come.
And if ye no rest may take,
All night minstrels for you shall wake.

IMMEDIATE PREDECESSORS OF CHAUCER.

ADAM DAVIE is supposed to have flourished about 1312. He was marshal of Stratford-le-bow, near London. His work consists of *Visions, The Battle of Jerusalem, The Legend of St. Alexius, Scripture Histories, Fifteen tokens before the Day of Judgment, Lamentations of Souls,* and his (if such it be) * principal poem, *The Life of Alexander the Great.* The subjoined extract of a passage in the last, describing a battle, is strikingly bold and animated.

Many landès, near and far,
Lesen her lord[1] in that war;
The earth quakèd of her[2] riding,
The weather thickèd of her crying;
The blood of hem,[3] that werein y-slawe,[4]
Ran by floodès to the lawe.[5]

ROBERT BASTON, a Carmelite friar of Scarborough, and a poet of the reign of Edward II. (1307-27), is mentioned as, while a prisoner to the Scots, having been compelled to write for his ransom a *Panegyric on Bruce.* Bale speaks of him as the author of *Poemata*

---
[1] Lost their lords. [2] Their. [3] Them. [4] Slain. [5] Low grounds.
* His claim to it seems questionable.

et Rythmi. His only extant poem is an account, in Latin hexameters, of *the siege of Sterling Castle.*

RICHARD ROLLE, an Augustinian hermit in Yorkshire, and a doctor of divinity, was a very popular and learned writer in Latin on theological subjects. The principal pieces in English ascribed to him, are a metrical paraphrase of a part of the *Book of Job*, of *The Lord's Prayer*, of *The Seven Penitential Psalms*, and a supposed translation of a poem (of the Latin original of which, if such there was,* he probably was the author), that treats, I. *of Man's Nature*, II. *of the World*, III. *of Death*, IV. *of Purgatory*, V. *of the Day of Judgment*, VI. *of the Torments of Hell*, VII. *of the Joys of Heaven.* Ritson enumerates no less than seventeen pieces attributed to this hermit.

[*What is in heaven.*]
[Spelling partly changed.]

There is life without ony death,
And there is youth without ony elde,
And there is all manner welthè to welde,¹
And there is rest without ony traváille,²
And there is peace without ony strife,
And there is all manner lyking of life,
And there is bright summer ever to see,
And there is never winter in that countrié,
And there is gret melody of aungelès song,
And there is praising hem³ among,
And there is ever perfect love and charitiè,
And there is wisdom without foloyé.

* Which Ritson doubts.
¹ Wield, manage. ² Labor. ³ Them.

Poets of the Catholic Period. 25

LAURENCE MINOT composed a series of short poems on the *Victories of Edward III*. His works are praised for the ease, variety, and harmony of their versification. He flourished about 1350.

A few years later, was written the *Vision of Piers Ploughman*, the reputed, but questionable author of which was ROBERT LANGLANDE, an English secular priest. The poem is diversified with satirical passages on all orders of men, particularly the religious. "The writer," however, says his Protestant editor,* "was neither a sower of dissensions, nor one who could be characterized by his countrymen as a heretic. No single important doctrine of the Popish religion is attacked." The degree of credibility due to the representations of a satirist, depends much upon his character and motives, and of these, in this instance, we have no certain knowledge. Warton, a Protestant, shrewdly remarks, " Our author, who probably could not get *preferment*, inveighs against the luxury and diversions of the prelates of his age." The lines of this poem in which Nature is supposed to send forth diseases at the command of conscience, appear to have suggested the sublime description of the lazar-house in Milton's *Paradise Lost*.

JOHN GOWER is supposed to have been born a few years before Chaucer, and about 1325. He is described as " A gentleman who held lands." Fifty of his French ballads remain, and are said to be more elegant and poetical than any of his subsequent English compositions. His three principal works are *Speculum*

* T. Wright, 1856.

Poets of the Catholic Period.

Meditantis in French; *Vox Clamantis* in Latin; and *Confessio Amantis* in English. The last contains more than 30,000 verses. Chaucer calls him "The moral Gower." While satisfied with being such, he is wise, impressive, and sometimes almost sublime.

He died in 1408, and was buried in St. Saviour's church, to the erection or decoration of which, he seems in some manner to have contributed, and in which his monument still remains.

[From the Episode of Rosiphele.]

[*Spelling partly changed.*]

And, as she cast her eye about,
She sigh,[1] clad in one suit, a rout
Of ladies, where they comen, ride,
Along under the wooddè side.
On fair, ambulend hors they set,
That were all white, fair and gret;
And everich one ride on side.
The sadels were of such a pride,
So rich sigh she never none,
With pearls and gold so well begone.[2]
In kirtels and in copès rich
They were clothèd all aliche,[3]
Departed[4] even of white and blewe;
With all lustès[5] that she knewe,
They were embroudred over all;
Her bodies weren long and small;

[1] Saw. [2] Painted over. [3] Alike. [4] Divided. [5] Lists, colors.

Poets of the Catholic Period. 27

The beáutee of hir[1] fair face
There may none earthly thing deface.
Corownès on their heads they bare,
As each of hem a quenè were;
That all the gold of Cresus' hall
The best coronal of all
Might not have bought after[2] the worth.
Thus comen they ridend forth.

GEOFFREY CHAUCER. The time and place of the birth of this eminent poet are uncertain. Recent researches appear to have disproved the earlier accounts of him, in several important particulars. Nothing is positively known of him until the autumn of 1359, when he was in the army with which Edward III. invaded France. In 1367, he was "valet of the king's chamber," and received from the crown a grant, for life, of an annual salary of 20 marks, equal, at present, to about 200*l*. About that time he married Philippa Roet, who was one of the ladies that attended on the queen, and is said to have been a sister of the wife of John of Gaunt, Duke of Lancaster. In 1372, he was joint envoy on a mission to the Duke of Genoa. In 1374 a pitcher of wine, daily, was granted to him, to be received from the king's butler, which was afterwards commuted into a pension of 20 marks, and he was appointed Comptroller of the Customs and Subsidy of Wools, etc., in the port of London. In the reign of Richard II., he appears to have, in 1378, been attached to the embassy for negotiating the king's marriage with a daughter of the French monarch, and, in the same year,

[1] Their. [2] According to.

he was sent on a mission to Lombardy. In 1382, he was appointed Comptroller of the Petty Customs in the port of London. In 1386, he was a member of Parliament. Towards the end of that year, he was superseded in both his offices. "His biographers," says Sir Harry Nicolas, "attribute Chaucer's dismissal to his having taken an active part in the dispute [in the reign of Richard II.] between the court and the citizens of London respecting the election of John of Northampton [who is said to have been attached to the doctrines of *Wickliffe*] to the mayoralty, in 1382 ; and they cite passages in the 'Testament of Love,' which they suppose shew that, in February, 1384, when Northampton was ordered to be arrested, a process issued against the poet, who fled for safety to the island of Zealand ; that he returned to England in 1386, and, on his arrival, was sent to the Tower ; that he remained in custody for three years, and was released about May, 1389 ; and that it was one condition of his pardon that he should impeach his former associates, to which term he ultimately yielded. These circumstances stand only on the authority of passages in the 'Testament of Love,' an allegorical composition, of which it is equally difficult to comprehend the meaning, or the purport."

"All these ingenious inferences and suppositions are, however, undoubtedly erroneous. Chaucer must have been in London from 1380 to May, 1388, as he regularly received his pension, half-yearly, at the Exchequer, with his own hands during that period;[*] and, so far from there being any record to justify such a construction of the 'Testament of Love,' it is certain

---

[*] Issue Rolls, from Easter, 3 Ric. II., to Easter, 11 Ric. II.

Poets of the Catholic Period. 29

that he held both his offices in the Customs from May, 1382, until about December, 1386; that in November, 1384, he was permitted to be absent from his duties on his own private affairs, for one month; that in February 1385, he obtained the further indulgence of being allowed to exercise his office of Comptroller of the Subsidies by deputy; and that, at the very moment when he is supposed to have been a prisoner in the Tower, he was sitting in Parliament. Though the cause of Chaucer's dismissal from his employments is not known, it is extremely likely that he became obnoxious to the ministers who had succeeded his patron, the Duke of Lancaster, in the government." In 1389, however, he was appointed clerk of the works at Wetminster, &c. He afterwards received from the King a grant for life of £20, and a tun of wine per annum, and, in 1398, letters of protection. In 1399, Henry of Bolingbroke, the son of his patron, having ascended the throne, his annuity of £20 was continued, and he was allowed 40 marks additional. In that year he obtained a lease by which the keeper of the chapel of "The Blessed Mary of Westminster," with the consent of the abbot and convent of that place, demised to him a tenement, situated in the garden of the said chapel, for 53 years, at the annual rent of £2 13s. 4d. It is extremely likely that, at the time of his death, which is said to have been the 25th of October, 1400, he was residing in this tenement, and, therefore, was buried in Westminster Abbey.

The site of what seems to have been his last domicile, shows that the Order to whom the convent belonged, did not regard him as hostile to either themselves, or their religion; and the interment of his remains in consecrated ground proves that, as death approached, he professed to be, in faith, not a Wicklevite, but a Catholic, and that such he was believed to have died. The purchasing, in his old age, of a lease-interest in a dwelling situated in the garden of a chapel and near a convent,* would seem to have been with a view to his leading a more strictly Catholic life. The court-favor which, for so long a period, he enjoyed in the reign of Richard II., evidently implies that, if (what does not appear) known to have joined the Northampton faction, or advocated their supposed Wicklevite tenets, he must, professedly at least, have abandoned the one, and recanted the other. It seems highly improbable that, by either word or deed, he should have abetted the cause of a party hostile to the court, at the imminent hazard, if not certainty, of being deprived of his lucrative appointments and influential position. His prayer, of twenty-three stanzas, to *The Blessed Virgin*, and his portrait by Occleve, painted from memory after his decease, which, as if to mark an habitual practice, represents him as holding a set of *rosary-beads*, little accord with Wickliffe's reputed sentiments respecting devotion to the Saints. Lydgate, a monk and poet, who knew him, calls him his "maister," and prays "God to yeve (give) his soule good rest," thereby signifying that he did not suppose him to have died a sectarian.

At the close of Chaucer's "Persones Tale," occurs an affecting paragraph,—the genuineness of which, as having been either endited, or dictated by him, though

---

* From the account of the lease the garden and chapel appear to have belonged to the convent.

Poets of the Catholic Period. 31

questioned, it seems unreasonable explicitly to deny,—wherein, after his having, from conscientious motives, regretted the composition of parts, at least, of his Canterbury Tales, and of some of his other works, he says, "Thank I Our Lord, and His blissful *Mother* and all the *Saints* in heaven, beseeching Them that They send me grace to bewail my guilts and to stodien [study?] to the salvation of my soul, and grant me grace of very *penance, confession,* and *satisfaction* to don (do) in this present life."

The *Canterbury Tales* form the most durable, though, in some respects, not most creditable, monument of his genius. Of his other poems the principal may be *The Flower and the Leaf.* He had no equal among the British poets that preceded Spenser, who terms his style "The pure well-head of English undefiled," and he is regarded as one of the great masters of his art. Nevertheless, it is no less surprising, than lamentable, that the author of so much that is pure and beautiful, should, at times, with what, we may resonably suppose, he, at a later period, would have gladly retracted, permit himself so pointedly to offend the moral delicacy of his readers. In this respect, however, he is far less culpable than some of his sectarian successors. He is claimed as "a reformer," from his exhibiting, not the great body, but certain individuals, of the religious order, as, by their conduct, dishonoring their profession; but where is the passage in which he attacks a Catholic doctrine?

[*Manner of reading his poetry.*]

By frequently changing the present pronunciation, as, by sounding the silent *e*, and *ed*, as the regular

Poets of the Catholic Period.

termination of the past tense and participle, and *es*, when denoting the genitive singular and the plural of nouns, his poetry and, possibly, that of most of the early British writers, as appears from specimens* in this volume, may be so read as, perhaps, much more frequently to please than offend the ear, and, if so read, is sometimes remarkable for euphony.

[From the Canterbury Pilgrimage.]

[*The Nun.*]

Ther was also a NONNE, a Prioresse,
That of hire¹ smiling was ful simple and coy;
Hire gretest othe n' as² but by Seint Eloy;
And she was clepèd Madame Eglentine.
Ful wel she sangè the servíce devine,
Entunèd in hire nose ful swetèly;
And Frenche she spake ful fayre and fetisly,³
After the scole of Stratford-attè-Bowe,
For Frenche of Paris was to hire unknowe.
At metè was she wel ytaughte withalle;
She lette no morsel from hire lippès falle,
Ne wette hire fingres in hire saucè depe:
Wel coude she carie a morsel, and wel kepe,
Thattè no drope ne fell upon hire brest.
*In curtesie was sette ful moche hire lest.*⁴

---

* The accentuated syllables in those specimens, having, with perhaps some exceptions, been (as the compiler supposes) either sounded, or both sounded and emphasized, as in the following line of Chaucer,
"Ful wel she sangè the servíce devine."
¹ Her. ² Not was. ³ Neatly. ⁴ Pleasure.

Poets of the Catholic Period. 33

Hire over-lippè ⁵ wipèd she so clene,
That in hire cuppè was no ferthing ⁶ sene
Of gresè whan she dronken hadde hire draught.
Ful semèly after hire mete she raught.⁷
And sikerly ⁸ she was of grete disport,
And ful plesánt, and amiable of port.
But, for to speken of hire consciénce,
She was so *charitable and so pitóus,*
She woldè wepe, if that she saw a mous
Caughte in a trappe, if it were ded or bledde.
Of smalè houndès hadde she that she fedde
With rosted flesh, and milk and wastel brede;
But sore wept she if on of hem were dede,
Or if men smote it with a yerdè ⁹ smert;
And all was consciénce and tendre herte.
Ful semèly hire wimple ¹⁰ ypinchèd was,
Hire nose tretis,¹¹ hire eyen grey as glas,
Hire mouth ful smale, and thereto soft and red.
But sikerly she hadde a fayre forehéd:
It was almost a spannè brode, I trowe:
For hardily she was not undergrowe.¹²

[*The Oxford Student.*]

A clerk ther was of Oxenforde also,
That unto logike haddé long ygo.
As lenè was his hors as is a rake,
And he was not right fat, I undertake;
But lokèd holwè ¹³ and thereto soberly.
Ful thredbare was his overest courtepy;¹⁴

⁵ Upper-lip. ⁶ Small spot. ⁷ Behaved. ⁸ Surely. ⁹ Rod.
¹⁰ Hood, or veil. ¹¹ Straight. ¹² Of low stature. ¹³ Hollow.
¹⁴ Uppermost short cloak.

2*

For him was lever han,[15] at his beddes hed,
A twenty bokes, clothèd in black or red,
Of Aristotle and his philosophie,
Than robès riche, or fidel, or sautrie.[16]
Of studie toke he mostè cure and hede.
Not a word spake he morè than was nede.
Souning in moral vertue was his speche;
And gladly wolde he lerne and gladly teche.

[*Chaucer's description of himself.*]

Til that our hoste to japen * he began,
And then at erst he lokèd upon me
And saidè thus: "What man art thou?" quod he:
"Thou lokèst as thou woldèst finde an hare;
For ever upon the ground I see thee stare.
Approchè nere, and loke up merily!
Now ware † you, sires, and let this man have place.
He semeth elvish by his contenance,
For unto no wight doth he daliance." ‡

[*Custance is banished from her husband, the King of Northumberland, and embarks, with her infant, in a rudderless ship.*]

[Spelling reduced.]

Wepen both young and old in all that place,
   When that the king this cursèd lettre sent;
And Custance, with a dedly palè face,
   The fourthè day towárd the ship she went.

---

[15] He would rather have.   [16] A musical string-instrument.
       * Jest.   † Beware.

‡ Another part of this description seems to imply that his figure was small, if not diminutive.

Poets of the Catholic Period.

But nathèless [17] she taketh in good entent
The will of Christ, and, kneeling on the strond,
She saydè, "Lord, ay welcome be thy sond!"[18]

He that me keptè from the falsè blame,
  While I was in the land amongès you,
He can me keep from harm and eke from shame,
  In the salt sea, although I see not how:
As strong as ever He was, He is yet now.
In Him trust I and in His mother dear:
That is to me my sail and eke my steer." [19]

Her little child lay weeping in her arm;
  And, kneeling piteously to him, she said,
" Peace, little son, I will do thee no harm."
With that her kerchief off her head she braid,[20]
And over his little eyèn she it laid,
And in her arm she lulleth it full fast,
And into the heaven her eyèn up she cast.

"Mother," quod she, "and maiden bright, Marý!
  Soth [21] is that, through wománnès eggèment,"[22]
Mankind was lorn[23] and damnèd aye to die,
  For which thy child was on a cross yrent:
Thy blissful eyèn saw all his tormént;
Then is there no comparison between
Thy woe and any woe man may sustain.

Thou saw'st thy child yslain before thine eyèn,
  And yet now liv'th my little child parfay:[24]
Now, Lady bright! to whom all woful crien,[25]
  Thou glory of womanhood, thou fairè May,

---

[17] Nevertheless. [18] Message. [19] Guide. [20] Took. [21] Truth.
[22] Incitement. [23] Lost. [24] By my faith. [25] Cry.

Poets of the Catholic Period.

Thou haven of refúte,[26] bright star of day!
Rue on my child, that, of thy gentillesse,
Ruest on every rueful in distress."

Therewith she lookèd backward to the land,
    And saidè " Farewell, husband ruthèless ! "
And up she rose and walketh down the strand
    Toward the ship ; her followeth all the press :[27]
And ever she pray'th her child to hold his peace,
And tak'th her leave, and, with a holy intent,
She blesseth her, and into the ship she went.

His admirable description of the *Parish Priest* would here be given, but for the excellent paraphrase of it by Dryden, which may be found among the selections from that poet in this volume.

[*From a Prayer to the Blessed Virgin, called " La Priere De Notre Dame," and " A.B.C."*]

I wotè well thou wilt been our succóur,
    Thou art so full of bounty in certáine,
For whan a soulè falleth in erróur,
    Thine pity goeth, and haleth him againe ;
Than[28] maketh thou his peace with his Soveráin,
And bringest him out of the crooked strete :
    Who so thee loveth shall not love in vaine,
That shall he find as he the life shall lete.[29]

Redresse me, Moder, and eke me chastise,
    For certainly my Fader's chastisíng,
Ne dare I not abiden in no wise,

---

[26] Refuge.   [27] Crowd.   [28] Then.   [29] Lose.

So hideous is His full reckeníng.
Moder, of whom our jóy̆ gan to spring,
Be ye mine judge and eke my soulès leech!
For ever in yoú is pity aboundíng,
To each that óf pity̆ will you beseech.

Sooth is, He ne gràúnteth no pity̆
Without thèé : for God of His goodnésse
Forgiveth none but it like unto thee : [30]
He hath thee made vicairè and maistrésse
Of all this world, and eke govèrnèresse
Of heavèn, and represseth His justíce
After thine will; and, therefore, in witnésse,
He hath thee crownèd in so royal wise.

JOHN BARBOUR is supposed to have been born about 1326. In 1357 he was archdeacon of Aberdeen. He was the author of a lost work, entitled, *The Brute*, probably another version of the story of Brutus of Troy. His sole remaining work is *The Bruce*, containing, in seven thousand rhymed couplets, a History of the transactions by which Robert I. asserted the independence of Scotland, and obtained its crown. It is difficult to say whether it ranks highest as a faithful history, or a graphic and descriptive poem. He died in 1396.

[*Apostrophe to Freedom.*]

[In modern spelling.]

Ah! Freedom is a noble thing.
Freedom makes man to have likeíng:
Freedom all solace to man gives:

---

[30] Except it please thee.

He lives at ease that freely lives.
A noble heart may have no ease,
Nor else nought that may him please,
If freedom fails : for free likeíng
Is yearnèd o'er all other thing,
Nor he that aye has livèd free,
May not know well the property,
The anger, nor the wretched doom,
That is couplèd to foul thraldóm.

[*From his graphic and spirited description of the Battle of Bannockburn.*]

[Spelling slightly changed.]

And they met them right hardily;
Sae that, at their assembly there,
Sic a frushing* of spears were,
That far away men might it hear:
While through the harness † burst the bleed
That till ‡ earth, down steamèd, gaed.§
There might men hear mony a dint
And weapons upon armour stint,
And see tumble knights and steeds,
And mony rich and royal weeds ‖
Defoullit foully under feet.
Some held on loft, some tint ¶ the seat.
Men heard nought but granes and dints,
That flew fire, as men flays flints.
They fought, ilk ane, sae eagerly,
That they *made nae noise nor cry,*
But dang on other with their might,

---

* Crushing. † Armour. ‡ To. § Went. ‖ Garments. ¶ Lost.

Poets of the Catholic Period. 39

With weapons that were burnist bright.
There might men see mony a steed
Flying astray, that lord had nane.

ANDREW OF WYNTOUN, prior of the monastery of St. Serf's in Lochleven, composed, in verse, a *Chronicle of Scotland*, which seems to have been completed between 1420 and 1424. His language is remarkably pure and his style often animated. As a historian he is highly valuable.

JAMES I. of Scotland, was born in 1395. The nineteen years of his life preceding 1424, he spent in England, as a prisoner to Henry IV. His only certain production is a poem called *The King's Quhair* (Book), in which he describes the circumstances of an attachment which he formed, while confined in Windsor Castle, to Jane Beaufort, a young English princess, whom he saw walking in the adjacent garden. This lady, a daughter of the Duke of Somerset, he afterwards married. He was assassinated in 1437. According to the historians of that age, he was a proficient in every branch of polite literature, in music, jurisprudence, and the philosophy of the times; and his dexterity in tilts and tournaments, in wrestling, archery, and the sports of the field, was perfectly unrivaled. His reign is said to have been equally honorable to himself and beneficial to his country.

The *King's Quhair* is full of simplicity and feeling, and, in poetical merit, is not inferior to any similar production of Chaucer. Two poems of a ludicrous cast, called *Christ's Kirk on the Green*, and *Peblis to the Play*, are also ascribed to this king. Bale speaks of his *Rythmi Latini*.

[From "The King's Quhair."]*
[Spelling partly changed.]

Now was there made, fast by the towris wall,
    A garden fair, and, in the corners, set
Ane arbour green, with wandis long and small
    Railèd about, and so with trèès set
    Was all the place, and hawthorn hedges knet,
That lyf[1] was nonè, walking there forby,
That might within scarce any wight espy.

So thick the boughis and the leavis green
    Beshaded all the alleys that were there,
And mids of every arbour might be seen
    The sharpè, sweetè, greenè juniper,
    Growing so fair with branches here and there,
That, as it seemèd to a lyf[1] without,
The boughis spread the arbour all about.

[*Having described the garden, and the entrance of the lady, he proceeds:*]

And in my head I drew right hastily,
    And eftèsoons[2] *I leant it out again,*
And saw her walk that very womanly,
    With no wight mo'[3] but only women twain.
    Then gan I study in myself, and sayn,
"Ah sweet! are ye a worldly créatúre
Or heavenly thing in likeness of natúre?

Or are ye god Cupídis own princéss,
    And comin are to loose me out of band?
Or are ye *very Nature, the goddéss,*

* From Chambers's Cyc. E. Lit.   [1] Person.   [2] Soon.   [3] More.

Poets of the Catholic Period. 41

That have depainted, with your heavenly hand,
This garden full of flowers as they stand?
What shall I think, alas! what reverence
Shall I mister⁴ unto your excellence?"

And when she walkèd had a little thraw,⁵
 Under the sweetè, greenè boughis bent,
Her fair, fresh face, as white as any snaw,
 She turnèd has and forth her wayis went:
But tho⁶ began my achès and tormént,
 To see her part and follow I na might:
Methought the day was turnèd into night.

In another stanza he says she had
 Beauty enough to make a world to doat.

In England, the chief immediate successors of Chaucer, were JOHN THE CHAPLAIN, a canon of Oseney, who, in 1410, translated into English verse the treatise of *Boëthius de Consolatione Philosophiæ;* THOMAS OCCLEVE,* whose most considerable poem is a version of *Egidius de Regimine Principium;* and JOHN LYDGATE. The last was a monk of the Benedictine Abbey of Bury, in Suffolk, who flourished about 1430. He is said to have opened a school, in his monastery, for teaching the sons of the nobility "the arts of versification and the elegancies of composition," and to have been, not only a poet and a rhetorician, but a geometrician, an astronomer, a theologist, and a disputant. Having studied at Oxford, he traveled in France and Italy,

---
⁴ Minister. ⁵ While. ⁶ Then.
* Flourished about 1420.

and returned a complete master of the language and literature of those countries. He is remarkable for versatility of talent and the great number of his poetical productions, the most esteemed of which may be the *Story of Thebes,* the *Fall of Princes,** the *History, Siege, and Destruction of Troy,** and a *Life of the Blessed Virgin.* His "Troy Book," containing about 28,000 verses, was finished in 1420. Its popularity was excessive, and continued, without much diminution, during at least two centuries. He is allowed to have improved the poetical language of his country, and, says Warton, "is the first of our writers, whose style is clothed with that perspicuity, in which the English phraseology appears, at this day, to an English reader." The time of his death is uncertain.

[From his " Testament."]

[*Christ describes His Sufferings.* †]

[Spelling partly changed.]

Behold, O man! lift up thine eye, and see
 What mortal pain I suffer'd for thy trespáce!
With piteous voice I cry, and say to thee,
 Behold my wounds, behold my bloody face!
 Behold the rebúkes, that do me so menáce,
Behold mine enmyes that do me so despise,
 And how that I, to réform thee to grace,
Was, like a lamb, offer'd in sacrifice!

* Said to be a translation. A poem entitled " The Temple of Glass," is supposed to have been written by either him, or STEPHEN HAWES.

† In what similar lament is this passage excelled?

Poets of the Catholic Period. 43

Behold the mynstrys,¹ which hád me in keepíng,
  Behold the pillar and the ropis strong,
Where I was bound, my sidès down bleedíng,
  Most felly beat with their scòórges long!
Behold the battle which I did underfong,²
  The brunt abiding of their mortál* emprise!
Through their accusing and their slanders wrong,
Was [I], like a lamb, offer'd in sacrifice.

Behold and see the hateful wretchedness,
  Put again me, to my confusìón,
Mine eyèn hid and blinded with darknéss,
  Beat and eke bobbid³ by fálse illusìón,
Salwèd⁴ in scorn by their false kneeling down!
Behold all this, and see the mortal guise,
  How I, alone, for man's savacìón,
Was, like a lamb, offer'd in sacrifice.

See my disciples, how they ha⁵ me forsake,
  And fro me fled, almost evérychóne,
See how they slept and list not with me wake!
  Of mortal dread they left me all alone,
Except my Mother and my cousin John,
My death complaining in most doleful wise:
  See fro my cross they woldè never gone,
Fro⁶ man's offense when I did sacrifice.

Behold the knights,⁷ which, by their froward chaunce,
  Sat for my clothès at the dice to play!
Behold my Mother, swouning for greváunce,
  Upon the cross when she sawhé⁸ me die!

¹ Ministers, officers.   ² Undertake.   * Deadly work.
⁸ Deceived.   ⁴ Saluted.   ⁵ Have.   ⁶ For.   ⁷ Soldiers.   ⁸ Saw

Behold the sepulchre in which my bonỳs lie,
Kept with strong watchè till I did arise!
Of hell gatés see how I *brak the key*,
And gave for man my blood in sacrifice!

Turn home again, thy sinnè do forsake,
  Behold and see if aught be left behind,
How I to mercy am ready thee to take;
  Give me thine heart and be no more unkind!
  Thy love and mine togidre do hem* bind,
And let hem† never partè in no wise:
  When thou wer lost, thy soul again to find,
My blood I offer'd for thee in sacrifice.

[*A pleasant retreat.*]

Till, at the last, among the bowès ‡ glade,
Of adventúre I caught a pleasaunt shade,
Full smooth, and plain and lusty for to seen,
And soft as velvet was the grassy green:
Where from my horse I did alight as fast,
And on a bough aloft his reinè cast.
So faint and mate § of weariness I was,
That I me laid adown upon the grass,
Upon a brinkè, shortly for to tell,
Beside the river of a crystal well;
And the watér, as I rehearsè can,
Like quick-silvér in hís streamés yran,
Of which the gravel and the brightè stone,
As any gold, against the sun yshone.

---

* Them.   † Them.   ‡ Boughs.   § Weak.

Poets of the Catholic Period. 45

In the reign of Henry VI., THOMAS CHESTRE translated, into English verse, the *Lay of Lanval;* and HUGH DE CAMPEDEN, the romance of *Sidrac.* Chestre's work is highly fanciful and entertaining.

The most interesting composition of this period, is the celebrated metrical *History of Sir William Wallace,* in eleven books, which appears to have been written, or, at least, made public, between about 1446 and 1471. Of the author, usually called HENRY THE MINSTREL, or, BLIND HARRY, nothing is known but that he was *blind from his birth,* composed this poem, and lived by reciting it, or parts of it, before company. It is said by himself to be founded on a narrative of the life of Wallace, written in Latin by one Blair,* chaplain to the Scottish hero, which, if it ever existed, is now lost. The chief materials, however, have evidently been the traditionary stories told respecting Wallace in the minstrel's own time. His poem, in various passages, proves him to have been a master of his art, and to deserve the popularity which he acquired among his countrymen, the Scotch, and which he continues to retain, after a lapse of more than three centuries.

[*The death of Wallace. Spelling partly changed.*]

Of men in arms led him a full great rout.
With a bauld sprite guid Wallace blent [b] about:
A priest he ask'd, for God that died on tree.
King Edward then commanded his clergy,

[b] Looked.
* According to another authority, he says that it was partly written by Thomas Gray.

Poets of the Catholic Period.

And said, "I charge you, upon loss of life,
Nane be sae bauld yon tyrant for to shrive.
He has reign'd long in contrar⁶ my highness."
A blyth bishóp soon, present in that place,
(Of Canterbury he then was righteous lord,)
Again' the king he made this richt⁷ recórd,
And said, "Myself shall hear his cónfessíon,
If I have micht,⁸ in contrar of thy crown.
An⁹ thou, through force, will stop me of this thing,
I vow to God, who is my righteous King,
That all Englánd I shall her¹⁰ interdict,
And make it known thou art a heretic.
The sacrament of kirk I shall him give :
Syne¹¹ take thy choice to starve, or let him live."
The king gart¹² charge they should the bishop ta,¹³.
But sad lords counselèd to let him ga.
All Englishmen said that his desire was right.
To Wallace then he rakit¹⁴ in their sijht,¹⁵
And sadly heard his cónfession till¹⁶ ane end :
Humbly to God his sprite he there commend,
Lowly him serv'd, with hearty dévotión
Upon his knees, and said ane orison.
A psalter-book Wallace had on him ever,
Fra his childhood fra it wald nocht dissever :
This grace he ask'd of Lord Cliffórd, that knight,
To let him have his psalter-book in sight :
He gart¹⁷ a priest it open before him hald,
While they till him had done all that they wald :
Stedfast he read for aught they did him there ;
Feil¹⁸ Southrons said that Wallace felt na sair.¹⁹

⁶ Against.   ⁷ Right.   ⁸ Might.   ⁹ If.   ¹⁰ Here?   ¹¹ So.
¹² Made.   ¹³ Take.   ¹⁴ Went.   ¹⁵ Sight.   ¹⁶ To.   ¹⁷ Made.
¹⁸ Many.   ¹⁹ Sorrowful.

Guid dévotíon sae was his béginníng,
Conteined[21] therewith, and fair was his endíng.

The blindness ascribed to this remarkable poet seems all but incredible.

A POETESS OF THE CONVENT.

About 1481, JULIANA BERNERS, a sister of Lord Berners, and Prioress of the nunnery of Sopewell, composed what is regarded as the great literary curiosity of the time, a work containing treatises on *hawking*, *hunting*, and *heraldry*, which, in 1486, was printed. A second edition has a treatise on *angling*, and a sort of lyrical epilogue to the treatise on hunting, which last is written in rhyme. Warton suspects this work to be a translation from the French and Latin, and Ashley remarks, "I think that these Religious translated the French or Latin books on hunting, war, &c., *to please their friends* who were professed sportsmen and warriors." It appears, from the following specimen, that our authoress, whether speaking, or not, in her own person, had remained long enough in the outer world to discover the usually chief passport to its favor.

[*From the epilogue.**]

A faithful friend I fain would find,
To find him there he might be found,

---

[21] Perhaps for "contained," or "conteyned," old Scottish words for "continued."

* In Ellis's Specimens. The spelling appears to have been partly changed.

But now is the world wext so unkind,
    That friendship is fall to the ground.
    Now a friend I have found
That I will neither ban ne [1] curse;
    But all friends in field or town,
Ever gramercy [2] mine own purse.

It fell by me, upon a time,
    As it hath doo [3] by many mo, [4]
My horse, my neat, my sheep, my swine,
    And all my goods they fell me fro:
I went to my friends and told them so,
    And home again they bade me truss.
I said again when I was wo, [5]
Ever gramercy mine own purse.

Cotemporary with this poetess, was WILLIAM OF NASSYNGTON, a proctor in the ecclesiastical court of York, supposed to have translated into English verse, about 1480, a Latin ESSAY ON "*The Trinity and Unity, with a declaration of God's works, and of the passion of Jesus Christ.*" About the same time, or in the reigns of Edwards IV. and V. (1461–83), flourished the minor English poets, JOHN HARDING the chronicler, JOHN SCOGAN, JOHN NORTON and GEORGE RIPLEY, writers on *Alchemy*. The last still maintains his reputation as a learned chemist of the lower age. He was a canon of the regular monastery of Bridlington, who had traveled much, and had studied in France and Italy. Pope Innocent VIII. absolved him from the observance of the rules of his order, that he might prosecute his

---

[1] Nor.   [2] Great thanks to.   [3] Done.   [4] More.   [5] Sorrowful.

Poets of the Catholic Period. 49

studies with more convenience and freedom. He at length became a Carmelite hermit, and such remained till he died, in 1490. His principal work is the *Compound of Alchemie*, written in octave verse.

JOHN KAY was appointed *Poet Laureate* to Edward IV., in whose reign the *first* mention is made of the king's poet under that appellation.

Of ROBERT HENRYSOUN, the most conspicuous, perhaps, of the Scottish poets of this period, there are no personal memorials, except that he was a schoolmaster at Dumfermline, is conjectured to have been a Benedictine monk, and died before 1508. He was the author of *The Testament and Complaint of Cresseide,** *The Abbey Walk*, the ballad of *Robene and Makyne*, and other poems. One of his thirteen fables, is the common story of *The Town Mouse and the Country Mouse*, which he treats with much humor and characteristic description, and concludes with the following moral:

> Blissed be simple life withouten dreid;[6]
> Blissed be sober feast in quietè:
> Wha has eneuch of no more has he neid,
> Though it be little into quantity.
> Grit[7] abundánce, and blind prosperity
> Oft timis make ane evil cónclusíon;
> The sweetest life, theirfor, in this countrý,
> Is of sickérness† with small póssessíon.

[6] Dread.   [7] Great.

* Found in Urry's edition of Chaucer, to whose *Troilus and Cresseide* it is a sequel.

† Security.

WILLIAM DUNBAR, "A poet," says Sir Walter Scott, "unrivaled by *any that Scotland has produced*," was born about 1465. Having taken the degree of A. M., at St. Andrew's, he seems to have traveled in the quality of a preaching Franciscan novice.[2] It is supposed that he was employed by James IV., in connection with various foreign embassies. In 1500, he received from that king a pension, and for some years subsequent to 1503, appears to have resided at court. He is said to have died either in, or about 1520, or 1530.

"In pieces of a didactic order," says Ellis,[3] "he is confessedly superior to all[4] who preceded, and to nearly all who have followed him: but his satires, his allegorical and descriptive poetry, and his tales, are all admirable, and full of fancy and originality." His chief allegorical poems are, *The Thistle and the Rose, The Golden Terge, and The Dance, or Procession of the Seven Deadly Sins.*

[From "The Golden Terge."]

[A vernal morning.]

Full angel-like thir[5] birdis[5] sang their hours,[7]
Within their curtains green, within their bowers,
   Appareled with white and red, with bloomys sweet;
Enammeled was the field with all colours,
The pearlit drops shook, as in silver showers,

---

[2] Friar, according to another account. [3] Specimens of E. E. Poets. [4] The Scottish poets. [5] These, or Those. [6] The spelling in these specimens appears to have been partly modernized. [7] Matins.

Poets of the Catholic Period. 51

While all in balm did branch and leavis fleit.[8]
Depart fra[9] Phœbus did Aurora greit;[10]
Her chrystal tears I saw hing on the flowers,
Which he, for love, all drank up with his heat.

[*From " Meditation written in winter."*]

I am assayed on every side.
Despair says aye, " In time provide,
   And get something whereon to leif:[11]
Or, with great trouble and mischief,
Thou shall intó this court abide."

And then says Age, " My friend, come near,
And be not strange I thee requeir;
   Come, brother, by the hand me take,
Remember, thou has 'compt to make
Of all the time thou spendit here."

Syne Deid[12] casts up his gatis wide,
Saying, " Thir[13] open shall thee 'bide :
   Albeit that thou were ne'er so stout,
Under this lintel shall thou lout :[14]
There is nane other way beside."

[*From " The Merle[15] and the Nightingale.*]

In May, as that Aurora did upspring,
   With crystal een chasing the cluddès[16] sable,
I heard a Merle with merry notis sing
   A sang of love, with voice right comfortáble,

---

[8] Float.   [9] Departed from.   [10] Weep.   [11] Live.   [12] Death.
    [13] These.   [14] Stoop.   [15] Blackbird.   [16] Clouds.

Poets of the Catholic Period.

Again' the orient beamís amiáble,
Upon a blissful branch of laurel green;
This was her sentence, sweet and délectáble,
"A lusty [17] life in Lovis [18] service been." [19]

Under this branch, ran down a river bright
Of balmy liquor, crystalline of hue,
Again' the heavenly azure skyis light,
Where did upon the tother side pursue
A Nightingale with sugared notis new,
Whose *angel-feathers* as the peacock shone :
This was her song, and of a sentence true,
"All love is lost but upon God alone."

[*This discussion of the comparative merits of earthly and spiritual affections, is continued through about a dozen stanzas.*]

Then said the Merle, "mine error I confess;
This frustis [20] love is all but vanity,
Blind ignorance me gave sic hardiness,
To argue so again' the verity.
Wherefore, I counsel every man that he
With love not in the feindis net be tone,*
But love the love that did for his love die.
All love is lost but upon God alone."

[*From "No Treasure without Gladness."*]

Be merry, man! and take not far in mind
The wavering of this wretchit world of sorrow;
To God be humble, and to thy friend be kind,

[17] Pleasant. [18] Love's. [19] Is. [20] Vain.
* Taken.

And with thy neighbours gladly lend and borrow;
His chance to-night, it may be thine to-morrow.
Be blithe in heart for any áventúre;
For oft with wysure[21] it has been said aforrow,[22]
Without gladnéss availis no treasúre.

Though all the werk[23] that ever had livand wight
  Were only thine, no more thy part does fall,
But meat, drink, clais,[24] and of the laif[25] a sight:
  Yet to the Judge thou shall give 'compt of all.
Ane reckoning right comes of ane ragment[26] small.
Be just, and joyous, and do none injúre,
And truth shall make thee strong as any wall.
Without gladnéss availis no treasúre.

A specimen of his graphic and spirited *Procession of the Seven deadly Sins* would here be given, were its Scottish, antiquated style to most readers much more intelligible.

GAWIN or GAVIN DOUGLAS, bishop of Dunkeld in Scotland, and son of Archibald, the great Earl of Angus, was born in 1474. The Earl of Angus, his nephew, married the queen-mother. After occupying a prominent place in the history of his country, he was compelled, by the persecution of the Duke of Albany, to seek for protection in England, where, in 1522, he died of the plague.

He excels as an allegorical and a descriptive poet. His chief original composition is *The Palace of Honour*, to which *The Pilgrim's Progress* " bears so strong a resem-

[21] Wisdom.   [22] Afore.   [23] Possessions.   [24] Clothes.
        [25] Remainder.   [26] Accompt.

blance, that Bunyan could scarcely have been ignorant of it."* His only other long original poem is *King Hart*. His most remarkable production is a *Translation of Virgil's Æneid* into Scottish verse, which he completed in eighteen months, at a time when no metrical version of a classic, except Boëthius, had appeared in English. The work is executed with equal spirit and fidelity, and is farther recommended by many beautiful specimens of original poetry, which, under the name of prologues, are prefixed to each of the thirteen books. His writings, however, too much abound with obsolete words, ever to regain their popularity.

[*From a description of May.*†]

And lusty Flora did her bloomès sprede
Under the feet of Phebus' sulyeart[1] steed :
The swardit[2] soil, enbrode[3] with selcouth[4] hues,
Wood and forést obumbrate[5] with the bews,[6]
Whais[7] blissful branches, portray'd on the ground
With shadows sheen, shew rochis[8] rubicund,
Towers, turrets, kirnals,[9] and pinnácles high
Of kirkis,[10] castles, and ilk fair citý :
Stood *paintit* every fane, phioll[11] and stage,
Upon the plain ground by their own umbráge.
The daisy did un-braid her crownel smale,
And every flower un-lappit[12] in the dale.
Sere downis small on dentilion[13] sprang,

[1] Sultry. [2] Turfed. [3] Embroidered. [4] Uncommon. [5] Shade.
[6] Boughs. [7] Whose. [8] Rocks. [9] Battlements. [10] Churches.
[11] Cupola. [12] Unfolded. [13] Dandelion.

* Chambers's Cyc. E. Lit.

† In Ellis's Specimens. The spelling is perhaps somewhat modernized.

The young, green, bloomit, strawberry leaves amang;
Gimp [14] gilliflowèrs their own leaves un-schet,[15]
Fresh primrose and the pourpour violet.

LAWRENCE WADE, a Benedictine monk of Canterbury, in 1497, translated into English verse the *Life of Thomas a Becket*, written, about 1180, in Latin.

BENEDICT BURGH, archdeacon of Colchester, about 1480, translated in the "royal stanza," the work called *Cato's Morals*.

WILLIAM CAXTON, the celebrated printer, besides his rhyming *Introductions and Epilogues*, is supposed to have written a poem of considerable length, entitled *The Werk of Sapience*, which, however, Ritson thinks is more justly to be ascribed to Lydgate. He died in 1491.

ROBERT FABIAN, who died about 1512, is classed as a poet, in consequence of the metrical prologues prefixed to his *Chronicle*.

HENRY BRADSHAW, a monk of the Benedictine monastery of St. Werberg, composed in stanzas, before 1500, a *Life of his Patroness-Saint*. His descriptions are often happy, and there is a tone of moral purity and rational piety in his thoughts, enriched by legendary lore, that renders many passages of his poem extremely interesting. The following specimen is from the description of the feast made by King Ulper, when his daughter, *St. Werberg*, took the veil.

[14] Pretty.   [15] Unshut.

The tables were covered with clothes of dyaper,
  Rychely enlarged with silver and with golde,
The cupborde, with plate, shyngyng fayre and clere ;
  Marshalles theyr offyces fulfylled manyfolde :
  Of myghty wyne plenty, both newe and olde,
  All maner kynde of meetès delicate,
  Whan grace was sayd, to them was préparate.

STEPHEN HAWES is supposed to have flourished about 1500. He was educated at Oxford, traveled in various countries, and became a complete master of French and Italian poetry. Before 1509, he had been groom of the chamber in the household of Henry VII. The time of his death is not known. He is said to have publicly confuted a *Lollard*. He was the author of *The Pastime of Pleasure*, finished in 1505-6, which Southey calls the best poem of his century, and of other poems. *The Temple of Glass* is supposed to have been written by either him or Lydgate. That he was superior to some of his immediate predecessors in harmonious versification, appears from the following and various other passages.

[*From " The Pastime of Pleasure."*]

Besydes this gyaunt, upon every tree
  I did see hanging many a goodly shielde,
Of noble knygtes, that were of his degree,
  Which he had slayne and murdred in the fielde.
  From farre this gyaunt I ryght well behelde,
  And towarde hym as I rode on my way,
  On his first heade I saw a banner gay.

Poets of the Catholic Period. 57

JOHN SKELTON was born probably about 1461. He was laureated at Oxford, called by Erasmus "The light and ornament of English scholars," at the accession of Henry VIII., whose tutor he had been, was created "Orator Royal," and, in 1499, was ordained priest. At length, however, his turbulent, irregular, and, in one respect, at least, highly criminal course, was such, that the bishop of Norwich is said to have severely censured, if not suspended, him. At one time, the humble client of Cardinal Woolsey, he subsequently assailed him in verses remarkable only for their vulgarity and virulence. Having fled to the Sanctuary at Westminster, he was there received and protected till he died in 1529. He was interred in consecrated ground, and must, therefore, before his death, have, at least, professed repentance and promised amendment.

His serious poems, as the elegy on the death of the *Earl of Northumberland*, the *Prayers to the Trinity*, etc., are those only, occasional passages in the others excepted, which, of all he wrote, a person of delicate taste in regard to either sentiment or expression, might possibly care to read. His attacks on the Cardinal and mendicant friars, may have disposed certain Protestant writers to treat his productions and their author with undue lenity. He seems, however, to have wanted neither genius nor learning.

In the preceding pages are noticed, perhaps, the principal British Catholic poets of those accounts of whom have reached us,* and who flourished within

---

* Superior to some of these may be considered the authors of some of the remains, the names of whom, at least as such, are unknown.

Poets of the Catholic Period.

what, in this work is termed, "The English Catholic period." They, and the others so noticed, are all presumed to have professed the ancient, national faith, inasmuch as none of them are said to have abandoned it, most of them died before "The Reformation" began, and the few who did not, are not known to have favored its views, and either died, or seem to have flourished, at too early a period, to have lived to witness their introduction, unless perhaps to a very limited extent, into their respective countries. Indeed it may be doubted if, in England, Henry VIII., before his marriage with Anne Boleyn, in 1533, tolerated any promulgator, or even advocate of its principles; and if, in Scotland, they found a convert before 1527.* It was not till 1560, that the Papal jurisdiction, in that kingdom, and, till 1534, in England, was by law abolished.†

Numerous poems by uncertain British authors,[1]

---

* About which time they were first introduced, by Patrick Hamilton, from Germany.

† Luther began to preach against certain reputed abuses in 1517, but did not openly separate from the Church till 1520. The only known dates, subsequent to 1517, of the deaths of any of these poets, are Douglas's, 1522, Dunbar's, either in or about 1520, or 1530, and Skelton's, 1529. Of those noticed subsequently to Burgh, who wrote as early as about 1480,§ the only one, the date of whose death is not known, is Hawes. He, however, is supposed to have flourished as early as about 1500. It is to be considered that Douglas is known, and Dunbar is said to have been of the religious order, and the interment of Skelton's remains in consecrated ground, proves that he was believed to have, in faith, at least, died a Catholic.

[1] Unless, as Hearne supposes, one R. Sheale composed "Chevy Chase."

§ The time of his death is not known.

Poets of the Catholic Period. 59

besides the Anglo-Saxon remains and the early Metrical Romances, before noticed, are referable to the " English Catholic period," to which class appear to pertain two of no little repute, *Chevy Chase*, and *The Nut-brown Maid*.

The number of itinerant and other professional reciters and singers of poetry in the middle, if not even later, ages, who, before books were common, in some measure, supplied the want of them, considered, it would seem as if much, if not, indeed, most of the popular British Catholic poetry of those times may have perished, as well as the names of many of its authors. At least, the present remains of it could' not possibly have satisfied the call for it, especially for that portion termed "Metrical Romances," which appear to have been composed chiefly for the above-mentioned performers. With the confiscation and plunder, in the reign of Henry VIII,[2] of the two great repositories of both manuscript and printed works, the monasteries and colleges, probably disappeared most of their literary treasures, portions of which are said to have been even used as fuel. "Whole libraries," says Cobbett,[3] " were scattered abroad, when they had robbed the covers of their *rich ornaments*."

[2] And perhaps subsequently.
[3] Hist. Reform. 6. " These men," says Chamberlain (Present State of Eng.), " under pretence of rooting out popery, superstition and idolatry, utterly destroyed these two noble libraries [of the University of Oxford] and embezzled, sold, burnt, or tore in pieces all those valuable books, which those great patrons of learning had been so diligent in procuring in *every country of Europe*." A few books were accidentally rescued from the *grocers*. " Whole ship-loads of manuscripts were sent as waste paper to foreign countries." White's Hist. of G. Brit., &c.

PART II.

CATHOLIC POETS OF THE SECOND PERIOD.*

SIR THOMAS MORE, the celebrated chancellor of Henry VIII, was born in 1430, and, in consequence of his disapproval of the divorce of that tyrant from his lawful wife, was, in 1535, executed. He was the author of a few small poems of considerable merit, one of which, it is supposed, may have suggested to Cowper the idea of his *John Gilpin*.

[*Fortune described.*]

Then, as a bait, she bringeth forth her ware,
   Silver and gold, rich pearl and precious stone,
On which the masèd† people gaze and stare,
   And gape therefor, as dogs do for the bone.

Fast by her side, doth weary labor stand,
   Pale fear, also, and sorrow all bewept;
Disdain and hatred, on that other hand,
   Eke restless watch, from sleep with travail kept.
   Before her standeth danger and envý,
   Flattery, deceit, mischief, and tyranný.

---

* Those who were both born in, and survived, "The English Catholic period," and those who were born after that period, and died before the commencement of the nineteenth century.
† Amazed.

JOHN HEYWOOD, styled "The epigrammatist," seems, at one time, to have been much admired by Henry VIII. According to Warton, however, he was "inflexibly attached to the Catholic cause," and, on the death of Queen Mary, left the kingdom. He composed various *Interludes*, or brief dramatic pieces; a long poem, called, *The Spider and The Fly;* a comic *Tale*, into which are interwoven all the proverbs of the English language; and six hundred *Epigrams*, interspersed with small *Tales* and *Fables*. He died, about 1565, at Mechlin. *a*. His son, as will subsequently appear, became a distinguished Jesuit.

JOHN BELLENDEN, was a native of Scotland. In his youth he served in the court, and was in great favor with James V. He was made canon of Ross, arch-deacon of Murray, took the degree of D. D. of the Sorbonne, and held the office of 'Clerk of Accounts,' or chief officer of the treasury. In the next reign he was a Lord of the Session. He, at length retired to Rome, where he died in 1550. He is described as, not only "A man of great parts, and one of the finest poets" which his country has produced, but "as a

a. The principal English poet of the reign of Henry VIII, perhaps, was the celebrated EARL OF SURREY, born in 1520, and beheaded in 1547. It would seem as if, in his last hours, he must, in desire at least, have returned to the Church, and not then adhered to a sect who acknowledged his royal persecutor and murderer as their spiritual head; especially as, though he had supported him in his claim on the Supremacy, on *all the other points*, says Lingard, he was a zealous patron of the ancient doctrines. What spiritual aid, if any, he received at the close of his life, does not appear.

Mary.

master of every branch of divine and human learning." His principal work is a translation of the *History of Hector Boece* from the Latin. Some of his poems are said to have been lost. Those found in his history are entitled, *The Proheme of the Cosmographie*, and *The Proheme of the History*, both of remarkable merit. Of the former the following is a specimen.

[VIRTUE SPEAKS.]

[*Spelling slightly changed.*]

My realm is set among my fois all,
Quhilkis¹ hes with me ane war continewal,
And evir still dois on my border ly;
And, though they may no wayis me ourthral,
They ly in wait, if any chance may fall,
Of me sum time to get the victory.
Thus is my life ane ithand² chevalry:
Labor me holdis strang as ony wall,
And nothing brekis me but slugardy.*

MARY, QUEEN OF SCOTS. This unfortunate Queen, of whom it has been said, no one ever beheld

---
¹ Who.   ² Busy.

* ALEXANDER BARCLAY, a Benedictine monk, and author of *The Castle of Labor*, *The Ship of Fools*, and other poems, would be noticed, as a Catholic poet, but for his apparently having joined, and, till he died, in 1552, adhered to the party who denied the Papal supremacy. The above-named poems, however, were written *long before* his supposed defection. He was one of the principal British poets of his time.

her person without admiration and love, or will read her history without sorrow, was born in 1542, and, on pretences which probably few writers, at this time, will venture to justify, was executed in 1588.*

She did not understand English, but composed verses in Latin and, with great facility, in French, of a pathetic passage in which the following sonnet is a translation.

> "Alas! what am I, and in what estate?
>   A wretched corse, bereavèd of its heart;
> An empty shadow, lost, unfortunate.
>   To die is now in life my only part.
> Foes to my greatness, let your envy rest!
>   In me no taste for grandeur now is found,
> Consum'd by grief, with heavy ills oppress'd,
>   Your wishes and desires will soon be crown'd.
> And you, my friends, who still have held me dear,
>   Bethink you that when health and heart are fled,
>   And every hope of future good is dead,
> 'Tis time to wish our sorrows ended here;
>   And that this punishment on earth is given,
> That my pure soul may rise to endless bliss in heaven."

JASPER HEYWOOD, the son of John Heywood, before noticed, was born in London and educated at Oxford. In 1558 he was recommended by Cardinal

---

* Her accomplished father, JAMES V, who was born in 1512 and died in 1542, is said to have been the author of two poems of a ludicrous cast, *The Gaberlunzieman*, and *The Jolly Beggar*, and, perhaps, others. He was a great patron of letters.

Pole, as a scholar, a disputant, and a Catholic, to be put in nomination for a fellowship of Trinity College, and, the same year, was appointed to one in All Souls. In 1562 he became a Jesuit at Rome. He afterwards, for seventeen years, held the theological chair at Dilling in Switzerland, and was so much distinguished as to have been promoted to the honor of D. D. and the "four vows." Having returned to England as a missionary, he was, for some time, imprisoned. At length he retired to Naples, where he died in 1597. He had the reputation of being an admirable Hebrew scholar. He translated, into English verse, the *Hercules Furens*, *Thyestes*, and *Troas*, of *Seneca*. Several of his poems are found in the *Paradise of Daintie Devices*, 1573.

ROBERT SOUTHWELL.

ROBERT SOUTHWELL was born at Horsham St. Faith's, about 1562. His father, a gentleman of opulence, married a lady of the court, who, according to More, had been Queen Elizabeth's instructress in Latin.

Having studied at Paris and Douay, he was sent to Rome, where, in 1578, before he had completed his seventeenth year, he became a member of the Society of Jesus. In 1584, he was ordained priest. In 1586, notwithstanding a law which threatened all members of his profession found in England *with death*, he returned thither as a missionary, and was appointed chaplain and confessor to the Countess of Arundel. In 1592 he was betrayed into the hands of his enemies, and committed to a dungeon in the Tower so filthy and noisome, that, when liberated for examination, his clothes were covered with vermin. After an imprisonment of three years with ten inflictions of the rack, he petitioned that either he might be brought to trial, or, at least, that his friends might be permitted to visit him. Cecil* is said to have replied to the effect, that, "if he was in so much haste to be hanged, he should have his desire." Be that as it may, on the 21st of February, 1594-5, he was placed at the bar. He pleaded not guilty to the charge of treason, but admitted that he was a priest, and had returned simply to administer the sacraments to those of his religion who might desire them, and perform the ordinary duties of a Catholic clergyman. A verdict of guilty, necessarily in accordance with the statute, was returned. At daybreak of the 22d, the jailer apprised him that he was to die that morning. Southwell embraced him and said, "You could not bring me more joyful tidings." Having arrived at the place of execution, and addressed the multitude, who by their silence and decorum, testified their admiration of the martyr, he prepared for his approaching end. At length the car was removed from under his feet. Even while suspended, he continued to beat his breast and make the sign of the cross. His behavior

---

* "As to his fortitude we have the [subjoined] admiring testimony of Cecil : ' Let antiquity boast of its Roman heroes and the patience of captives in torments. There is one Southwell, a Jesuit, who, thirteen times most cruelly tortured, cannot be induced to confess anything, not even the color of the horse, whereon, on a certain day, he rode, lest from such indication, his adversaries might conjecture in what house, or in company of what Catholics, he that day was.' Moore." *Turnbull's* Southwell.

had such an effect on the spectators, that when, in terms of his sentence, the executioner wished to cut him down alive,* neither they nor the magistrate who superintended the judicial murder, would permit him so to do. His body was emboweled and quartered.

In the course of his speech he said, "As regards the Queen [Elizabeth], to whom I have neither done nor wished any evil, I have daily prayed for her, and now, with all my heart, do pray, that He [God] may grant that she may use the ample gifts wherewith He has endowed her, to the glory of His name. I deliver my soul into the hands of my Creator. For what may be done to my body I have no care. I die because I am a Catholic priest, elected into the Society of Jesus in my youth; *nor has any other thing*, during the last three years in which I have been imprisoned, *been charged against me.*" The fortitude with which he endured the tortures of the rack, was, perhaps, even more admirable than that with which he met death. While subjected to them, he maintained an inflexible silence, and his tormentors affirmed that he resembled a post rather than a man. It is said that after death his countenance exhibited no change, neither did the halter leave its ordinary marks of discoloration; that, when his body was partitioned, his heart leaped from the dissector's hand, and, by its throbbing, seemed to repel the flames, as if expressing with the Psalmist, "My heart shall exult in the living God." One of his

---

* The ancient sentence, under which he was executed, required that he "should be hanged, but taken down alive, and then that his bowels should be taken out and burned before his face." Penn. Cyc.

sisters is supposed to have wrought, with some of his relics, several cures on persons afflicted with diseases, which had baffled the skill of the physicians.

The following account of the sufferings of the imprisoned Catholic priests, occurs in one of his letters. " What was given them to eat, was so little in quantity, and withal so filthy and nauseous, that the very sight of it was enough to turn their stomachs. The labors to which they obliged them were continual and immoderate, and no less in sickness than in health; for with hard blows and stripes, they forced them to accomplish their tasks, how weak soever they were. Some are there hung up whole days by the hands, in such a manner that they can but just touch the ground with the tips of their toes. This purgatory we are looking for every hour, in which the executioners exercise all kinds of torments. But come what pleaseth God, we hope we shall be able to bear all in Him that strengthens us."

The copies of his works a few years since known to exist, were the remnant of at least *twenty-four* editions. A reprint of his poems has recently appeared. Says Sir Edgerton Brydges, " A deep moral pathos, illumined by fervent piety, marked everything that Southwell wrote. There is something singularly simple, chaste, eloquent, and fluent in his diction, on all occasions."

[*From his piece entitled,* " *The author to his loving cousin.*"]

" Poets, by abusing their talents, and making the follies and feignings of love the customary subject of their base endeavors, have so discredited this faculty, that a poet, a lover, and a liar, are by many reckoned but three words of one signification. The devil, as he affecteth deity and seeketh to have all the compliments of divine honor applied to his service, so hath he, among the rest, possessed also most poets with idle fancies. And, because the best course to let them see the error of their works, is to weave a new web in their own loom, I have here laid a few coarse threads together, to invite some skillfuller wits to go forward in the same, or to begin some finer piece, wherein it may be seen how well verse and virtue suit together. With many good wishes I send you these few ditties."

[*From " Content and Rich."*]

I dwell in Grace's court,
    Enriched with virtue's rights;
Faith guides my wit, Love leads my will,
    Hope all my mind delights.

My conscience is my crown,
    Contented thoughts my rest;
My heart is happy in itself,
    My bliss is in my breast.

My wishes are but few,
    All easy to fulfil;
I make the limits of my power
    The bounds unto my will.

I feel no care of coin,
    Well-doing is my wealth;
My mind to me an empire is,
    While grace affordeth health.

Southwell.

Spare diet is my fare,
 My clothes more fit than fine;
I know I feed and clothe a foe
 That pampered would repine.

To rise by others' fall,
 I deem a losing gain;
All states with others' ruins built
 To ruin run amain.

[*From " The Image of Death."*]

I often look upon a face
 Most ugly, grisly, bare and thin;
I often view the hollow place
 Where eyes and nose had sometime been;
I see the bones across that lie;
Yet little think that I must die.

I read the label underneath,
 That telleth me whereto I must;
I see the sentence, eke, that saith,
 Remember, man, thou art but dust:
But yet, alas! but seldom I
Do think, indeed, that I must die.

Continually, at my bed's head,
 A hearse doth hang, which doth me tell
That I, ere morning, may be dead,
 Though now I feel myself full well.
But yet, alas! for all this I
Have little mind that I must die.

If none can 'scape death's dreadful dart,
   If rich and poor his beck obey,
If strong, if wise, if all, do smart,
   Then I to 'scape shall have no way:
Oh grant me grace, O God! that I
My life may mend, since I must die.

[From "St. Peter's Complaint."]

When, traitor to the Son, in Mother's eyes
   I shall present my humble suit for grace,
What blush can paint the shame that will arise,
   Or write my inward feelings on my face?
Might she the sorrow with the sinner see,
Though I'm despised, my grief might pitied be.

O sister nymphs!* the sweet renownèd pair,
   That bless Bethania bounds with your abode;
Shall I infect that sanctifièd air,
   Or stain those steps where Jesus breathed and trod?
No, let your prayers perfume that sweetened place;
Turn me, with tygers, to the wildest chace.

Could I revivèd Lazarus behold,
   The third of that *sweet trinity of saints*,
Would not astonished dread my senses hold?
   Ah yes! my heart even with his naming faints:
I seem to see a messenger from hell,
That my preparèd torments comes to tell.

With mildness, Jesu, measure mine offence,
   Let true remorse thy due revenge abate,

---

* Mary and Martha.

Let tears appease, when trespass doth increase,
    Let pity temper thy deserved hate,
Let grace forgive, let love forget my fall!
With fear I crave, with hope I humbly call.

[*From "Mary Magdalen's Complaint at Christ's Death."*]

    O true life! sith* Thou hast left me,
        Mortal life is tedious;
    Death it is to live without Thee,
        Death of all most odious.
    Turn again, or take me to Thee,
    Let me die, or live Thou in me!

    O my soul! that did unloose thee
        From thy sweet captivity,
    God, not I, did still possess thee,
        His, not mine, thy liberty:
    Oh! too happy thrall thou wert,
    When thy prison was His heart.

[*From "Love's servile Lot."*]

She shroudeth vice in virtue's veil,
Pretending good in ill;
She offereth joy, affordeth grief,
A kiss where she doth kill.

A honey-shower rains from her lips,
Sweet lights shine in her face;
She hath the blush of virgin's mind,
The mind of viper's race.

* Since.

She makes thee seek, yet fear to find,
To find, but not enjoy;
In many frowns some gliding smiles
She yields, to more annoy.

She letteth fall some luring baits
For fools to gather up;
To sweet, to sour, to every taste,
She tempereth her cup.

With soothèd words enthrallèd souls
She chains in servile bands;
Her eye in silence hath a speech
Which eye best understands.

Her little sweet hath many sours,
Short hap immortal harms;
Her loving looks are murdering darts,
Her songs bewitching charms.

Her diet is of such delights
As please till they be past;
But then the poison kills the heart
That did entice the taste.

Plough not the seas, sow not the sands,
Leave off your idle pain;
Seek other mistress for your minds:
Love's service is in vain.

[*From " Times go by turns."*]

Not always fall of leaf, nor ever spring,
  Not endless night, nor yet eternal day;

The saddest birds a season find to sing,
  The roughest storm a calm may soon allay.
Thus, with succeeding turns, God tempereth all,
That man may hope to rise, yet fear to fall.

[*From " New Prince, new Pomp."*]

Weigh not his crib, his wooden dish,
  Nor beasts that by Him feed;
Weigh not his mother's poor attire,
  Nor Joseph's simple weed.

This stable is a Prince's court,
  The crib his chair of state;
The beasts are parcel of his pomp,
  The wooden dish his plate.

The persons in that poor attire
  His royal liveries wear;
The Prince Himself is come from heaven;
  This pomp is praisèd there.

[*From " At Home in Heaven."*]

Fair soul! how long shall veils thy graces shroud?
  How long shall this exile withold thy right?
When will thy sun disperse his mortal cloud,
  And give thy glories scope to blaze their light?
Oh that a star, more fit for angels' eyes,
Should pine on earth, not shine above the skies!

Thy ghostly* beauty offered force to God;
  It chainèd Him in links of tender love;

---
* Spiritual.

It won his will with man to make abode ;
   It stayed his sword, and did his wrath remove ;
It made the vigour of his justice yield,
And crownèd Mercy empress of the field.

This lulled our heavenly Samson fast asleep,
   And laid Him in our feeble nature's lap ;
This made Him under mortal load to creep,
   And in our flesh His Godhead to enwrap;
This made Him sójourn with us in exíle,
And not disdain our titles in His style.

[*From " Stanzas on the death of Mary, Queen of Scots."*]

Some things more perfect are in their decay,
   Like spark that going out gives clearest light ;
Such was my hap, whose doleful dying-day
   Began my joy, and termèd Fortune's spite.

Alive a Queen, now dead I am a Saint ;
   Once Mary called, my name now Martyr is ;
From earthly reign debarrèd by restraint,
   In lieu whereof I reign in heavenly bliss.

Rue not my death, rejoice at my repose ;
   It was no death to me, but to my woe :
The bud was opened to let out the rose ;
   The chains unloosed to let the captive go.

[*From "Life's Death, Love's Life."*]

Life out of earth hath no abode,
   In earth love hath no place ;
Love settled hath her joys in heaven,
   In earth life all her grace.

Mourn, therefore, no true lover's death,
   Life only him annoys;
And when he taketh leave of life,
   Then love begins his joys.

[*From "Fortune's Reach."*]

To beauty's fading bliss I am no thrall;
   I bury not my thoughts in metal mines;
I aim not at such fame as feareth fall;
   I seek and find a light that ever shines,
Whose glorious beams display such heavenly sights,
As yield my soul the sum of all delights.

[*From " Of the Blessed Sacrament of the Altar."*]

To ravish eyes, here heavenly beauties are;
   To win the ear, sweet music's sweetest sound;
To lure the taste, the angels' heavenly fare;
   To soothe the scent, divine perfumes abound.

Here, to delight the will, true wisdom is;
   To woo the will, of every good the choice;
For memory a mirror showing bliss;
   Here all that can both sense and soul rejoice.

The God of hosts in slender host doth dwell,
   Yea, God and man with all to either due;
That God that rules the heavens and rifled hell,
   That man whose death did us to life renew.

[*From " The Death of Our Lady."*]

Weep, living things! of life the mother dies;

The world doth lose the sum of all her bliss,
The queen of earth, the empress of the skies;
  By Mary's death *mankind an orphan is.*
Let nature weep, yea, let all graces moan;
Their glory, grace, and gifts die all in one.

Prayer.

It is the spirit with reverence must obey
  Our Maker's will, to practice what He taught;
Make not the flesh thy counsel when thou pray,
  'Tis enemy to every virtuous thought.

Even as Elias, mounting to the sky,
  Did cast his mantle to the earth behind,
So, when the heart presents the prayer on high,
  Exclude the world from traffic with the mind.

Nothing more grateful in the highest eyes,
  Nothing more firm in danger to protect us,
Nothing more forcible to pierce the skies,
  And not depart till mercy do respect us;
And, as the soul life to the body gives,
So prayer revives the soul, by prayer it lives.

[*Detached Passages.*]

The fairest flowers have not the sweetest smell;
A seeming heaven proves oft a damning hell.

Of mirth to make a trade may be a crime,
But tirèd sprites for mirth must have a time.

Life saved by sin is purchase dearly bought.

THOMAS LODGE.

THOMAS LODGE was of a Lincolnshire family, and was born probably about 1556. In 1573, he was entered at Oxford, where he took one degree and seems to have been distinguished as a scholar, a wit and a poet. He subsequently accompanied Captain Clarke in a voyage, and, also, Captain Cavendish. He speaks of having been in the Straits of Magellan, " in which," he says, " to the southward, many wonderous iles, many strange fishes, many monstrous Patagones withdrew my senses." In 1584 he was an actor. He also wrote for the stage, and appears to have studied law. At length, having studied medicine and taken the degree of M. D. at Avignon, he settled in London, where he soon rose into notice and seems to have obtained a lucrative practice. Besides the plays, *Wounds of the Civil War*, and, conjointly with R. Greene, *A Looking-Glass for London*, he composed *a volume of poems, a treatise on the plague, translations of Josephus and Seneca*, and other works. From the story of his *Rosalind*, an admired novel, Shakspeare constructed his *As You Like It*. He died of the plague in 1625. Tributes were paid to his memory by many of his contemporary poets, who have characterized him as a man of very considerable genius.

[*A Solitary life commended.*]

At peep of day, when, in her crimson pride,
  The morn bespreads with roses all the way,
Where Phœbus' coach with radiant course must glide,

The hermit bends his humble knees to pray;
Blessing that God, whose bounty did bestow
Such beauties on the earthly things below.

Whether, with solace tripping on the trees
   He sees the citizens of forest sport,
Or, midst the wither'd oak, beholds the bees
   Intend their labor with a kind consórt,
Down drop his tears, to think how they agree,
While men alone with hate inflaméd be.

Sweet solitary life, thou true repose,
   Wherein the wise contemplate Heaven aright,
In thee no dread of war or worldly foes,
   In thee no pomp seduceth mortal sight,
In thee no wanton cares to win with words,
Nor lurking toys, which city life affords.

[*Human miseries.*]

The judgment seat hath brawls, honor is hated,
   The soldier's life is daily thrall to danger,
The merchant's bag by tempest is abated,
   His stock still serves for prey to every stranger,
The scholar with his knowledge learns repent;
Thus each estate in life is discontent.

[*Advice to Sons.*]

In choice of thrift let honor be your gain,
   Win it by virtue and by manly might;
In doing good esteem thy toil no pain,

Protect the fatherless and widow's right:
Fight for thy faith, thy country, and thy king;
For why? this thrift will prove a blessed thing.

In choice of friends, beware of light belief,
   A painted tongue may shroud a subtle heart;
The Syren tears do threaten mickle grief.
   Foresee, my sons, for fear of sudden smart;
Chuse in your wants, and he that friends you then,
When richer grown, befriend you him again.

Learn, with the ant, in summer to provide,
   Drive, with the bee, the drone from out the hive;
Build, like the swallow, in the summer tide;
   Spare not, too much, my sons, but sparing thrive;
Be poor in folly, rich in all but sin;
So by your death your glory shall begin.

[*From "Diana's Epitaph."*]

All ye that fix your eyes upon this tomb,
   Remember this, that beauty fadeth fast,
That honors are enthrall'd to hapless doom,
   That life hath nothing sure, but soon doth waste:
So live you then, that, when your years are fled,
Your glories may survive when you are dead.

"In Lodge," says Sir E. Brydges, "we find whole pastorals and odes which have all the ease, polish and refinement of a modern author."

WAS SHAKSPEARE A CATHOLIC?

[*From " Historical Memoirs of the English Catholics," by C. Butler.*]

"May the writer premise a suspicion, which from internal evidence he has long entertained, that Shakspeare was a Roman Catholic? Not one of his works contains the slightest reflection on popery, or on any of its practices, or any eulogy on the Reformation. His panegyric on Queen Elizabeth is cautiously expressed, while Queen Katharine [the repudiated Catholic wife of her father] is placed in a state of veneration; and nothing can exceed the skill with which Griffith draws the panegyric of Wolsey. The ecclesiastic is never presented by Shakspeare in a degrading point of view. The jolly monk, the irregular nun, never appear in his dramas. Is it not natural to suppose that the topics on which, at that time, those who criminated popery loved so much to dwell, must have often attracted his notice, and invited him to employ his muse upon them, as subjects likely to engage the favorable attention both of the sovereign and the subject? Does not his abstinence from these justify a suspicion that a Catholic feeling witheld him from them? This conjecture acquires additional confirmation from the undisputed fact that the *father* of the poet lived and died in communion with the Church of Rome."

In his "Midsummer-night's Dream," we find the subjoined commendation of the life of virginal and religious celibacy:

"Thrice blessèd they, that master so their blood
To undergo such maiden pilgrimage."

He makes Hamlet invoke the protection of the angels, brings his father's ghost from Purgatory, and perhaps it is difficult to conceive a Protestant dramatist of that period causing ISABELLA, the *conventual* novice in "Measure for Measure," to be, as such, addressed as she is by LUCIO, or exhibiting her as a lovely example of female purity, without his having first divested her of the conventual character, should it, in any work upon which his scenes might have been founded, have been ascribed to her.

[LUCIO TO ISABELLA.]

"Hail Virgin, if you be; as those cheek-roses
Proclaim you are no less!
I hold you as a thing *ensky'd* and *sainted*,
By your renouncement an immortal spirit,
And to be talk'd with in sincerity,
As with a saint." *Act* 1. 5.

What Protestant would probably have represented a disembodied soul * as lamenting that it had left the world "unanel'd," that is, without having received the Catholic sacrament of "extreme unction"? These and other, in his dramas, apparent manifestations of a Catholic sentiment in their author, are the more remarkable, as not only unnecessary, but, doubtless, much less likely to have pleased than offended the Protestant and, perhaps, larger and certainly more influential part of his theatrical auditory.

* In "Hamlet."

We have the high, Protestant authority of Mr. Gifford,* the late eminent editor of the English "Quarterly Review," for believing that PHILIP MASSINGER, the greatly distinguished and principal tragic poet of the reign of James I, was a Catholic convert. Nevertheless, as the evidence in regard to his and Shakspeare's supposed catholicity, is merely, however strongly, presumptive, no specimens of their poetry will here be given.†

HENRY CONSTABLE.

HENRY CONSTABLE was born about 1566. He took his A. B. at Cambridge in 1579. He was noted as a sonneteer. He is supposed to have been the Henry Constable, who, for his zeal in the Catholic cause, was long obliged to live in a state of banishment, and, having privately returned to London, was imprisoned in the tower.

The most striking of his productions is *The Shepherd's Song of Venus and Adonis*, which is thought far to excel Shakspeare's on the same subject, at least in taste and natural touches. The following specimen is

---

* His words, as cited in Lardner's Cyc., are, " A close and repeated perusal of Massinger's works, has convinced me that he was a Catholic."

† BENJAMIN JONSON, their celebrated fellow-dramatist and cotemporary, was a Catholic convert, but is said to have at length apostatized. Some, however, and perhaps all, of his principal dramas, were composed while he is confessed to have adhered to the Catholic communion, and the same may possibly be true of many, if not most, of his minor poems. His apostasy was perhaps the result of his aspiring to *court-favor*.

from his *Diana,* a collection of sonnets, &c., published in 1594.

[*Love's Troubles.*]

To tread a maze that never shall have end;
  To burn in sighs and starve in daily tears;
To climb a hill, and never to descend;
  Giants to kill, and quake at childish fears;
To pine for food, and watch the Hesperian tree;
  To thirst for drink, and nectar still to draw;
To live accurst, whom men hold blest to be;
  And weep those wrongs which never creature saw;
If this be love, if love in these be founded,
My heart is love, for these in it are grounded.

JAMES SHIRLEY.

JAMES SHIRLEY, one of the great English dramatic poets, was born in London in 1594. Designed for orders in the established church, he was educated first at Oxford, where archbishop Laud refused to ordain him on account of his appearance being disfigured by a mole on his left cheek. He afterwards took the degree of A. M. at Cambridge, and officiated as curate at St. Albans. Having embraced the Catholic communion, he there lived as a teacher, but, at length, settled in London and became a voluminous dramatic writer. When the civil war broke out, he took the field under his patron, the Earl of Newcastle. After the cessation of that struggle, he was forced to betake himself to his former occupation of teacher. In 1666, the great fire of London drove him and his family from their home, and, shortly afterwards, both he and his wife died on the same day.

"His better characters," says Hallam, "express pure thoughts in pure language." Campbell speaks of "the airy touches of his expression, the delicacy of his sentiments, the beauty of his similes," his "polished and refined dialect," and his language as sparkling "with the most exquisite images."

Besides his *thirty-nine plays*,[*] in one of which occurs *Death's final Conquest*, his, perhaps, finest lyrical production, he composed a small volume of miscellaneous poems.

The Garden.

This garden does not take my eyes,
   Though here you show how art of men,
Can purchase nature at a price
   Would stock old Paradise again.

These glories while you dote upon,
   I envy not your spring, nor pride.
Nay! boast the summer all your own,
   My thoughts with less are satisfied.

Give me a little plot of ground,
   Where, might I with the sun agree,
Though every day he walk his round,
   My garden he should seldom see.

---

[*] See note 2 to the Notice of Dryden.

Those tulips, that such wealth display
   To court my eye, shall lose their name;
Though now they listen, *as if they*
   Expected I should praise their flame.

But I would see myself appear,
   Within the violet's drooping head,
On which a melancholy tear
   The discontented Morn hath shed.

Within their buds let roses sleep,
   And virgin lilies on their stem,
Till sighs from lovers glide and creep
   Into their leaves, to open them.

In the centre of my ground compose
   Of bays and yews my summer room,
Which may, so oft as I repose,
   Present my arbour and my tomb.

No birds shall live within my pale,
   To charm me with their shames of art,
Unless some wandering nightingale,
   Come here to sing and break her heart.

Death's Final Conquest.[*]

The glories of our blood and state
   Are shadows, not substantial things;
There is no armour against fate;
   Death lays his icy hand on kings.

---

[*] Said to have been a favorite poem with Charles II.

        Sceptre and crown
        Must tumble down,
And in the dust be equal made,
With the poor crooked scythe and spade.

Some men with swords may reap the field,
    And plant fresh laurels where they kill;
But their strong nerves at last must yield,
    They tame but one another still.
        Early or late
        They stoop to fate,
And must give up their murmuring breath,
When they, pale captives, creep to death.

The garlands wither on your brow,
    Then boast no more your mighty deeds;
Upon death's purple altar now
    See, where the victim bleeds!
        Your heads must come
        To the cold tomb:
Only the actions of the just,
Smell sweet and blossom in the dust.

JOHN DIGBY.

JOHN DIGBY, an English nobleman, was educated at Oxford. In 1606 he was knighted by James I., who subsequently sent him as ambassador to Spain, to the Archduke Albert, and to the Emperor. On his return from Spain, whither, in 1622, he had gone to negotiate the marriage of Prince Charles with the Infanta, he was created Earl of Bristol. In the civil troubles he was exiled, and died in Paris in 1653.

He was the author of verses on *The Death of Sir Henry Unton*, and other poems,* and translated *Du Moulin's Defense of the Catholic Faith*.

SIR KENELME DIGBY.

SIR KENELME DIGBY, one of the most noted and remarkable men of his time, was born at Gothurst, in 1603. He was educated at Oxford, where his tutor used to compare him, probably for the universality of his genius, to the celebrated Picus de Mirandola. Having left the university, he traveled in France, Spain, and Italy. On his return he was, while a minor, knighted by the king, and subsequently appointed a gentleman of the bedchamber, a commissioner of the navy, and a governor of Trinity House. In 1628, he went as admiral to the Mediterranean, and won great honor by his bravery and conduct at Algiers, in rescuing many English slaves, and in attacking the Venetian fleet in the bay of Scanderoon. His conversion to the Catholic Church from the Church of England, seems to have been first publicly professed in 1636. In 1638, he published, at Paris, *A Correspondence with a Lady about the Subject of Religion.* In 1651, *Letters between Lord George Digby and Sir Kenelme Digby, Knight, concerning Religion*, were published in London. HIS OPPONENT IN THIS CONTROVERSY SUBSEQUENTLY BECAME A CATHOLIC. In 1639, Sir Kenelme and Sir Walter Montague

---

* The compiler has met with no specimen of them.

were employed by the Queen to endeavor to persuade the Catholics to contribute liberally in aid of the King, (Charles I,) which object they are said to have effected. At the commencement of the civil war he was imprisoned by the Parliament, but, in 1643, was set at liberty. During his confinement he composed observations on *Brown's Religio Medici* and a portion of *Spenser's Fairy Queen*. Having retired to France, he there completed and published several philosophical works.* On his visiting England, in order to compound for his estate, he was, by the parliament, not only ordered to withdraw, but told that, if he should at any time return without leave, he should forfeit both life and estate. Thereupon, he again went to France, where by Henrietta, dowager-queen of England, to whom he had for some time been chancellor, he was very kindly received, and, not long afterwards, was sent by her into Italy. He, at length, ventured to return to England, and was supposed to have been engaged in a project for reconciling the Catholics to the administration of Cromwell. Having returned from the Continent in 1661, he reappeared and was well received at the English Court. In the first settlement of the Royal Society he was appointed a member of the Council. One of his discourses, "Concerning the Vegetation of Plants," was in that year printed. In 1654 he published a translation, which he had made from the Latin, and called, *A Treatise of adhering to God*. He died, 11th June, 1665.

* Entitled, "A Treatise on the Nature of Bodies;" "A Treatise declaring the Operations and Nature of Man's Soul, out of which the Immortality of Reasonable Souls is evinced;" and "Institutionum Peripateticarum libri quinque, cum Appendice Theologica de Origine Mundi."

Davenant.

Wood calls him "A magazine of all the arts." His cotemporary, Lord Clarendon, says, "He was very eminent throughout the whole course of his life; of a very extraordinary person and presence, which drew the eyes of all men upon him, which were more fixed by a wonderful grace of behavior, a flowing courtesy and civility, and such a volubility of language as surprised and delighted. In a word, he had all the advantages that nature and art and an excellent education could give him."

Of a poem ascribed to him, Ellis cites the following passage:

" Fame, honor, beauty, state, trains, blood, and birth,
Are but the fading blossoms of the earth.
I would be great, but that the sun doth still
Level his rays against the highest hill;
I would be high, but see the proudest oak
More subject to the rending thunder-stroke;
I would be wise, but that the fox I see
Suspected guilty, while the ass goes free;
I would be fair, but see that champion proud,
The brightest sun, oft setting in a cloud.

SIR WILLIAM DAVENANT.

SIR WILLIAM DAVENANT, the son of a "sufficient vintner" in Oxford, was born in 1605. In 1621, he was entered at Lincoln College, Oxford, but appears to have soon left it and become first page to Frances, Duchess of Richmond. His patron was the celebrated Fulk

Greville, in whose family he lived until that nobleman was assassinated, in 1628. In 1629, he produced his first play. The next eight years of his life were spent in a constant attendance upon the court, where he seems to have been a special favorite. In 1638 he was appointed poet-laureate. He was subsequently manager of Drury-Lane, but having entered into the commotions and intrigues of the civil war, he was apprehended and confined in the Tower. He, at length, escaped to France, where he appears to have remained till the Queen sent over to the Earl of Newcastle a quantity of military stores, when he resolved to return. He was appointed by the Earl, Lieutenant-General of Ordnance, and distinguished himself so much in the cause of the royalists, that he was knighted for his skill and bravery. The time of his *conversion to the Catholic faith* is supposed to have been about the year 1646. On the decline of the royal cause he returned to France, where he partly wrote *Gondibert*, a heroic and his principal poem, which he subsequently continued under confinement and condemnation. In the summer, however, of that year, he was concerned in a very important negotiation, and by the Queen dispatched to England with a letter of credit to the King. His next step was to sail for Virginia, as a colonial projector; but the vessel in which he had embarked, was captured by a parliamentary ship of war, and he was lodged in prison at Cowes. In 1650 he was removed to the Tower. His life was considered in danger, but he was released after a confinement of two years.

His operas and comedies were the first pieces brought out on the English stage after the Restoration. He effected two great improvements in theatrical representations, the regular introduction of female players, and the use of movable scenery and appropriate decorations. It seems not improbable that he was, at length, driven, as a writer and manager, to the stage * for a maintenance, the King being in no condition fully to provide for many whom he might have wished to oblige.

He died in 1668, and was buried in Westminster Abbey. Inscribed upon his tomb are the words,

"O, rare Sir William Davenant."

Besides *Gondibert, Madagascar*, and other poems, he was the author of *twenty-five dramatic pieces*. His poems are remarkable for moral purity, originality, and, their date considered, for correctness and elegance. Dryden remarks that he was first taught by Davenant to admire Shakspeare, and that he " found " him " of so quick a fancy," that nothing " was proposed to him in which he could not suddenly produce a thought extremely pleasant and surprising." The notice of him in the *Biographia Britannica*, alluding to his letter to Whitlocke, says that it " would have secured him the reputation of the politest pen of the times, if nothing of his had remained besides." Southey calls him a man "of great and indubitable genius," and remarks that he and his cotemporary, Sir John Davis, " avoiding equally the opposite faults of too artificial and too careless a style, wrote in numbers which, for precision, and clearness, and felicity, and strength, have never been surpassed." Says Sir Walter Scott, "A single poet, Sir William Davenant, made a meritorious effort to rescue poetry from becoming the mere handmaid of pleasure, and to

---

* See note 2 to the Notice of Dryden.

restore her to her natural rank in society, as an auxiliary of religion and virtue. Few poems afford more instances of vigorous conception, and even of felicity of expression, than *Gondibert*."

The profession of the Catholic faith by Davenant and his cotemporary convert, Sir Kenelme Digby, at a period when that profession necessitated, in a great degree, the forfeiture of public favor, and, perhaps, royal patronage, and subjected them to the possibility of legal prosecutions,* may be regarded as satisfactory evidence of their sincerity.

The Restoration having deprived Milton of his public employments, and exposed him to danger, by the interest of Davenant and Marvell he was included in the general amnesty.

[FROM "GONDIBERT."]

[*Rhodalind described.*]

Her father's prosperous palace was the sphere
   Where she to all with heavenly order moved;
Made rigid virtue so benign appear,
   That 'twas, without religion's aid, beloved.

Her looks like empire shewed, great above pride,
   Since pride ill counterfeits excessive height;
But nature published what she fain would hide,
   Who for her deeds, not beauty, loved the light.

Her mind, scarce to her feeble sex akin,
   Did, as her birth, her right to empire show;

---

* Under the statutes enacted against Catholics.

Seemed careless outward when employed within ;
Her speech, *like lovers'* * *watched,* was *kind and low*

[*Birtha described.*]

Whilst her great mistress, Nature, thus she tends,
   The busy household waits no less on her ;
By secret law each to her beauty bends,
   Though all her lowly mind to that prefer.

Gracious and free she breaks upon them all
   With morning looks ; and they, when she does rise,
Devoutly at her dawn in homage fall,
   And droop, like flowers, when evening shuts her eyes.

She ne'er saw courts, yet courts could have undone
   With untaught looks, and an unpractised heart.
Her nets the most prepared could never shun,
   For nature spread them in the scorn of art.

She never had in busy cities been,
   Ne'er warmed with hopes, nor e'er allayed with fears ;
Not seeing punishment, could guess no sin,
   And, sin not seeing, ne'er had use of tears.

And, as kind Nature, with calm diligence,
   Her own free virtue silently employs,
Whilst she unheard does ripening growth dispense,
   So were her virtues busy without noise.

[*Praise, Prayer, and Penitence.*]

Praise is devotion fit for mighty minds,
   The differing world's agreeing sacrifice,

---

* Lovers' *speech* watched.

Where Heaven divided faiths united finds;
But prayer, in various discord, upward flies.

For prayer the ocean is where diversly
    Men steer their course, each to a several coast;
Where all our interests so discordant be,
    That half beg winds by which the rest are lost.

By penitence when we ourselves forsake,
    'Tis but in wise design on piteous Heaven:
In praise we nobly give what God may take,
    And are, without a beggar's blush, forgiven.

[*The temples of Prayer, Penitence, and Praise, as dedicated by Astragon, described.*]

The temple built for prayer can neither boast
    The builder's curious art, nor does declare,
By choice materials, he intended cost;
    To show that nought should need to tempt to prayer.

No bells are here; unhinged are all the gates;
    Since craving in distress is natural,
All lies so ope that none for entrance waits;
    And those whom faith invites can need no call.

The great have by distinction here no name;
    For all so covered come in grave disguise,
To show none come for decency or fame,
    That all are strangers to each other's eyes.

Since the required extreme of penitence
    Seems so severe, this temple * was designed,

---

* Of Penitence.

Solemn and strange without, to catch the sense,
    And dismal showed within, to awe the mind.

Of sad, black marble was the outward frame,
    A mourning monument to distant sight;
But by the largeness, when you near it came,
    It seemed the palace of eternal night.

Hither a loud bell's tone rather commands,
    Than seems to invite the persecuted ear;
A summons Nature hardly understands,
    For few and slow are those who enter here.

Within a dismal majesty they find;
    All gloomy, great, all silent does appear,
As Chaos was ere the elements were designed:
    Man's evil fate seems hid and fashioned here.

Black curtains hide the glass, whilst, from on high,
    A winking lamp still threatens all the room,
As if the lazy flame just now would die;
    Such will the sun's last light appear at doom.

[*Temple of Praise.*]

Dark are all thrones to what this temple seemed,
    Whose marble veins outshined heaven's various bow;
And would, eclipsing all proud Rome esteemed,
    To northern eyes like eastern mornings show.

In statue o'er the gate God's favorite king,
    The author of celestial praise, did stand;
His quire, that did his sonnets set and sing,
    In niches ranged, attended either hand.

Tapers and lamps are not admitted here;
   Those but with shadows give false beauty grace,
And this victorious glory can appear
    Unvailed* before the sun's meridian face.

[*Picture of the Ascension in this temple.*]

And know, lost Nature! this resemblance was
   Thy frank Redeemer in ascension shown;
When hell He conquered in thy desperate cause,
   Hell, which before man's common grave was grown.

The holy mourners, who this Lord of Life
   Ascending saw, did seem with Him to rise,—
So well the painter drew their passions' strife,—
   To follow Him with bodies, as with eyes.

[*Scripture and its abuse.*]

But here the soul's chief book did all precede,
   Our map towards heaven, to common crowds denied,
Who proudly aim to teach ere they can read;
   And all must stray where each will be a guide.

About this sacred, little book did stand
   Unwieldy volumes, and in number great;
And long it was since any reader's hand
   Had reached them from their unfrequented seat.

For a deep dust, which time does softly shed
   Where only time does come, their covers bear;
On which grave spiders streets of webs had spread,
   Subtle and slight, as the grave writers were.

* Undiminished.

In these Heaven's holy fire does vainly burn,
    Nor warms, nor lights, but is in sparkles spent;
Where froward authors with disputes have torn
    The garment, seamless as the firmament.

[*Books.*]

———————— Gold of the dead,
Which time does still disperse, but not devour.

[*Truth.*]

Truth, the discovery made by traveling minds.

[*Secret love discovered.*]

Her face, o'ercast with thought, does soon betray
    The assembled spirits, which his eyes detect
By her pale looks; as, by the milky-way,
    Men first did the assembled stars suspect.

Or, as a prisoner, that in prison pines,
    Still, at the utmost window, grieving lies;
Even so her soul, imprisoned, sadly shines—
    As if it watched for freedom—at her eyes.

[*From " The Christian's Reply to the Philosopher."*]

The good in graves, as heavenly seed, are sown,
    And, at the saints' first spring, the general doom,
Will rise not by degrees, but fully blown;
    When all the angels to their harvest come.

God bred the arts, to make us more believe,
    By seeking Nature's covered mysteries,

His darker works; that faith might thence conceive
    He can do more than what our reason sees.

Frail life! in which through mists of human breath
    We grope for truth and make our progress slow,
Because by passion blinded, till by death,
    Our passions ending, we begin to know.

O harmless death! whom still the valiant brave,
    The wise expect, the sorrowful invite,
And all the good embrace, who know the grave
    A short, dark passage to eternal light.

Epitaph on Mrs. Cross.

Within this hallowed ground this seed is sown
Of such a flower, though fallen ere fully blown,
As will, when doom, the *saints' first spring*, appears,
Be sweet as those which heaven's choice bosom wears.
As calm in life as others in death's shade,
So silent that her tongue seemed only made
For precepts, weighed as those in wisest books:
Yet nought that silence lost us, for her looks
Persuaded more than others by their speech:
Yet more by deeds than words she loved to teach.

Song.

The lark now leaves his watery nest,
    And climbing shakes his dewy wings;
He takes this window for the East,
    And, to implore your light, he sings.
Awake! awake! the moon will never rise
Till she can dress her beauty at your eyes.

The merchant bows unto the seaman's star,
  The ploughman from the sun his season takes;
But still the lover wonders what they are,
  Who look for day before his mistress wakes.
Awake! awake! look through your veils of lawn,
Then draw your curtains, *and begin the dawn!*

WILLIAM HABINGTON.

WILLIAM HABINGTON was born, in 1605, of a Catholic family in Worcestershire, and educated at Paris and St. Omer's. His literary attainments recommended him to the favor of Charles I., at whose command he wrote a *History of Edward IV.* He also composed *Observations upon History*, and *The Queen of Aragon*, a play which was acted at court. Twenty years before his death he published his *Poems*. His life seems to have glided quietly away, cheered by the society and affection of his "Castara," as his wife, a daughter of Lord Powis, is called in his verses. He died in 1654.

His poetry is tender, often elegant, and remarkable for the delicacy with which, pure in an age of license, it treats erotic subjects. Southey calls him an " amiable man and irreproachable poet."

His father was implicated in Babington's Conspiracy; his uncle suffered death for his share in it; and his mother is said to have written the famous letter to Lord Monteagle, which is supposed to have averted the gun-powder plot. Milner, however, says that, according to a certain authority, Tresham wrote it, and if so, seems to think it was dictated by Cecil.

Castara.

Like the violet, which alone
    Prospers in some happy shade,
My Castara lives unknown,
    To no looser eye betrayed.

She obeys with speedy will,
    Her grave parents' wise commands,
And so innocent, that ill
    She nor acts nor understands.

She her throne makes reason climb,
    While wild passions captive lie;
And, each article of time,
    Her pure thoughts to Heaven fly.

Upon Beauty.

[A Sonnet.]

Castara, see that dust the sportive wind
So wantons with. 'Tis haply all you'll find
Left of some beauty, and how still it flies,
To trouble, as it did in life, our eyes!
O empty boast of flesh! though our heirs gild
The far-fetched Phrygian marble, which shall build
A burthen to our ashes, yet will death
Betray them to the sport of every breath.
Dost thou, poor relic of our frailty, still
Swell up with glory? Or is it thy skill
To mock weak man, whom every wind of praise
Into the air doth 'bove his centre raise?
If so, mock on, and tell him that his lust
To beauty's madness, for it courts but dust.

Habington.

[*From " Cupio Dissolvi."*]

The soul which doth with God unite,
Those gaieties how doth she slight
   Which o'er opinion sway !
Like sacred virgin's wax, which shines
On altars or on martyrs' shrines,
   How doth she burn away !

How soon she leaves the pride of wealth,
The flatteries of youth and health
   And fame's more precious breath ;
And every gaudy circumstance
That doth the pomp of life advance,
   At the approach of death !

The cunning of astrologers
Observes each motion of the stars,
   Placing all knowledge there ;
And lovers, in their mistress' eyes,
Contract those wonders of the skies,
   And seek no higher sphere.

But he whom heavenly fire doth warm
And 'gainst these powerful follies arm,
   Doth soberly disdain
All these fond, human mysteries,
As the deceitful and unwise
   Distempers of our brain.

He, as a burden, bears his clay,
Yet vainly throws it not away,
   On every idle cause ;

But with the same untroubled eye,
Can or resolve to live or die,
   Regardless of th' applause.

[*From "Non Nobis Domine."*]

No laurel wreath about my brow!
   To Thee, my God! all praise! whose law
The conquered doth and conqueror bow:
For both dissolve to air, if Thou
   Thy influence withdraw.

[*From "Nox nocti indicat scientiam."*]

For the bright firmament
   Shoots forth no flame
So silent, but is eloquent
   In speaking the Creator's name.

No unregarded star
   Contracts its light
Into so small a character,
   Remov'd far from our human sight.

But, if we steadfast look,
   We shall discern
In it, as in some holy book,
   How men may heavenly knowledge learn.

Thus, those celestial fires,
   Though seeming mute,
The fallacy of our desires
   And all the pride of life confute.

For they have watched since first
    The world had birth,
And found sin in itself accurst,
    And nothing permanent on earth.

[*The Pomp without the Spirit of devotion.*]

To the cold, humble hermitage,
Not tenanted but by discolored age,
Or youth enfeebled by long prayer
And tame with fasts, the Almighty doth repair;
But, from the lofty gilded roof,
Stained with some *pagan* fiction, keeps aloof,
Nor the gay landlord deigns to know,
Whose buildings are, like monsters, but for show.

[*From " Of True Delight."*]

The rose yields her sweet blandishment,
    Lost in the folds of lovers' wreaths:
The violet enchants the sense,
    When early in the spring she breathes.

But winter comes, and makes each flower
    Shrink from the pillow where it grows;
Or an intruding cold hath power
    To scorn the pérfume of the rose.

Our senses, like false glasses, show
    Smooth beauty where brows wrinkled are,
And make the cozened fancy glow:
    Chaste Virtue's only true and fair.

[*From " To a Tomb."*]

What horror at thy sight shoots through each sense!
How powerful is thy silent eloquence
Which never flatters!   Thou instruct'st the proud
That their swoll'n pomp is but an empty cloud,
Slave to each wind; the fair, those flowers they have
Fresh in their cheek, are *strewed upon a grave.*
Thou tell'st the rich their idol is but earth;
The vainly pleased, that syren-like their mirth
Betrays to mischief, and that only he
Dares welcome death, whose aims at virtue be.

[*From " Laudate Dominum de Cœlis."*]

   You spirits! who have thrown away
   That envious weight of clay,
      Which your celestial flight denied;
   Who, by your glorious troops supply
   The wing'd hiérarchy,
      So broken in the angel's pride;

   O you! whom your Creator's sight
   Inebriates with delight,
      Sing forth the triumphs of his name!
   All you enamour'd souls, agree,
   In a loud symphony,
      To give expression to your flame!

   While we, who to earth contract our hearts,
   And only study arts
      To shorten the sad length of time,

In place of joys, bring humble fears,
For hymns, repentant tears,
   And a new sigh for every crime.

SIR ASTON COKAIN.

SIR ASTON COKAIN was born at Ashbourn, in 1608. He was educated at both Oxford and Cambridge. Having continued, for some time, at the Inns of Court, he traveled with Sir Kenelme Digby, and, on his return, married. He appears to have led a retired life upon his estate, and during the civil wars, to have suffered much for his religion. He is said to have been regarded by many as "an ingenious gentleman, a good poet, and a great lover of learning." His book, entitled, *Poems of Divers Sorts*, appeared in 1658. He died in 1683.

To Plautia.

I can behold thy golden hair,
And for the owner nothing care;
Thy starry eyes can look upon,
And be mine own when I have done;
Can view the garden of thy cheeks,
And slight the roses there as leeks;
My liberty thou canst not wrong
With all the magic of thy tongue;
For thou art false and wilt be so,
I else no other fair would woo.
Away! therefore; tempt me no more!
I'll not be won with all thy store.

5*

RICHARD CRASHAW.

RICHARD CRASHAW, an eminent religious poet, was the son of a clergyman, who officiated at the Temple Church in London. The date of his birth is not known, but, according to a recent notice of him, may have been about 1616. In 1637, he became a fellow at Cambridge. His bachelor's degree was taken in 1633. He is said to have been an eloquent and a powerful preacher.

During the Great Rebellion, in 1644, he was ejected from his fellowship, for not complying with the rules of the Parliamentary army. Having embraced the Catholic faith, he went to Paris,[*] where, through the friendship of Cowley, the poet, he obtained the notice of the Queen, Henrietta Maria, and was by her recommended to persons of influence at Rome. There he is said to have become Secretary to Cardinal Palotta. He was for some time a Canon of the church of Loretto. He died about 1650.

In 1646 appeared his English poems, consisting of *Steps to the Temple*, *The Delights of the Muses*, and *Carmen Deo Nostro*. His numerous Latin Poems, including a few in Greek, are entitled *Poemata Latina*, and *Epigrammata Sacra*. They contain the well-known verse, relating to the miracle of changing water into wine:

Lympha[†] pudica Deum vidit et erubuit.
"The conscious water [‡] saw its God and blushed."[§]

---

[*] According to Turnbull. Chamber's Cyc. E. Lit. seems to imply that his removal to Paris preceded his conversion.
[†] *Nympha* in Turnbull's Ed.
[‡] "*Modest Water*" in Chalmers's Biog. Dic.
[§] This translation is ascribed to Dryden.

His imagination was fertile and various, and his verse is sometimes highly musical. "His devotional strains and lyric raptures," says one of his biographers, "evince the highest genius." He was an accomplished scholar, and an excellent translator, and is said to have been skilled in music, drawing and painting.

Cowley, a Protestant,* honored his memory with a monody, in which he says,

> " Poet and saint! to thee alone are given
> The two most sacred names of earth and heaven.
> Pardon, my mother church, if I consent
> That angels led him when from thee he went;
> For even in error sure no danger is,
> When joined with so much piety as his;
> And I, myself, a Catholic will be
> So far, at least, great saint, *to pray to thee.*"

His friend, Car, thus speaks of his disregard of bodily comforts:

> " What he might eat or wear he took no thought;
> His needful food he rather found than sought;
> He seeks no downs, no sheets, his bed's still made;
> If he can find a chair, or stool, he's laid."

[*From* "*Hymn to the name of Jesus.*"]

I sing the name which none can say,
But touch'd with an interior ray;
The name of our new peace, our good,
Our bliss, and supernatural blood:

---

* "Cowley designed to imitate his friends, Woodhead and Crashaw, in their happy retreats, but was prevented by death." *Note* in Butler's Lives.

The name of all our lives and loves.
Hearken and help, ye holy doves!
The high-born brood of day; you bright,
Candidates of blissful light,
The heirs elect of love; whose names belong
Unto the everlasting life of song.

Fair, flowery name! in none but thee
And thy nectareal fragrancy,
  Hourly there meets
 A *universal synod of all sweets*,
 By whom it is definèd thus;
  That no perfume
  Forever shall presume
 To pass for odoriferous,
But such alone whose sacred pedigree
Can prove itself some kin, sweet name, to thee.
 Sweet name! in thy each syllable,
 A thousand blest Arabias dwell.

Oh, that it were as it was wont to be!
When thy old friends of fire, all full of thee,
Fought against frowns with smiles; gave glorious chase,
To persecutions; and, against the face
Of death and fiercest dangers, durst, with brave
And sober face, march on to meet a grave.
On their bold breasts about the world they bore thee,
 And to the teeth of hell stood up to teach thee;
In centre of their inmost souls they wore thee,
 Where racks and torments strived in vain to reach thee.

  [*From his translation of "Dies Iræ."*]
 O that trump! whose blast shall run
 An even sound with the circling sun,

And urge the murmuring grave to bring
Pale mankind forth to meet his King.

O that book! whose leaves so bright
Will set the world in severe light:
O that Judge! whose hand, whose eye
None can endure, yet none can fly.

But Thou giv'st leave, dread Lord! that we
Take shelter from Thyself in Thee,
And, with the wings of Thine own dove,
Fly to the sceptre of soft love.

[*From " On a Prayer-Book, sent to Mrs. M. R."*]

Lo, here a little volume, but great book!
It is, in one choice handful, heaven, and all
Heaven's royal host, encamped thus small
To prove that true schools use to tell,
A thousand angels in one point can dwell.

It is an armory of light:
Let constant use but keep it bright,
   You'll find it yields,
To holy hands and humble hearts,
   More swords and shields,
Than sin hath snares, or hell hath darts.

[*From " On the Glorious Assumption of the Blessed Virgin."*]

Hark! She is called, the parting hour is come;
Take thy farewell, poor wòrld! heaven must go home,
A piece of heavenly light, purer and brighter
Than the chaste stars whose choice lamps come to
    light her,

While through the crystal orbs, clearer than they,
She climbs, and makes a far more milky-way.

    Hail, holy Queen of humble hearts!
    We in thy praise will have our parts;
      Thy sacred name shall be
      Thyself to us, and we
With holy cares will keep it by us:
      We, to the last,
      Will hold it fast,
And no ASSUMPTION shall deny us.
      All sweetest showers
      Of fairest flowers
We'll strew upon it;
    Though our sweetness cannot make
    It sweeter, they may take
Themselves new sweetness from it.

    Live! crown of women, Queen of men;
    Live! mistress of our song; and when
    Our weak desires have done their best,
    Sweet angels, come and sing the rest.

[*From " The office of the Holy Cross."*]

[Christ's Victory.]

    Christ, when he died,
      Deceived the cross,
    And on death's side
      Threw all the loss:
    The captive world awaked, and found
    The prisoner loose, the jailor bound.

O dear and sweet dispute
'Twixt death's and love's far different fruit!
　Different as far
　As antidotes and poisons are.
　By that first fatal tree
　Both life and liberty
　　Were sold and slain;
By this they both look up and live again.

　O, strange mysterious strife
　Of open death and hidden life!
　When on the cross my king did bleed,
　Life seemed to die, death died indeed.

[From " A Song."]

Lord! when the sense of Thy sweet grace
Sends up my soul to seek Thy face,
Thy blessed eyes breed such desire,
I die in love's delicious fire.
O love! I am thy sacrifice;
Be still triumphant, blessed eyes,
Still shine on me, fair suns! that I
Still may behold, though still I die:
For, while Thou sweetly slayest me,
Dead to myself, I live in Thee.

Temperance, or the Cheap Physician.

Go! now, and, with some daring drug,
Bait the disease, and, while they tug,
Thou, to maintain their precious strife,
Spend the dear treasure of thy life.

Go! take physic, doat upon
Some big-named compositión,
The oraculous doctors' mystic bills,
Certain hard words made into pills;
And what, at last, shall get by these?
Only a costlier disease.
That which makes us have no need
Of physic, that's physic indeed.
Wouldst see a man all his own wealth,
His own physic, his own health,
A happy soul, that, all the way
To heaven, hath a summer's day?
Wouldst see a nest of roses grow
In a bed of reverend snow?
In sum, wouldst see a man that can
Live to be old, and still a man?
This rare one, reader, wouldst thou see?
Hark, hither! and thyself be he!

[*From " To the Morning."*]
[Penance for sleep.]

What succor can I hope the Muse will send,
Whose drowsiness hath wronged the Muse's friend?
What hope, Aurora, to propitiate thee,
Unless the Muse sing my apology?
O! in that morning of my shame, when I
Lay folded up in sleep's captivity,
How at the sight didst thou draw back thine eyes
Into thy modest veil! how didst thou rise
Twice dyed in thine own blushes, and didst run
To draw the curtains and awake the sun?
Bright lady of the morn, pity doth lie
So warm in thy soft breast, it cannot die;

Have mercy, then, and when he next doth rise,
O meet the angry god, invade his eyes,
And stroke his radiant cheeks; one timely kiss
Will kill his anger, and revive my bliss.
So to the treasure of thy pearly dew
Thrice will I pay three tears, to show how true
My grief is; so my wakeful lay shall knock
At th' oriental gates, and duly mock
The early lark's shrill orisons, to be
An anthem at the day's nativity.
And the same rosy-fingered hand of thine,
That *shuts night's dying eyes*, shall open mine.

St. Theresa.

What soul soe'er, in any language, can
Speak Heaven like hers, is my soul's countryman.

[*From "On Hope."*]

Dear Hope! earth's dowry and Heaven's debt,
The entity of things that are not yet:
   Fair cloud of fire! both shade and light,
   Our life in death, our day in night:
Fates cannot find out a capacity
     Of hurting thee.
From thee their thin dilemma with blunt horn
Shrinks, like the sick moon at the wholesome morn.

   Faith's sister! nurse of fair desire!
   Fear's antidote! a wise, a well-stayed fire,
     Tempered 'twixt cold despair and torrid joy,
Queen-regent in young Love's minority!
     Though the vexed chymic vainly chases
     His fugitive gold through all her faces,

And love's more fierce, more fruitless fires assay
   One face more fugitive than they,
True Hope's a glorious huntress, and her chase
The God of nature in the field of grace.

On Nanus.

[Apparently from the Greek.]

High mounted on an ant, Nanus, the tall,
Was thrown, alas! and got a deadly fall.
Under the unruly beast's proud feet he lies,
All torn; with much ado, yet, ere he dies,
He strains these words : "Base envy, do laugh on!
Thus did I fall, and thus fell Phaeton."

[*From " Description of a Religious House."*]

Out of Barclay.

No roofs of gold o'er riotous tables shining,
Whole days and suns devoured with endless dining;
No sails of Tyrian silk, proud pavements sweeping,
Nor ivory couches, costlier slumbers keeping;
Our lodgings hard and homely as our fare,
That chaste and cheap, as the few clothes we wear;
A hasty portion of prescribèd sleep;
Obedient slumbers that can wake and weep;
And work for work, not wages; let to-morrow's
New drops wash off the sweat of this day's sorrows:
A long and daily-dying life, which breathes
A respiration of reviving deaths.
But neither are there those ignoble stings
That nip the bosom of the world's best things;

No cruel guard of diligent cares, that keep
Crowned woes awake, as things too wise for sleep:
But reverend discipline, and religious fear,
And soft obedience, find sweet biding here;
Silence and sacred rest, peace and pure joys;
Kind loves keep house, lie close, and make no noise;
And room enough for monarchs, while none swells
Beyond the kingdom of contented cells.

[*From " Epitaph on Mr. Ashton."*]

Sermons he heard, yet not so many
As left no time to practice any:
He heard them reverently, and then
His practice preached them o'er again.

Flowers.

So have I seen, to dress their mistress, May,
Two silken, sister flowers consult, and lay
Their bashful cheeks together: newly they
Peeped from their buds, showed *like the garden's
eyes*
Scarce waked:* like was the crimson of their joys;
Like were the pearls they wept; so like, that one
Seemed but the other's kind reflectión.

Power of Love.

[Printed, in the Paris edition, beneath a picture of a heart with a padlock, inscribed, " Non vi."]

'Tis not the work of force, but skill,
To find the way into man's will.

'Tis love alone can hearts unlock:
Who knows the word, he needs not knock.

[*The Author's Motto.*]*

Live, Jesus, live! and let it be
My life to die for love of Thee.

SIR EDWARD SHERBURNE.

SIR EDWARD SHERBURNE was born in London, in 1618. At the death of his father, he succeeded him in the clerkship of the royal ordnance, but the Rebellion prevented his long retaining it.† Being a Catholic, he was ejected in 1642, and harassed by a long and expensive confinement. On his release he determined to follow the fortunes of the king, who made him his Commissary General of the Artillery. In this post he witnessed the battle of Edge-hill, and afterwards attended the king at Oxford, where he was made Master of Arts, and remained till that city was surrendered to the parliamentary forces. He was subsequently plundered of all his property. In 1651 he published his *Poems* and *Translations*, and, from March 1654 to 1659, visited various parts of the continent, as a traveling

---

* These lines are so placed in Turnbull's edition, that it seems somewhat doubtful whether he supposed they were Crashaw's, or a borrowed motto. They are, however, presumed to be his.

† "He was the principal person concerned in drawing up the 'Rules, Orders, and Instructions' given to the Ordnance in 1683, which, with very few exceptions, are those by which it is now governed." *Chalmers's* Biog. Dic. 1816.

tutor. At the Restoration he recovered his clerkship, and, in 1682, was knighted. As, however, he could not take the oaths at the Revolution, he left his public employment, and, by this step, sacrificed his property to his principles. He died in 1702.

He seems to have owed much of his reputation to his translations, among which are those of the *Medea, Phædra and Hippolitus,* and *Troades of Seneca,* and of the philosophical poem of *Manilius.* The last was honored with the special approbation of the Royal Society. "His poems," says Ellis, "exhibit marks of considerable genius."

Mary weeping for Jesus Lost.

Blest Virgin! who, in tears half drowned,
Griev'st that thy Son cannot be found,
The time will come when men shall hear thee
Complain that He is too, too near thee;
When, in the midst of hostile bands,
With piercèd feet and nailèd hands,
Advanced upon a cursèd tree,
His naked body thou shalt see,
As void of coverture as friends,
But what kind Heaven in pity lends;
Thy soul will then abhor the light,
And think no grief worse than His sight.

The Message.

Dear Saviour! That my love I might make known
To Thee, I sent more messengers than one.
My heart went first, but came not back; my will
I sent Thee next, and that staid with Thee still;

Then, that the better Thou might'st know my mind,
I sent my intellect; that too staid behind.

Good Friday.

This day, Eternal Love, for me
  Fast nailed unto a cursed tree,
Rending His fleshy veil, did, through His side,
  A way to Paradise provide.
This day, Life died, and, dying, overthrew
  Death, sin, and Satan too.
    O happy day!
    May sinners say:
But day can it be said to be,
  Wherein we see
The bright sun of celestial light,
O'ershadow'd with so black a night!

"And they laid Him in a manger."

See! heaven's sacred Majesty
Humbled beneath poverty,
Swaddled up in homely rags,
On a bed of straw and flags.
He, whose hands the heavens display'd
And the world's foundation laid,
From the world's almost exil'd,
Of all ornaments despoil'd:
Pérfumes bathe Him not, new-born,
Persian mantles not adorn.

Where, O Royal Infant! be
The ensigns of Thy Majesty?

Where 's Thy angel-guarded throne,
Whence Thy laws Thou didst make known?
Laws which heaven, earth, hell obey'd.
These, ah! these, aside He laid;
Would the emblem be of pride
By humility outvied.

A Sylvan Scene.

[From the Italian of Girolamo Preti.)

The flowers which on its fertile borders grow,
As if in love with their own beauty, show,
Bending their fragrant tops and slender stems,
Narcissus-like, to gaze on the clear streams,
Where, limned in water-colors to the life,
They see themselves, and raise a pleasing strife
In the deluded sense, at the first view,
To judge which flowers are counterfeit, which true.
On the left hand of this transparent flood,
Fringing the plain's green verge, there stands a wood,
Whose close-weaved branches a new heaven present,
And to the sight form a green firmament;
In which, like fixèd stars, we might espy
Gold-colored apples glitter to the eye;
No vulgar birds there make their mean abodes,
But wingèd heroes, music's demigods.

A maid in love with a youth blind of one eye.

Though a sable cloud benight
One of thy fair twins of light,
Yet the other brighter seems
As't had robbed its brother's beams,

Or both lights to one were run,
Of two stars now made one sun.
Close the other too, and all
Thee the God of Love will call.

[*From Antipater Sidonius.*]

This tomb Maronis holds, o'er which doth stand
A bowl carved out of flint by Mentor's hand.
The tippling crone while living, death of friends
Ne'er touched, nor husband's, nor dear children's ends.
This only troubles her, now dead, to think
The monumental bowl should have no drink.

[*From Cassimir.*]

Whilst timorous Ana led his martial band
'Gainst the invaders of his native land,
Thus he bespake his men before the fight:
"Courage my mates! let's dine; for we, to-night,
Shall sup in heaven." * *   This having said,
Soon as the threatening ensigns were displayed,
And the loud drums and trumpets had proclaimed
Defiance 'twixt the hosts, he, who ne'er shamed
At loss of honor, fairly ran away;
When, being asked how chanced he would not stay
And go along with them to sup in heaven;
"Pardon me, friends!" said he, "I *fast* this even."

[*Cupid dislodged.*]

Naked Love did to thine eye,
Chloris, once, to warm him, fly;
But its subtle flame and light
Scorched his wings and spoiled his sight.

Sherburne.

Forced from thence he went to rest
In the soft couch of thy breast,
But there met a frost so great
As his torch extinguished straight.

When poor Cupid, thus constrained
His cold bed to leave, complained,
"'Las! what lodging's here for me,
If all ice and fire she be!"

The Fountain.

Stranger, whoe'er thou art, that stoop'st to taste
These sweeter streams, let me arrest thy haste;
    Nor of their fall
    The murmurs (though the lyre
    Less sweet be) stand to admire:
    But, as you shall
    See from this marble tun
    The liquid crystal run,
    And mark withall
    How fixt the one abides,
    How fast the other glides,
Instructed thus, the difference learn to see
'Twixt mortal life and immortality.

Magdalen.

The proud Egyptian queen her Roman guest,
  To express her love, in height of state and pleasure,
With pearl, dissolv'd in gold, did feast,—
  Both food and treasure.

And now, dear Lord! Thy lover, on the fair
  And silver table of Thy feet, behold!
Pearl, in her tears, and, in her hair,
  Offers Thee gold.

JOHN DRYDEN.

"Thou great High-Priest of all the Nine."
Churchill on Dryden.

JOHN DRYDEN is supposed to have been born at Aldwinckle, in 1631.* His father is said to have been a strict Puritan.

In 1650 he was sent to Cambridge, where he resided about seven years. He took the degree of A. B., and, by dispensation, was made A. M. In 1657, he settled in London. At the death of Cromwell, in 1658, he became a public candidate for fame, by his *Heroic Stanzas on the late Lord Protector*, in which, prophetic of future excellence, occurs the sublime passage,

" His grandeur he derived from Heaven alone,
    For he was great ere fortune made him so;
And wars, like mists, that rise against the sun,
    Made him but greater seem, not greater grow."

In 1660, however, appeared his *Astræa Redux*, a poem celebrating the "Restoration," and the return of Charles II. In 1662 he composed several short poems, and was elected a member of the Royal Society. At or about the same time, he began to write for the stage.

---

* The exact time and place of his birth seem not to have been ascertained.

Of his *seven and twenty dramas*[2] produced during a period of about thirty years, the best, as splendid literary works at least, are, perhaps, *All for Love*, and *Don Sebastian*.

In 1665 he married the Lady Elizabeth Howard, a daughter of the Earl of Berkshire. The unhappy life which he led with her, may account for the apparently imbittered feeling with which he occasionally speaks of marriage.* Her wayward disposition, however, is supposed to have been the effect of a disordered imagination, as shortly after his death she became insane.

In 1667 he published *Annus Mirabilis*, one of his longest and most elaborate poems. Every stanza presents some strong thought, or vivid description. In that year, or the next, appeared his *Essay on Dramatic Poesy*, especially remarkable for its celebrated account of Shakspeare. In 1670, he was made Poet-laureate and Royal Historiographer. He had, nevertheless, critics to endure and rivals to oppose. The principal wits of the nobility were the Earl of Rochester and the Duke of Buckingham. The former set up Elkanah Settle as his competitor, and, by the Duke and his satirical coadjutors, he was ridiculed in *The Rehearsal*, a farce. His hour of triumph, however, was near. In

---

[2] The stage, for a long period, appears to have been the most, if not only, available resource for such of the English poets as endeavored to subsist by their writings. Some of the great English dramatic poets were also actors, as Shakspeare, Jonson, and others.

* The following epitaph is ascribed to him :
> Here lies my wife, here let her lie ;
> Now she's at rest, and so am I.

It does not, however, appear in Scott's edition of his works.

1681 he published *Absalom and Achitophel.* The success of this bold political poem was almost unprecedented. He was now elevated above all his poetical cotemporaries. Shortly afterwards he renewed his attack on the Earl of Shaftesbury ("Achitophel") in *The Medal,* a poem abounding in strokes of both humorous and serious satire. A second part of *Absalom and Achitophel* appeared, which was mostly written by Nahum Tate. Dryden contributed about two hundred lines, in which the characters of his rivals, Settle and Shadwell, under the names of "Doeg" and "Og" are drawn with a power of personal ridicule, which, perhaps, no other writer has ever equaled. The same may be said of the description of Shadwell in his *Mac Flecknoe,* published in 1682. In that year was also published his *Religio Laici,* a poem, in some respects, of great excellence, written to defend the Church of England against the dissenters, yet regarded as evincing in its author a bias to the Catholic doctrines. To those doctrines, soon after the accession of James II., in 1685, he declared himself a convert. "The conversion," says Johnson, "of such a man at such a time, was not likely to pass uncensured. The clamor seems to have been long continued. It is some proof of Dryden's sincerity in his new religion that he taught it to his sons." "If," remarks Sir Walter Scott, "we are to judge of Dryden's sincerity in his new faith by the determined firmness with which he retained it, we must allow him to have been a martyr, or, at least, a confessor in the Catholic cause. The Catholic religion, and the consequent disqualifications, was an insurmountable obstacle to his holding any office under government; and his adherence to it, with all the poverty, reproach, and even persecution which followed the profession, argued a deep and substantial conviction of the truth of the doctrines which it inculcated."* Mitford says, that Malone entertains no doubt of his sincerity, and proceeds to remark that "the integrity of such a man as Dryden is not to be sullied by suspicions that rest on what, after all, might prove a fortuitous coincidence of circumstances."

These observations are the more satisfactory as coming from Protestant writers. In a well-known passage in *The Hind and The Panther*, alluding to his conversion, he exclaims,

"*Good life* be now my task, my *doubts* are done."

The subject of his *Threnodia Augustalis*, a poem, in which there are fine passages, was the death of Charles II. He undertook the defense of a paper, written by the Duchess of York, stating the motives which had induced her to become a Catholic, and was answered by Stillingfleet. The most remarkable literary result, however, of his change of religion, was *The Hind and The Panther*, a poem, in which the main Catholic argument is fully stated. It appears to have been composed in 1686 and 1687. "The wit in this poem," says the eminent Protestant writer, Hallam, "is sharp, ready and pleasant; the reasoning is sometimes admirably close and strong; it is the energy of Bossuet in verse." It was widely dispersed and eagerly read.

* Sir Walter Scott elsewhere says: "We find that Dryden's conversion was not of that sordid kind which is the consequence of a strong temporal interest; for he had expressed intelligibly the imagined *desiderata* which the Church of Rome alone pretends to supply, long before that temporal interest had an existence."

The birth of the young prince drew from him his *Britannia Rediviva*. His *Ode to the Memory of Miss Anne Killigrew*, Dr. Johnson regarded as the noblest which the English language had ever produced.

The Revolution of 1688 deprived Dryden of his places of poet-laureate and royal historiographer. He could not hold them as being a Catholic. The want, however, of independent income seems to have but stimulated his faculties. Between 1689 and 1698, besides several plays,* one of which, *Don Sebastian*, is perhaps his greatest, he gave to the world versions of Juvenal,† Persius, and Virgil. In 1692 was published his *Eleonora*, a poem which abounds in original and beautiful thought. In 1697 appeared his celebrated *Ode for St. Cecilia's Day*, commonly called "Alexander's Feast." It was followed by a few small pieces, and his, perhaps, most popular work, the *Fables*, published in 1699. In an epistolary poem to Congreve, he says,

> Unprofitably kept at Heaven's expense,
> I live a rent-charge on His providence;

and, in a dedication, speaks of his "sickly age, worn out with study, and oppressed by fortune, without other support than the constancy and patience of a Christian." The consequence of neglecting an inflammation of his feet was a mortification, of which he died on the 1st of May, 1700.‡ He seems to have been sensible till nearly

---

* Want having probably driven him again to the stage.

† In translating Juvenal he was assisted. A translation of Bouhour's Life of St. Francis Xavier is ascribed to him.

‡ Scott and Mitford: Johnson says, 1701.

his last moments. He died in the profession of the Catholic faith, with submission and entire resignation to the Divine will.*

In disposition and moral character Dryden is represented as most amiable. He declares, however, that he was not one of those whose sprightly sayings diverted company. One of his censurers makes him remark of himself,

"To writing bred, I knew not what to say."

By Congreve,† who spoke from observation, he is described as "very modest and very easily to be discountenanced, in his approaches to his equals or superiors." In his youth he appears to have been handsome.‡ He is said to have been short of the middle height, and, at a more advanced age, corpulent and florid.

In the preceding pages, many of his compositions, in both verse and prose, have not been noticed.

[*From "The Hind and The Panther."*]

[The Hind represents the Catholic Church; the Panther, the Church of England. As a controversial poem, this piece has no equal, and is no less remarkable for power of expression than of reasoning. Some of the happiest of Dryden's satirical efforts are its episodes descriptive of Luther, Bishop Burnet, and the Sects.]

---

* Scott. Mitford.
† As cited by Johnson.
‡ Milbourne, his enemy, apostrophizing him, 1690, says,

"Still smooth as when, adorn'd with youthful pride,
For thy dear sake, the blushing virgins died."

A milk-white Hind, immortal and unchanged,
Fed on the lawns and in the forest ranged;
Without unspotted, innocent within,
She feared no danger, for she knew no sin.
Yet had she oft been chased with horns and hounds,
And Scythian shafts; and many wingéd wounds
Aimed at her heart; was often forced to fly,
And doomed to death, though fated not to die.   *   *

   Panting and passive, now she ranged alone,
And wandered in the kingdoms once her own.
The common hunt, though from their rage restrained
By sovereign power, her company disdained;
Grinned as they passed, and with a glaring eye,•
Gave gloomy signs of secret enmity.
'Tis true, she bounded by and tripped so light,
They had not time to take a steady sight;
For truth has such a face and such a mien,
As to be loved needs only to be seen.   *   *

   The Panther, sure the noblest next the Hind,
And fairest creature of the spotted kind;
Oh, could her inborn stains be washed away,
She were too good to be a beast of prey.   *   *
If, as our dreaming Platonists report,
There could be spirits of a middle sort,
Too black for heaven, and yet too white for hell,
Who just dropped half-way down, nor lower fell;
So poised, so gently she descends from high,
It seems a soft dismission from the sky.
Her house not ancient, whatsoe'er pretence
Her clergy-heralds make in her defence;
A second century not half-way run,
Since the new honors of her blood begun.   *   *

Dryden.

Her front erect with majesty she bore,
The crosier wielded and the mitre wore:
Her upper part of decent discipline
Showed affectation of an ancient line,
And fathers, councils, church, and church's head
Were on her reverend phylactèries read.
But what disgraced and disavowed the rest,
Was Calvin's brand, that stigmatized the beast.   * *

Such is her faith; where good cannot be had,
At least she leaves the refuse of the bad,
Nice in her choice of ill, though not of best,
And least deformed, because reformed the least.
In doubtful points betwixt her differing friends,
Where one for substance, one for sign contends,
Their contradicting terms she strives to join;
Sign shall be substance, substance shall be sign.
A real presence all her sons allow,
And yet 'tis flat idolatry to bow,
Because the Godhead's there, they know not how.
Her novices are taught, the bread and wine
Are but the visible and outward sign,
Received by those who in communion join,
But the inward grace, or the thing signified,
His blood and body, who to save us died;
The faithful this thing signified receive;
What is 't those faithful then partake or leave?
For, what is signified and understood
Is, by her own confession, flesh and blood:
Then, by the same acknowledgment, we know
They take the sign and take the substance too.
The literal sense is hard to flesh and blood,
But nonsense never can be understood.   * *

Still, she 's the fairest of the fallen crew,
No mother more indulgent, but the true.
   Fierce to her foes, yet fears her force to try,
Because she wants innate authority;
For how can she constrain them to obey,
Who has herself cast off the lawful sway?
Rebellion equals all, and those who toil
In common theft, will share the common spoil.
Let her produce the title and the right
Against her own superiors first to fight;
If she reform by text, e'en that 's as plain
For her own rebels to reform again.
*As long as words a different sense will bear
And each may be his own interpreter,
Our airy faith will no foundation find,
The* WORD *'s a weather-cock for every wind.*

      *   *   *   *

The wretched Panther cries aloud for aid
To church and councils, whom she first betrayed;
No help from fathers' or tradition's train;
Those ancient guides she taught us to disdain,
And by that scripture, which she once abused
To reformation, stands herself accused.
What bills for breach of laws can she prefer,
Expounding which she owns herself may err? * *
If doubts arise, she slips herself aside,
And leaves the private conscience for the guide:
If then that conscience set the offender free,
It bars her claim to church authority.
How can she censure, or what crime pretend
But scripture may be cónstrued to defend?
Even those, whom for rebellion she transmits
To civil power, her doctrine first acquits;

Because no disobedience can ensue
Where no submission to a judge is due ;
Each judging for himself by her consent,
Whom, thus absolved, she sends to punishment. * *
   Of all the tyrannies on human kind,
The worst is that which persecutes the mind.
Let us but weigh at what offence we strike ;
'Tis but because we cannot think alike.
In punishing of this we overthrow
The law of nations and of nature too.
Beasts are the subjects of tyrannic sway,
Where still the stronger on the weaker prey ;
Man only of a softer mould is made,
Not for his fellows' ruin, but their aid ;
Created kind, beneficent and free,
The noble image of the Deity. * *

[*In the following admired passage Dryden speaks of his recent conversion.*]

   What weight of ancient witness can prevail
If private reason hold the public scale?
But, gracious God! how well dost thou provide
For erring judgments an unerring guide !
Thy throne is darkness in the abyss of light,
A blaze of glory that forbids the sight.
O teach me to believe Thee thus concealed,
And search no farther than Thyself revealed ;
But her alone for my director take
Whom Thou hast promised never to forsake !
My thoughtless youth was winged with vain desires ;
My manhood, long misled by wandering fires,

Followed false lights, and, when their glimpse was gone,
My pride struck out new sparkles of her own.
Such was I, such by nature still I am ;
Be Thine the glory and be mine the shame !
Good life be now my task, my doubts are done.
What more could fright my faith than Three in One?
Can I believe eternal God could lie
Disguised in mortal mould and infancy?
That the great Maker of the world could die?
And, after that, trust my imperfect sense,
Which calls in question His omnipotence?
Can I my reason to my faith compel,
And shall my sight, and touch, and taste rebel?
Superior faculties are set aside ;
Shall their subservient organs be my guide?
Then let the moon usurp the rule of day,
And winking tapers shew the sun his way ;
For what my senses plainly can perceive,
I need no revelation to believe.
Can they who say the Host should be descried
By sense, define a body glorified?
Impassible, and penetrating parts?
Let them declare by what mysterious arts
He shot that body through the opposing might
Of bolts and bars, impervious to the light. * *
For since thus wondrously He passed, 'tis plain
One single place two bodies did contain ;
And sure the same Omnipotence as well
Can make one body in more places dwell. * *

   'Tis urged, again, that faith did first commence
By miracles, which are appeals to sense,
And thence concluded that our sense must be
The motive still of credibility ;

For latter ages must on former wait,
And what began belief, must propagate.
But winnow well this thought, and you shall find
'Tis light as chaff that flies before the wind.
Were all those wonders wrought by power Divine,
As means, or ends, of some more deep design?
Most sure as means, whose end was this alone,
To prove the Godhead of the Eternal Son.
God thus asserted, man is to believe
Beyond what sense and reason can conceive,
And, for mysterious things of faith, rely
On the proponent, Heaven's authority.
If then our faith we for our guide admit,
Vain is the farther search of human wit;
As when the building gains a surer stay
We take the unuseful scaffolding away.
Reason by sense no more can understand;
The game is played into another hand. * *
In the same vessel which our Saviour bore,
Himself the pilot, let us leave the shore. * *
Could He His Godhead veil with flesh and blood,
And not veil these again to be our food? * *
And, if He can, why all this frantic pain
To construe what His clearest words contain,
And make a riddle what He made so plain?
To take up half on trust, and half to try,
Name it not faith, but bungling bigotry.
Both knave and fool the merchant we may call,
To pay great sums and to compound the small;
For who would break with Heaven and would not
    break for all?
Rest then, my soul, from *endless anguish* freed,
Nor sciences thy guide, nor sense thy creed. * *

[*The true guide.*]

HIND. I then affirm that this unfailing guide
In Pope and General Councils must reside;
Both lawful, both combined; what one decrees
By numerous votes the other ratifies:
On this undoubted sense the Church relies.* *
The sacred books, you say, are full and plain,
And every needful point of truth contain;
All who can read interpreters may be:
Thus, though your several churches disagree,
Yet every saint has to himself alone
The secret of this philosophic stone.* *
Ruled by the scripture and his own advice,
Each has a blind by-path to Paradise.* *
 For did not Arius first, Socinus now,
The Son's eternal Godhead disavow?
And did not these, by gospel texts alone,
Condemn our doctrine and maintain their own?
Have not all heretics the same pretence
To plead the scriptures in their own defence?
How did the Nicene council then decide
That strong debate? was it by scripture tried?
No, sure; to that the rebel would not yield;
Squadrons of texts he marshaled in the field.* *
The good old bishops took a simpler way;
Each asked but what he heard his father say,
Or how he was instructed in his youth,
And by tradition's force upheld the truth.
 The Panther smiled at this; and when, said she,
Were those first councils disallowed by me?
Or where did I at sure tradition strike,
Provided still it were apóstolic?

Friend, said the Hind, you quit your former ground,
Where all your faith you did on scripture found:
Now 'tis tradition joined with holy writ;
But thus your memory betrays your wit.
   No, said the Panther; for in that I view
When your tradition's forged, and when 'tis true.
I set them by the rule, and, as they square,
Or deviate from undoubted doctrine there,
This oral fiction, that old faith declare.
   HIND. The Council steered, it seems, a different course;
They tried the scripture by tradition's force;
But you tradition by the scripture try;
Pursued by sects, from this to that you fly,
Nor dare on one foundation to rely.
The word is then deposed, and, in this view,
You rule the scripture, not the scripture you.
Thus said the dame, and smiling thus pursued:
I see tradition then is disallowed,
When not evinced by scripture to be true,
And scripture as interpreted by you.
But here you tread upon unfaithful ground,
Unless you could infallible expound;
Which you reject as odious popery,
And throw that doctrine back with scorn on me.
Suppose we on things traditive divide,
And both appeal to scripture to decide;
By various texts we both uphold our claim,
Nay, often ground our titles on the same.
After long labor lost and time's expense,
Both grant the words and quarrel for the sense.
Thus all disputes forever must depend,
For no dumb rule can controversies end.

Thus, when you said, tradition must be tried
By sacred writ, whose sense yourselves decide,
You said no more, but that yourselves must be
The judges of the scripture sense, not we.
Against our church-tradition you declare,
And yet your clerks would sit in Moses' chair;
At least 'tis proved against your argument,
The rule is far from plain, where all dissent.

   If not by scriptures, how can we be sure,
Replied the Panther, what tradition's pure? * *

   How, but by following her, replied the Dame,
To whom derived from sire to son they came;
Where every age does on another move,
And trusts no farther than the next above;
Where all the rounds like Jacob's ladder rise,
The lowest hid in earth, the topmost in the skies.

   Sternly the savage did her answer mark,
Her glowing eyeballs glittering in the dark,
And said but this: Since lucre was your trade
Succeeding times such dreadful gaps have made,
'Tis dangerous climbing; to your sons and you
I leave the ladder and its omen too. * *

   HIND. As for your answer 'tis but barely urged:
You must evince tradition to be forged,
Produce plain proofs, unblemished authors use,
As ancient as those ages they accuse.* *
Then, for our interest, which is named alone
To load with envy, we retort your own.
For, when traditions in your faces fly,
Resolving not to yield you must decry.
As, when the case goes hard, the guilty man
Excepts and thins his jury all he can;
So, when you stand of other aid bereft,

Dryden.

You to the twelve apostles would be left.
Your friend, the Wolf,* did with more craft provide,
To set those toys, traditions, quite aside,
And fathers, too, unless when, reason spent,
He cites them but sometimes for ornament. * *
The private spirit is a better blind
Than all the dodging tricks your authors find:
For they, who left the scripture to the crowd,
Each for his own peculiar judge allowed;
The way to please them was to make them proud.*
Well may they † argue, nor can you deny,
If we must fix on church authority,
Best on the best, the fountain, not the flood;
That must be better still, if this be good.* *
Shall she command who has herself rebelled?
Is Antichrist by Antichrist expelled?* *
Why all these wars to win the book, if we
Must not interpret for ourselves, but she?
Either be wholly slaves, or wholly free.* *

 Thus she; nor could the Panther well enlarge
With weak defence against so strong a charge;
But said: For what did Christ his word provide,
If still his Church must want a living guide?
And if all saving doctrines are not there,
Or sacred penmen could not make them clear,
From after ages we should hope in vain
For truths which men inspired could not explain.
 Before the word was written, said the Hind,
Our Saviour preached His faith to human kind;

---

* Presbyterian.
† Dissenters from the church of England.

From His apostles the first age received
Eternal truth, and what they taught believed,
Thus, by tradition faith was planted first,
Succeeding flocks succeeding pastors nursed.
This was the way our wise Redeemer chose,
Who sure could all things for the best dispose,
To fence His fold from their encroaching foes.
He could have writ Himself, but well foresaw
The event would be like that of Moses' law;
Some difference would arise, some doubts remain,
Like those which yet the jarring Jews maintain.
No written laws can be so plain, so pure,
But wit may gloss, and malice may obscure.* *
Thus faith was, ere the written word appeared,
And men believed, not what they read, but heard.
But since the apostles could not be confined
To these or those, but severally designed
Their large commission round the world to blow,
To spread their faith, they spread their labours too.
Yet still their absent flock their pains did share;
They hearkened still, for love produces care.
And as mistakes arose, or discords fell,
Or bold seducers taught them to rebel,
As charity grew cold, or faction hot,
Or long neglect their lessons had forgot,
For all their wants they wisely did provide,
And preaching by epistles was supplied.
So, great physicians cannot all attend,
But some they visit, and to some they send.
Yet all those letters were not writ to all;
Nor first intended but occasional,
Their absent sermons; nor, if they contain
All needful doctrines, are those doctrines plain.

Clearness by frequent preaching must be wrought;
They writ but seldom, but they daily taught:
And, what one saint has said of holy Paul,
"He darkly writ," is true applied to all.
For this obscurity could Heaven provide
More prudently than by a living guide,
As doubts arose, the difference to decide?
A guide was therefore needful, therefore made;
And, if appointed, sure to be obeyed.
Thus, with due reverence to the apostles' writ,
By which my sons are taught, to which submit,
I think, those truths, their sacred works contain,
The Church alone can certainly explain;
That following ages, leaning on the past,
May rest upon the primitive at last.
Nor would I thence the word no rule infer,
But none without the church interpreter;
Because, as I have urged before, 'tis mute,
And is itself the subject of dispute.
But what the apostles their successors taught,
They to the next, from them to us is brought,
The undoubted sense which is in scripture taught.
From hence the Church is armed, when errors rise,
To stop their entrance, and prevent surprise.* *
By these* all festering sores her councils heal,
Which time or has disclosed, or shall reveal;
For discord cannot end without a last appeal.
Nor can a council national decide,
But with subordination to her guide,
Much less the scripture; for suppose debate
Betwixt pretenders to a fair estate,
Bequeathed by some legátor's last intent;

* Means previously mentioned.

(Such is our dying Saviour's testament ;)
The will is proved, is opened, and is read ;
The doubtful heirs their differing titles plead ;
All vouch the words their interest to maintain,
And each pretends by those his cause is plain.
Shall then the testament award the right?
No, that's the Hungary for which they fight.* *
The sense is intricate, 'tis only clear
What vowels and what consonants are there.
Therefore 'tis plain, its meaning must be tried
Before some judge appointed to decide.* *

    The dame, who saw her fainting foe retired,
With force renewed to victory aspired ;
And, looking upward to her kindred sky,
As once our Saviour owned His Deity,
Pronounced His words, "She whom you seek am I."
Nor less amazed this voice the Panther heard,
Than were those Jews to hear a God declared.
Then thus the matron modestly renewed :
Let all your prophets and their sects be viewed,
And see to which of them yourselves think fit
The conduct of your conscience to submit.
Each proselyte would vote his doctor best,
With absolute exclusion to the rest;
Thus would your Polish diet disagree
And end, as it began, in anarchy.* *
To church-decrees your articles require
Submission modified, if not entire.
Homage denied, to censure you proceed :
But, when Curtana* will not do the deed,

  * *Curtana.*] The name of King Edward the Confessor's sword without a point, an emblem of mercy, which is carried before the king and queen, at their coronation.

You lay that pointless clergy-weapon by,
And to the laws, your sword of justice fly.
Now this your sects the more unkindly take,
(Those prying varlets hit the blots you make,)
Because some ancient friends of yours declare,
Your only rule of faith your scriptures are,
Interpreted by men of judgment sound,
Which every sect will for themselves expound;
Nor think less reverence to their doctors due
For sound interpretation, than to you.* *
I pass the rest, because your church alone
Of all usurpers best could fill the throne.
But neither you, nor any sect beside,
For this high office can be qualified.
For that which must direct the whole must be
Bound in one bond of faith and unity;
But all your several churches disagree.* *
In short, in doctrine, or in discipline,
Not one reformed can with another join;
But all from each, as from damnation, fly,
No union they pretend, but in non-popery.
Nor, should their members in a synod meet,
Could any church presume to mount the seat,
Above the rest, their discords to decide;
None would obey, but each would be the guide;
And, face to face, dissensions would increase,
For only distance now preserves the peace.
All, in their turns, accusers and accused,
Babel was never half so much confused;
What one can plead, the rest can plead as well;
For amongst equals lies no last appeal,
And all confess themselves are fallible.
Now, since you grant some necessary guide,

All who can err are justly laid aside;
Because a trust so sacred to confer
Shows want of such a sure interpreter;
And how can he be needful who can err? * *
Dumb you were born indeed, but, thinking long,
The Test,* it seems, at last has loosed your tongue;
And, to explain what your forefathers meant,
By real presence in the sacrament,
After long fencing, pushed against a wall,
Your salvo come's that He's not there at all:
There changed your faith, and what may change may fall.
Who can believe what varies every day,
Nor ever was, nor can be at a stay? * *

   Then, granting that unerring guide we want,
That such there is you stand obliged to grant:
Our Saviour else were wanting to supply
Our needs, and obviate that necessity.
It then remains, that church can only be
The guide which owns unfailing certainty.* *
But this annexed condition of the crown,
Immunity from errors, you disown.
For petty royalties you raise debate,
But this unfailing, universal state
You shun, nor dare succeed to such a glorious weight;
And for that cause those promises detest
With which our Saviour did His Church invest;
But strive to evade, and fear to find them true,
As conscious they were never meant to you:
All which the Mother-Church asserts her own,
And with unrivaled claim ascends the throne.

   * The Test Act, passed in 1672-3, enjoined the abjuration of the Real Presence in the sacrament.

So, when of old the Almighty Father sate
In council, to redeem our ruined state,
Millions of millions, at a distance round,
Silent the sacred consistory crowned :
All prompt, with eager pity, to fulfil
The full extent of their Creator's will.
But, when the stern conditions were declared,
A mournful whisper through the host was heard,
And the whole hiérarchy, with heads hung down,
Submissively declined the ponderous proffered crown.
Then, not till then, the eternal Son from high
Rose in the strength of all the Deity;
Stood forth to accept the terms, and underwent
A weight which all the frame of heaven had bent,
Nor he Himself could bear, but as Omnipotent.

  Now,* to remove the least remaining doubt,
That e'en the blear-eyed sects may find her out,
Behold what heavenly rays adorn her brows,
What from his wardrobe her Beloved allows.* *
Behold what marks of majesty she brings,
Richer than ancient heirs of eastern kings.
Her right hand holds the sceptre and the keys,
To show whom she commands, and who obeys;
With these to bind, or set the sinner free,
With that to assert spiritual royalty.

  One in herself not rent by schism, but sound,
Entire, one solid, shining diamond,
Not sparkles shattered into sects like you,
One is the Church, and must be to be true;
One central principle of unity,
As undivided, so from errors free;

    * Marks of the true church from the Nicene Creed.

As one in faith, so one in sanctity.* *
   Thus one, thus pure, behold her largely spread,
Like the fair ocean from her mother-bed;
From east to west triumphantly she rides;
All shores are watered by her swelling tides,
The gospel's sound, diffused from pole to pole,
Where winds can carry, and where waves can roll;
The self-same doctrine of the sacred page
Conveyed to every clime in every age.* *
Thus, of three marks which in the creed we view,
Not one of all can be applied to you;
Much less the fourth. In vain, alas! you seek
The ambitious title of apóstolic:
Godlike descent! 'tis well your blood can be
Proved noble in the third or fourth degree:
For, all of ancient that you had before,
(I mean what is not borrowed from our store,)
Was error fulminated o'er and o'er;
Old heresies condemned in ages past,
By care and time recovered from the blast.
   'Tis said with ease, but never can be proved,
The Church her old foundations has removed,
And built new doctrine on unstable sands;
Judge that, ye winds and rains! you proved her, yet she stands.
Those ancient doctrines charged on her for new,
Show, when, and how, and from what hands they grew.
We claim no power, when heresies grow bold,
To coin new faith, but still declare the old.* *
To prove tradition new, there's somewhat more
Required, than saying, 'twas not used before.* *
   Thus what you call corruptions, are, in truth,
The first plantations of the gospel's youth;

Dryden.

Old standard faith; but cast your eyes again,
And view those errors which new sects maintain,
Or which of old disturbed the Church's peaceful reign:
And we can point each period of the time
When they began, and who begot the crime;
Can calculate how long the eclipse endured,
Who interposed, what digits were obscured;
Of all which are already passed away,
We know the rise, the progress, and decay.
   Despair at our foundations then to strike,
Till you can prove your faith apóstolic;
A limpid stream drawn from the native source;
Succession lawful in a lineal course.
Prove any church, opposed to this our head,
So one, so pure, so unconfinedly spread,
Under one chief of the spirítual state,
The members all combined and all subordinate.
Show such a seamless coat, from schisms so free,
In no communion joined with heresy.
If such a one you find, let truth prevail;
Till when, your weights will in the balance fail.* *
But if you cannot think, (nor sure you can
Suppose in God what were unjust in man,)
That He, the fountain of eternal grace,
Should suffer falsehood, for so long a space,
To banish truth, and to usurp her place;
That seven successive ages should be lost,
And preach damnation at their proper cost;
That all your erring ancestors should die,
Drowned in the abyss of deep idolatry;
If piety forbid such thoughts to rise,
Awake, and open your unwilling eyes!
God hath left nothing for each age undone,

From this to that wherein He sent his Son.* *
   [*Some of the causes of unbelief.*]
   By education most have been misled;
So they believe, because they so were bred.* *
The rest I named before, nor need repeat;
But interest is the most prevailing cheat,
The sly seducer both of age and youth;
They study that and think they study truth.* *
Add long prescription of established laws,
And pique of honour to maintain a cause,
And shame of change, and fear of future ill,
And zeal, the blind conductor of the will;
And chief, among the still-mistaking crowd,
The fame of teachers, obstinate and proud,
And, more than all, the private judge allowed;
Disdain of fathers, which the dance began;
The clown unread, and half-read gentleman.* *
   [*Dryden again speaks of his conversion.*]
If joys hereafter must be purchased here
With loss of all that mortals hold so dear,
Then welcome *infamy* and *public shame*,
And last, *a long farewell to earthly fame!*
'*Tis said with ease, but, Oh, how hardly tried
By haughty souls, to human honour tied!
O sharp convulsive pangs of agonizing pride!*
Down then, thou rebel, never more to rise,
And what thou *didst, and dost, so dearly prize,
That fame, that darling fame, make that thy sacrifice.*
'Tis nothing thou hast given; then add thy tears
For a long race of unrepentant years:
'Tis nothing yet, yet all thou hast to give:
Then add those may-be years thou hast to live:
Yet nothing still: then, poor and naked, come,

Thy Father will receive His unthrift home,
And thy blest Saviour's blood discharge the mighty sum.

[*Luther described.*]

Though our lean faith these rigid laws has given,
The full-fed Mussulman goes fat to heaven;
For his Arabian prophet with delights
Of sense allured his eastern proselytes.
The jolly Luther, reading him, began
To interpret scriptures by his Alcoran;
To grub the thorns beneath our tender feet,
And make the paths of Paradise more sweet;
Bethought him of a wife, ere half-way gone,
For 'twas uneasy traveling alone;
And, in this masquerade of mirth and love,
Mistook the bliss of heaven for bacchanals' above.

[*Description of the Sects under the figures of various animals.*]

The bloody Bear, an independent beast,[1]
Unlicked to form, in groans her hate exprest.
Among the timorous kind, the quaking Hare[2]
Professed neutrality, but would not swear.
Next her, the buffoon Ape,[3] as atheists use,
Mimicked all sects, and had his own to choose.
The bristled baptist Boar,[4] impure as he,
But whitened with the foam of sanctity,
With fat pollutions filled the sacred place
And mountains leveled, in his furious race.
But since the mighty ravage, which he made
In German forests, had his guilt betrayed,
With broken tusks and with a borrowed name,

---

[1] The Independents.   [2] The Quakers.   [3] The Free-thinkers.
[4] The Anabaptists.

He shunned the vengeance, and concealed the shame;
So lurked in sects unseen. With greater guile,
False Reynard [b] fed on consecrated spoil;
The graceless beast by Athanasius first
Was chased from Nice, then, by Socinus nursed,
His impious race their blasphemy renewed,
And nature's King through nature's optics viewed.
Reversed they viewed Him, lessened to their eye,
Nor in an Infant could a God descry:
New swarming sects *to this obliquely tend,*
Hence they began, and here they all will end.
More haughty than the rest, the wolfish race, [c]
Never was so deform'd a beast of grace!
——————————but his rough crest he rears
And pricks up his *predestinating* ears.
His wild, disordered walk, his haggard eyes,
Did all the bestial citizens surprise.*   *
These are the chief; to number o'er the rest,
And stand, like Adam, naming every beast,
Were weary work: nor will the Muse describe
A slimy-born and sun-begotten tribe,
Who, far from steeples and their sacred sound,
In fields their sullen cónventícles found.
These gross, half animated, lumps I leave;
Nor can I think what thoughts they can conceive.
But if they think at all, 'tis sure no higher
Than matter, put in motion, may aspire;
Souls that can scarce ferment their mass of clay:
So drossy, so divisible are they,
As would but serve pure bodies for allay:
Such souls as shards produce, such beetle things

[b] The Unitarians.   [c] The Presbyterians.

Dryden.

As only buzz to heaven with evening wings;
Strike in the dark, offending but by chance;
Such are the blindfold blows of ignorance.
They know not beings, and but hate a name;
To them the Hind and Panther are the same.* *

[*Bishop Burnet described.*]

A portly prince, and goodly to the sight,
He seemed a son of Anach for his height;
Like those whom stature did to crowns prefer,
Black-browed and bluff, like Homer's Jupiter.* *
A theologue more by need than genial bent,
By breeding sharp, by nature confident.
Interest in all his actions was discerned;
More learned than honest, more a wit than learned.
Or forced by fear, or by his profit led,
Or both conjoined, his native clime he fled;[7]
But brought the virtues of his heaven along,
A fair behaviour and a fluent tongue.
And yet, with all his arts, he could not thrive,
The most unlucky parasite alive.
Loud praises to prepare his paths he sent,
And then himself pursued his compliment;
But by reverse of fortune chased away,
His gifts no longer than their authors stay.* *
Oft has he flattered and blasphemed the same,
For in his rage he spares no sovereign's name.
The hero and the tyrant change their style
By the same measure that they frown or smile.
When well received by hospitable foes,
The kindness he returns, is to expose.
For courtesies, though undeserved and great,

---

[7] He was a native of Scotland.

No gratitude in felon-minds beget.* *
His praise of foes is venemously nice,
So touched, it turns a virtue to a vice.* *
Seven sacraments he wisely does disown,
Because he knows *confession stands for one.** *
Prompt to assail, and careless of defense,
Invulnerable in his impudence,
He dares the world ; and, eager of a name,
He thrusts about and justles into fame.
Frontless and satire-proof, he scours the streets
And runs an Indian-muck at all he meets ;
So fond of loud report, that, not to miss
Of being known, (his last and utmost bliss,)
He rather would be known for what he is.
Such was and is the captain of the Test,[8]
Though half his virtues are not here exprest.

Religio Laici.

[This admired poem was written before his conversion, but is supposed to have evinced, in its author, a bias to the Catholic doctrines.]

Dim as the borrowed light of moon and stars
To lonely, weary, wandering travelers,
Is reason to the soul : and, as on high
Those rolling fires discover but the sky,
Not light us here ; so reason's glimmering ray
Was lent, not to assure our doubtful way,
But guide us upward to a better day.
And, as those nightly tapers disappear

---

[8] The "Test Act," which enjoined the abjuration of the Real Presence in the Sacrament,—an act for the passage of which, the words of the poet seem to imply, this bishop was either the prime mover, or the leading advocate.

When day's bright lord ascends our hemisphere;
So pale grows reason at religion's sight,
So dies and so dissolves in supernatural light.
Some few, whose lamp shone brighter, have been led
From cause to cause, to nature's secret head,
And found that one First Principle must be:
But what, or who, that universal He;
Whether some soul encompassing this ball,
Unmade, unmoved, yet making, moving all;
Or various atoms' interfering dance
Leaped into form, the noble work of chance;
Or this great All was from eternity;
Not even the Stagirite* himself could see,
And Epicurus guessed as well as he.
As blindly groped they for a future state,
As rashly judged of Providence and fate;
But least of all could their endeavors find
What most concerned the good of human kind;
For happiness was never to be found,
But vanished from them like enchanted ground.
One thought content the good to be enjoyed;
This every little accident destroyed:
The wiser madmen did for virtue toil,
A thorny, or, at best, a barren soil:
In pleasure some their glutton souls would steep,
But found their line too short, the well too deep,
And leaky vessels which no bliss could keep.
Thus anxious thoughts in endless circles roll,
Without a centre where to fix the soul:
In this wild maze their vain endeavors end;
How can the less the greater comprehend,

* Aristotle.

Or finite reason reach infinity?
For what could fathom God were more than He.
  The Deist thinks he stands on firmer ground;
Cries "Εὕρηκα!"[1] the mighty secret's found:
God is that spring of good; supreme and best;
We made to serve, and in that service blest.
If so, some rules of worship must be given,
Distributed alike to all by Heaven;
Else God were partial and to some denied
The means His justice should for all provide.
This general worship is to praise and pray;
One part to borrow blessing, one to pay:
And when frail nature slides into offence,
The sacrifice for crimes is penitence.
Yet since the effects of Providence, we find,
Are variously dispensed to human kind;
That vice triumphs, and virtue suffers here,
A brand that sovereign justice cannot bear;
Our reason prompts us to a future state,
The last appeal from fortune and from fate,
Where God's all-righteous ways will be declared;
The bad meet punishment, the good reward.
  Thus, man by his own strength to heaven would soar,
And would not be obliged to God for more.
Vain, wretched creature, how art thou misled,
To think thy wit these god-like notions bred!
These truths are not the product of thy mind,
But dropt from heaven, and of a nobler kind.
Revealed Religion first informed thy sight,
And Reason saw not, till Faith sprung the light.
Hence all thy natural worship takes the source;
'Tis revelation what thou think'st discourse.
Else how com'st thou to see these truths so clear,

[1] Eureka, (I have discovered it.)

Which so obscure to heathens did appear?
Not Plato these, nor Aristotle found,
Nor he [1] whose wisdom oracles renowned.
Hast thou a wit so deep, or so sublime,
Or canst thou deeper dive, or higher climb?
Canst thou by reason more of Godhead know
Than Plutarch, Seneca, or Cicero?
          [*The Bible.*]
Whether from length of time its worth we draw,
The world is scarce more ancient than the law:
Heaven's early care prescribed for every age,
First in the soul, and after in the page.
Or, whether more abstractedly we look,
Or on the writers, or the written book,
Whence, but from Heaven, could men unskilled in arts,
In several ages born, in several parts,
Weave such agreeing truths? or how, or why
Should all conspire to cheat us with a lie?
Unasked their pains, ungrateful their advice,
Starving their gain, and martyrdom their price.
If on the book itself we cast our view,
Concurrent heathens prove the story true:
The doctrine, miracles: which must convince,
For Heaven in them appeals to human sense.
And, though they prove not, they confirm the cause,
When what is taught agrees with nature's laws.
    Then for the style, majestic and divine,
It speaks no less than God in every line;
Commanding words; whose force is still the same
As the first fiat that produced our frame.
All faiths beside, or did by arms ascend,
Or sense indulged has made mankind their friend;

---

[1] Socrates.

This only doctrine does our lusts oppose,
Unfed by nature's soil in which it grows;
Cross to our interests, curbing sense and sin,
Oppressed without, and undermined within,
It thrives through pain; its own tormentors tires,
And with a stubborn patience still aspires.
To what can reason such effects assign,
Transcending nature, but to laws divine?
But stay: the deist here will urge anew,
No supernatural worship can be true:
Because a general law is that alone
Which must to all, and everywhere, be known;
A style so large as not this book can claim,
Nor aught that bears revealed religion's name.
'Tis said the sound of a Messiah's birth
Is gone through all the habitable earth:
But still that text must be confined alone
To what was then inhabited and known:
And what provision could from thence accrue
To Indian souls and worlds discovered new?
In other parts, it helps, that ages past
The scriptures there were known, and were embraced,
Till sin spread once again the shades of night:
What's that to these who never saw the light?

   Of all objections this indeed is chief
To startle reason, stagger frail belief.
We grant, 'tis true, that Heaven from human sense
Has hid the secret paths of Providence:
But boundless wisdom, boundless mercy, may
Find e'en for those bewildered souls a way;
If from His nature foes may pity claim,
Much more may strangers who ne'er heard His name.
And though no name be for salvation known,

But that of His Eternal Son's alone;
Who knows how far transcending goodness can
Extend the merits of that Son to man?
Who knows what reasons may His mercy lead,
Or ignorance invincible may plead?
Not only charity bids hope the best,
But more the great apostle has expressed:
That, if the Gentiles, whom no law inspired,
By nature did what was by law required
They, who the written rule had never known,
Were to themselves both rule and law alone:
To nature's plain indictment they shall plead;
And by their conscience be condemned or freed.
Most righteous doom! because a rule revealed
Is none to those from whom it was concealed.

[*Tradition.*]
Must all tradition, then, be set aside?
This to affirm were ignorance or pride.
Are there not many points, some needful sure
To saving faith, that scripture leaves obscure?
Which every sect will wrest a several way,
For what one sect interprets all sects may.
We hold, and say we prove from scripture plain,
That Christ is God; the bold Socinian
From the same scripture urges He's but man.
Now what appeal can end the important suit?
Both parts talk loudly, but the rule is mute.

[*The Bible in the hands of the ignorant and fanatical.*]
The book thus put in every vulgar hand,
Which each presumed he best could understand,
The common rule was made the common prey,
And at the mercy of the rabble lay;
The tender page by horny fists was galled,

And he was gifted most that loudest bawled ;
The spirit gave the doctoral degree,
And every member of a company,
Was of his trade and of the Bible free.
Each was ambitious of the obscurest place,
No measure ta'en from knowledge, all from grace.
Study and pains were now no more their care ;
Texts were explained by fasting and by prayer.
This was the fruit the private spirit brought,
Occasioned by great zeal and little thought.
While crowds unlearned, with rude devotion warm,
About the sacred viands buzz and swarm ;
The fly-blown text creates a crawling brood,
And turns to maggots what was meant for food.
A thousand daily sects uprise and die ;
A thousand more the perished race supply :
So, all we make of Heaven's discovered will,
Is not to have it, or to use it ill.* *
What then remains, but, waiving each extreme,
The tides of ignorance and pride to stem?
Neither so rich a treasure to forego,
Nor proudly seek beyond our power to know :
For 'tis not likely we should higher soar
In search of Heaven, than all the Church before.
Faith is not built on disquisitions vain ;
The things we must believe are few and plain.
The unlettered Christian, who believes in gross,
Plods on to heaven, and ne'er is at a loss :
For the strait gate would be made straiter yet,
Were none admitted there but men of wit.

[*From " Absalom and Achitophel."*]

[The subject of this celebrated Political poem is the conspiracy of the Earl of Shaftesbury and others, in the reign of Charles II., to place the Duke of Monmouth, the eldest of the king's sons, on the throne.]

[*The Duke of Monmouth, as "Absalom," described.*]
Early in foreign fields he won renown,
With kings and states allied to Israel's * crown :
In peace the thoughts of war he could remove,
And seemed as he were only born for love.
Whate'er he did was done with so much ease,
In him alone 'twas natural to please :
His motions all accompanied with grace ;
And Paradise was opened in his face.
    What cannot praise effect in mighty minds,
When flattery soothes and when ambition blinds?
    Surrounded thus with friends of every sort
Deluded Absalom forsakes the court,
Impatient of high hopes, urged with renown,
And fired with near possession of a crown.
The admiring crowd are dazzled with surprise,
And on his goodly person feed their eyes :
His joy concealed, he sets himself to show,
On each side bowing popularly low :
His looks, his gestures, and his words he frames,
And with familiar ease, repeats their names.
Youth, beauty, graceful action, seldom fail,
But common interest always will prevail ;
And pity never ceases to be shown
To him who makes the people's wrongs his own.

[*The Earl of Shaftesbury, as "Achitophel," described.*†]
[From the same.]
Some by their friends, more by themselves thought wise,

  * England's.
  † This specimen and other passages in the writings of Dryden, place him in the first rank of delineators of character.

Opposed the power to which they could not rise.
Some had in courts been great, and thrown from thence,
Like fiends were hardened in impenitence.
Some, by their monarch's fatal mercy, grown
From pardoned rebels kinsmen to the throne,
Were raised in power and public office high;
Strong bands, if bands ungrateful men could tie.

  Of these the false ACHITOPHEL was first,
A name to all succeeding ages curst:
For close designs and crooked counsels fit;
Sagacious, bold, and turbulent of wit;
Restless, unfixed in principles and place;
In power unpleased, impatient of disgrace;
A fiery soul, which, working out its way,
Fretted the pigmy body to decay,
And o'erinformed the tenement of clay.
A daring pilot in extremity;
Pleased with the danger when the waves went high,
He sought the storms; but, for a calm unfit,
Would steer too nigh the sands to boast his wit.
Great wits are sure to madness near allied,
And thin partitions do their bounds divide;
Else why should he, with wealth and honor blest,
Refuse his age the needful hours of rest?
Punish a body which he could not please?
Bankrupt of life, yet prodigal of ease:
And all, to leave what with his toil he won
To that unfeathered, two-legged thing, a son.
In friendship false, implacable in hate,
Resolved to ruin, or to rule the state,
To compass this, the triple bond * he broke,

---

* The alliance of England with Sweden and Holland.

And fitted Israel* for a foreign yoke:
Then, seized with fear, yet still affecting fame,
Usurped a patriot's all-atoning name;
So easy still it proves, in factious times,
With public zeal to cancel private crimes.
How safe is treason, and how sacred ill,
Where none can sin against the people's will!
Where crowds can wink, and no offence be known,
Since in another's guilt they find their own!
Yet fame deserved no enemy can grudge;
The statesman we abhor, but praise the judge;
Unbribed, unsought, the wretched to redress,
Swift of dispatch and easy of access.
Oh! had he been content to serve the crown
With virtues only proper to the gown;
Or had the rankness of the soil been freed
From cockles that oppressed the noble seed.
But wild ambition loves to slide, not stand,
And fortune's ice prefers to virtue's land.
Achitophel, grown weary to possess
A lawful fame, and lazy happiness,
Disdained the golden fruit to gather free,
And lent the crowd his arm to shake the tree.

[*Villiers, Duke of Buckingham*,† as "*Zimri*," *described.*]
[From the same].

Some of their chiefs were princes of the land;
In the first rank of these did ZIMRI stand;
A man so various that he seemed to be

---

* England.

† A principal author of "The Rehearsal," in which Dryden was ridiculed.

Not one, but all mankind's epitome :
Stiff in opinions, always in the wrong,
Was everything by starts and nothing long ;
But, in the course of one revolving moon,
Was chymist, fiddler, statesman and buffoon ;
Then all for women, painting, rhyming, drinking,
Besides ten thousand freaks that died in thinking.
Blest madman ! who could every hour employ
With something new to wish, or to enjoy.
Railing and praising were his usual themes,
And both, to show his judgment, in extremes.
In squandering wealth was his peculiar art,
Nothing went unrewarded but desert :
Beggared by fools, whom still he found too late,
He had his jest, and they had his estate.
He laughed himself from court, then sought relief
By forming parties, but could ne'er be chief.
Thus wicked but in will, of means bereft,
He left not faction, but of that was left.

[" *Doeg,*" * *described.*]
[From the same.]

DOEG, though without knowing how or why,
Made still a blundering kind of melody,
Free from all meaning, whether good or bad,
And, in one word, heroically mad.
Spiteful he is not, though he wrote a satire,

* Elkanah Settle, one of Dryden's poetical rivals. Neither he, nor Shadwell and Flecknoe, may have merited the castigation inflicted in this and the two next pieces, which are here introduced chiefly as exemplifications of Dryden's unrivaled satiric power. As ludicrous pictures, they will, at least, serve to amuse.

For still there goes some thinking to ill-nature.
He needs no more than birds and beasts to think,
All his occasions are to eat and drink.
Let him be gallows-free, by my consent,
And nothing suffer, since he nothing meant;
Hanging supposes human soul and reason;
This animal's below committing treason.
Railing in other men may be a crime,
But ought to pass for mere instinct in him:
Instinct he follows, and no farther knows,
For to write verse with him is to transpose.
Let him rail on, let his invective muse
Have four and twenty letters to abuse,
Which if he jumbles to one line of sense,
Indict him of a capital offense.

[" Og," * described.]

[From the same.]

With all this bulk there's nothing lost in OG,
For every inch that is not fool is rogue.
With wealth he was not trusted, for Heaven knew
What 'twas of old to pamper up a Jew.
Thou art of lasting make, like thoughtless men,
A strong nativity but for the pen;
Eat opium, mingle arsenic with thy drink,
Still thou may'st live, avoiding pen and ink.
Rhyme is the rock on which thou art to wreck,
'Tis fatal to thy fame and to thy neck.
DOEG to thee, thy painting is so coarse,
A poet is, though he's the poet's horse.

* Thomas Shadwell, another poetical rival of Dryden.

A double noose thou on thy neck dost pull,
For writing treason and for writing dull.

[*From* "*Mac Flecknoe.*" [1]]

[This poem has been called " The sublime of satire."]

All human things are subject to decay,
And, when fate summons, monarchs must obey.
This FLECKNOE found, who, like Augustus, young
Was called to empire, and had governed long ;
In prose and verse, was owned, without dispute,
Through all the realms of Nonsense absolute.
This aged prince, now flourishing in peace,
And blessed with issue of a large increase ;
Worn out with business, did at length debate
To settle the succession of the state ;
And pondering which of all his sons was fit
To reign, and wage immortal war with wit,
Cried, 'Tis resolved ; for nature pleads that he
Should only rule who most resembles me.
SHADWELL alone my perfect image bears,
Mature in dulness from his tender years ;
Shadwell alone, of all my sons, is he
Who stands confirmed in full stupidity.
The rest to some faint meaning make pretence,
But Shadwell never deviates into sense :
Some beams of wit on other souls may fall,
Strike through, and make a lucid interval,
But Shadwell's genuine night admits no ray ;
His rising fogs prevail upon the day.
Besides, his goodly fabric fills the eye,[2]

---

[1] i. e. Son of Flecknoe.
[2] He was remarkable for his corpulency.

And seems designed for thoughtless majesty;
Thoughtless as monarch oaks, that shade the plain,
And, spread in solemn state, supinely reign.
   Here stopped the good, old sire, and wept for joy,
In silent raptures of the hopeful boy.
All arguments, but most his plays, persuade,
That for anointed dulness he was made.
Now empress Fame had published the renown
Of Shadwell's coronation through the town.
The hoary prince in majesty appeared,
High on a throne of his own labours* reared;
At his right hand our young Ascanius sat,
Rome's other hope, and pillar of the state;
His brows thick fogs, instead of glories, grace,
And lambent dulness played around his face.
As Hannibal did to the altars come,
Sworn by his sire, a mortal foe to Rome,
So Shadwell swore, nor should his vow be vain,
That he to death true dulness would maintain,
And, in his father's right and realm's defence,
Ne'er to have peace with wit, nor truce with sense.
The king himself the sacred unction made,
As king by office, and as priest by trade;
In his sinister hand, instead of ball,
He placed a mighty mug of potent ale.
His temples last with poppies were o'erspread,
That nodding seemed to consecrate his head.
Just at the point of time, if fame not lie,
On his left hand twelve reverend owls did fly:
So Romulus, 'tis sung, by Tiber's brook,
Presage of sway from twice six vultures took.

* Writings.

The admiring throng loud acclamations make,
And omens of his future empire take.
The sire then shook the honours of his head
And from his brows damps of oblivion shed
Full on the filial dulness. Long he stood,
Repelling from his breast the angry god;
At length burst out, in this prophetic mood,
" Heavens bless my son! from Ireland let him reign
To far Barbadoes on the western main.
Success let others teach; learn thou from me
Pangs without birth and fruitless industry:
Let 'Virtuosos'[4] in five years be writ,
Yet not one thought accuse thy toil of wit.
Nor let false friends seduce thy mind to fame
By arrogating Jonson's hostile name:[5]
Thou art my blood, where Jonson has no part;
What share have we in nature and in art?
Where did his wit on learning fix a brand
And rail at arts he did not understand?
When did his muse from Fletcher scenes purloin,
As thou whole Etheredge dost transfuse to thine?
But so transfused as oil and waters flow;
His always floats above, thine sinks below.
Like mine thy gentle numbers feebly creep;
Thy tragic muse gives smiles, thy comic sleep;
With whate'er gall thou sett'st thyself to write,
Thy inoffensive satires never bite."

    He said; but his last words were scarcely heard;
For Bruce and Longvil[6] had a trap prepared,
And down they sent the yet declaiming bard.

[4] "The Virtuoso" is the title of a play by Shadwell.
[5] He affected the character of Ben Jonson.
[6] Characters in Shadwell's "Virtuoso."

Sinking he left his drugget robe behind,
Borne upwards by a subterranean wind.
The mantle fell to the young prophet's part,
With double portion of his father's art.

[*From " The Medal."*]
[Character of the Earl of Shaftesbury.]

A martial hero first, with early care,
Blown, like a pigmy by the winds, to war ;
A beardless chief, a rebel ere a man,
So young his hatred to his prince began.
Next this, (how wildly will ambition steer !)
A vermin wriggling in the Usurper's * ear.
Bartering his venal wit for sums of gold,
He cast himself into the saint-like mould ;
Groaned, sighed, and prayed, while godliness was gain,
The loudest bag-pipe of the squeaking train.
Power was his aim ; but thrown from that pretence,
The wretch turned loyal in his own defence,
Behold him now exalted into trust ;
His counsel's oft convenient, seldom just.
E'en in the most sincere advice he gave,
He had a grudging still to be a knave.
The frauds he learned in his fanatic years,
Made him uneasy in his lawful gears.
At best as little honest as he could,
And, like white witches, mischievously good.
To his first bias longingly he leans,
And rather would be great by wicked means.

[*Apostrophe to Shaftesbury.*]
But thou, the pander of the people's hearts,

* Cromwell's.

O crooked soul, and serpentine in arts,
What curses on thy blasted name will fall!
Which age to age their legacy shall call.
Religion thou hast none; thy mercury
Has passed through every sect, or theirs through thee.
Yet, should thy crimes succeed, should lawless power
Compass those ends thy greedy hopes devour,
Thy canting friends thy mortal foes would be,
Thy God and theirs will never long agree;
For thine, if thou hast any, must be one
That lets the world and human-kind alone;
A jolly god, that passes hours too well,
To promise heaven, or threaten us with hell:
A tyrant theirs; the heaven their priesthood paints
A cònventìcle of gloomy, sullen saints;*
A heaven, like Bedlam, slovenly and sad,
Foredoomed for souls with false religion mad.

[*From " Eleonora."*]

[The subject of this panegyric, perhaps the most beautiful ever composed on any one of her sex, was the Countess of Abingdon. The date of it being subsequent to that of Dryden's conversion, the presumption is that she was a Catholic.]

As when some great and gracious monarch dies,
Soft whispers, first, and mournful murmurs, rise
Among the sad attendants; then the sound
Soon gathers voice, and spreads the news around,
Through town and country, till the dreadful blast
Is blown to distant colonies at last,
Who then, perhaps, were offering vows in vain,
For his long life, and for his happy reign:

---

* The sectarian fanatics.

So slowly, by degrees, unwilling fame
Did matchless Eleonora's fate proclaim,
Till public as the loss the news became.
  The nation felt it in the extremest parts,
With eyes o'erflowing and with bleeding hearts;
But most the poor, whom daily she supplied,
Beginning to be such, but when she died.
For, while she lived, they slept in peace by night,
Secure of bread, as of returning light;
And with such firm dependence on the day,
That need grew pampered, and forgot to pray;
So sure the dole, so ready at their call,
They stood prepared to see the manna fall.
Of her five talents other five she made;
Heaven, that had largely given, was largely paid:
Nor did her alms from ostentation fall,
Or proud desire of praise; the soul gave all.
Want passed for merit at her open door:
Heaven saw, He safely might increase His poor,
And trust their sustenance with her so well,
As not to be at charge for miracle.
None could be needy, whom she saw or knew;
All in the compass of her sphere she drew.
The distant heard, by fame, her pious deeds,
And laid her up for their extremest needs;
A future cordial for a fainting mind;
For, what was ne'er refused, all hoped to find,
Each in his turn: the rich might freely come,
As to a friend; but to the poor, 'twas home.
For zeal like hers her servants were too slow;
.She was the first, where need required, to go.
    Yet, was she not profuse; but feared to waste,
And wisely managed, that the stock might last;

That all might be supplied, and she not grieve,
When crowds appeared, she had not to relieve:
Which to prevent she still increased her store;
Laid up, and spared, that she might give the more.

    Now, as all virtues keep the middle line,
Yet somewhat more to one extreme incline,
Such was her soul; abhorring avarice,
Bounteous, but almost bounteous to a vice:
Had she given more, it had profusion been,
And turned the excess of goodness into sin.

    These virtues raised her fabric to the sky;
For that, which is next heaven, is charity.
But, as high turrets for their airy steep
Require foundations in proportion deep;
So low did her secure foundation lie,
She was not humble, but humility.
Scarcely she knew that she was great or fair,
Or wise, beyond what other women are,
Or, which is better, knew, but never durst compare.
For, to be conscious of what all admire,
And not be vain, advances virtue higher.
But still she found, or rather thought she found
Her own worth wanting, others' to abound;
Ascribed above their due to every one,
Unjust and scanty to herself alone.

    Such her devotion was, as might give rules
Of speculation to disputing schools.
Business might shorten, not disturb her prayer;
Heaven had the best, if not the greatest share.
An active life long orisons forbids;
Yet still she prayed, for still she prayed by deeds.

    Her every day was sabbath, only free
From hours of prayer, for hours of charity.

Such as the Jews from servile toil released,
Where works of mercy were a part of rest;
Such as blest angels exercise above,
Varied with sacred hymns and acts of love.
All this she practiced here, that, when she sprung
Amidst the choirs, at the first sight she sung;
Sung, and was sung herself in angels' lays;
For, praising her, they did her Maker praise.
All offices of heaven so well she knew,
Before she came, that nothing there was new;
And she was so familiarly received
As one returning, not as one arrived.

   A wife as tender, and as true withall,
As the first woman was before her fall:
Made for the man, of whom she was a part,
Made to attract his eyes and keep his heart;
A second Eve, but by no crime accurst,
As beauteous, not as brittle as the first.
Had she been first, still Paradise had been,
And death had found no entrance by her sin.
So she not only had preserved from ill
Her sex and ours, but lived their pattern still.

   Love and obedience to her lord she bore;
She much obeyed him, but she loved him more:
Not awed to duty by superior sway,
But taught by his indulgence to obey.

   Though all these rare endowments of the mind
Were in a narrow space of life confined,
The figure was with full perfection crowned;
Though not so large an orb, as truly round.
   AS WHEN IN GLORY, THROUGH THE PUBLIC PLACE,*

---

* As a similitude, this passage has been regarded as the finest in the English language.

The spoils of conquered nations were to pass,
And but one day for triumph was allowed,
The consul was constrained his pomp to crowd;
And so the swift procession hurried on,
That all, though not distinctly, might be shown:
So, in the straitened bounds of life confined,
She gave but glimpses of her glorious mind,
And multitudes of virtues passed along,
Each pressing foremost in the mighty throng,
Ambitious to be seen, and then make room
For greater multitudes that were to come.
As precious gums are not for lasting fire,
They but perfume the temple and expire;
So was she soon exhaled, and vanished hence,
A short, sweet odour, of a vast expense.
One sigh did her eternal bliss assure;
So little penance needs, when souls are almost pure.*

 Let this suffice: nor thou, great saint, refuse
This humble tribute of no vulgar muse;
Who, not by cares, or wants, or age deprest,
Stems a wild deluge with a dauntless breast;
And dares to sing thy praises in a clime
Where vice triumphs and virtue is a crime;
Where e'en to draw the picture of thy mind
Is satire on the most of human kind.
 Be what and where thou art; to wish thy place
Were in the best presumption more than grace.
Thy relics (such thy works of mercy are)
Have, in this poem, been my holy care.
As earth thy body keeps, thy soul the sky,
So shall this verse preserve thy memory;
For thou shalt make it live, because it sings of thee.

    * She died suddenly.

Dryden.

[*From " Ode to the Memory of Miss Anne Killigrew."*]

[This ode Dr. Johnson calls the noblest which the English language has ever produced.]

Thou youngest virgin-daughter of the skies,
    Made in the last promotion of the blest;
Whose palms, new plucked from Paradise,
In spreading branches more sublimely rise,
    Rich with immortal green, above the rest:
Whether, adopted to some neighbouring star,
    Thou roll'st above us, in thy wandering race;
Or, in procession fixed and regular,
    Mov'st with the heaven's majestic pace;
    Or, called to more superior bliss,
Thou tread'st with seraphims the vast abyss:
Whatever happy region is thy place,
Cease thy celestial song a little space!
Thou wilt have time enough for hymns divine,
    Since heaven's eternal year is thine.
Hear, then, a mortal muse thy praise rehearse,
    In no ignoble verse;
But such as thy own voice did practice here,
    When thy first fruits of poesy were given,
To make thyself a welcome inmate there,
    While yet a young probationer
    And candidate of heaven.

    If by traduction came thy mind,
    Our wonder is the less to find
A soul so charming from a stock so good;
Thy father was transfused into thy blood:

So wert thou born into a tuneful strain,
An early, rich, and inexhausted vein.
    But, if thy preëxisting soul
        Was formed, at first, with myriads more,
It did through all the mighty poets roll,
        Who Greek or Latin laurels wore,
And was that Sappho last, which once it was before.
    If so, then cease thy flight, O heaven-born mind!
Thou hast no dross to purge from thy rich ore:
    Nor can thy soul a fairer mansion find,
    Than was the beauteous frame she left behind:
Return to fill or mend the choir of thy celestial kind!

Thy brother angels, at thy birth,
    Strung each his lyre, and tuned it high,
    That all the people of the sky
Might know a poetess was born on earth:
    And then, if ever, mortal ears
    Had heard the music of the spheres.

O gracious God! how far have we
Prophaned Thy heavenly gift of poesy?
What can we say to excuse our second fall?
Let this, Thy vestal, Heaven, atone for all:
    Her Arethusian stream remains unsoiled;
Her wit was more than man, her innocence a child.

    Art she had none, yet wanted none;
        For nature did that want supply;
    So rich in treasures of her own,
        She might our boasted stores defy.
Such noble vigour did her verse adorn,
    That it seemed borrowed where 'twas only born.
Each test and every light her muse will bear,

Though Epictetus with his lamp were there.
E'en love (for love sometimes her muse exprest)
Was but a lambent flame which played about her breast;
    Light as the vapours of a morning dream:
So cold herself, while she such warmth exprest,
    'Twas Cupid bathing in Diana's stream.

Born to the spacious empire of the Nine,
One would have thought she should have been content
To manage well that mighty government;
    But what can young, ambitious souls confine?
    To the next realm she stretched her sway,
    For painture near adjoining lay.
Her pencil drew whate'er her soul designed,
And oft the happy draught surpassed the image in her mind:
    The sylvan scenes of herds and flocks
    And fruitful plains and barren rocks;
    Of shallow brooks that flowed so clear,
    The bottom did the top appear;
    Of deeper too and ampler floods
    Which, as in mirrors, showed the woods;
    The ruins too of some majestic piece
    Boasting the power of ancient Rome or Greece;
What nature, art, bold fiction, e'er durst frame,
Her forming hand gave feature to the name.

Thus, nothing to her genius was denied;
    But, like a ball of fire the further thrown,
    Still with a greater blaze she shone,
And her bright soul broke out on every side.

When in mid-air the golden trump shall sound
    To raise the nations under ground;

When, in the valley of Jehosophat,
The judging God shall close the book of fate;
  And there the last assizes keep
  For those who wake and those who sleep;
The sacred poets first shall hear the sound
And foremost from the tomb shall bound,
For they are covered with the lightest ground;
And straight, with inborn vigor, on the wing,
Like mounting larks, to the new morning sing.
There thou, sweet saint, before the choir shall go,
As harbinger of heaven, the way to show,
The way which thou so well hast learnt below.

[*From " Epitaph on Miss Mary Frampton."*]

Below this marble monument is laid
All that heaven wants of this celestial maid.
Preserve, O sacred tomb, thy trust consigned;
The mould was made on purpose for the mind:
And she would lose, if, at the latter day,
One atom could be mixed of other clay.
Such were the features of her heavenly face,
Her limbs were formed with such harmonious grace,
So faultless was the frame, as if the whole
Had been an emanation of the soul,
Which her own inward symmetry revealed,
And like a picture shone, in glass annealed;
Or, like the sun eclipsed, with shaded light;
Too piercing else to be sustained by sight.
All white, a virgin saint, she sought the skies:
For marriage, though it sullies not, it dyes.
High though her wit, yet humble was her mind;
As if she would not, or she could not find

How much her worth transcended all her kind.
Yet she had learned so much of heaven below,
That when arrived she scarce had more to know;
But only to refresh the former hint,
And read her Maker in a fairer print.
So pious, as she had no time to spare
For human thoughts, but was confined to prayer,
Yet, in such charities she passed the day,
'Twas wondrous how she found a time to pray.
A soul so calm, it knew not ebbs or flows,
Which passion could but curl, not discompose;
A female softness, with a manly mind;
A daughter duteous, and a sister kind;
In sickness patient, and in death resigned.

[*From "Epitaph on Mrs. Paston."*]

Heaven's image was in her so well exprest,
Her very sight upbraided all the rest.

On Milton.

Three poets, in three distant ages born,
Greece, Italy, and England, did adorn.
The first in loftiness of thought surpassed;
The next in majesty; in both the last.
The force of Nature could no further go;
To make a third, she joined the other two. *

---

* Malone regards these verses as an amplification of the following by Selvaggi:

Græcia Mœonidem jactet sibi, Roma Maronem; Anglia Miltonem jactat utrique parem.

[*From "Alexander's Feast, or the Power of Music," an ode for St. Cecilia's day.*]

    'Twas at the royal feast, for Persia won
        By Philip's warlike son,
      Aloft, in awful state,
      The godlike hero sate
        . On his imperial throne.
    His valiant peers were placed around,
Their brows with roses and with myrtles bound;
    So should desert in arms be crowned.
The lovely Thais by his side
Sate like a blooming, Eastern bride,
In flower of youth and beauty's pride.
    Happy, happy, happy pair!
      None but the brave,
      None but the brave,
    None but the brave deserves the fair.

Timotheus, placed on high
    Amid the tuneful quire,
    With flying fingers touched the lyre;
The trembling notes ascend the sky
    And heavenly joys inspire.
The listening crowd admire the lofty sound;
A present deity! they shout around;
A present deity! the vaulted roofs rebound.

---

* "In lyrical power Dryden must be allowed to have no equal. *Alexander's Feast*, is sufficient to show his superiority in that brilliant Department." Sir Walter Scott.

St. Cecilia, from her assiduity in singing the divine praises, in which she is said to have often joined instrumental music with vocal, is regarded as the patroness of church-music.

      With ravished ears
      The monarch hears,
      Assumes the god,
      Affects to nod,
  And seems to shake the spheres.

The praise of Bacchus then the sweet musician sung,
  Of Bacchus ever fair and ever young;
    The jolly god in triumph comes;
    Sound the trumpets; beat the drums;
    Flushed with a purple grace,
    He shows his honest face:
Now, give the hautboys breath; he comes, he comes!
    Bacchus, ever fair and young,
    Drinking joys did first ordain;
    Bacchus' blessings are a treasure,
    Drinking is the soldier's pleasure;
        Rich the treasure,
        Sweet the pleasure,
  Sweet is pleasure after pain.

  Soothed with the sound, the king grew vain;
    Fought all his battles o'er again;
And thrice he routed all his foes; and thrice he
      slew the slain.
    The master saw the madness rise,
  His glowing cheeks, his ardent eyes;
And, while he heaven and earth defied,
Changed his hand, and checked his pride.
      He chose a mournful muse,
      Soft pity to infuse:
He sung Darius, great and good,
    By too severe a fate

Fallen, fallen, fallen, fallen,
Fallen from his high estate,
And weltering in his blood:
Deserted, at his utmost need,
By those his former bounty fed,
On the bare earth exposed he lies,
With not a friend to close his eyes.
With downcast looks the joyless victor sate,
Revolving, in his altered soul,
The various turns of chance below,
And, now and then, a sigh he stole,
And tears began to flow.

The mighty master smiled, to see
That love was in the next degree;
'Twas but a kindred sound to move;
For pity melts the mind to love.
Softly sweet, in Lydian measures,
Soon he soothed his soul to pleasures;
War, he sung, is toil and trouble,
Honour, but an empty bubble;
Never ending, still beginning,
Fighting still, and still destroying;
If the world be worth thy winning;
Think, O think it worth enjoying!
Lovely Thais sits beside thee,
Take the good the gods provide thee.
The many rend the skies with loud applause;
So love was crowned, but music won the cause.
The prince, unable to conceal his pain,
Gazed on the fair
Who caused his care,
And sighed and looked, sighed and looked,

Dryden.

Sighed and looked, and sighed again.
At length, with love and wine at once oppressed,
The vanquished victor sunk upon her breast.

Now strike the golden lyre again;
A louder yet, and yet a louder strain.
Break his bands of sleep asunder,
And rouse him, like a rattling peal of thunder.
    Hark! hark! the horrid sound
      Has raised up his head,
      As awaked from the dead,
    And, amazed, he stares around.
    Revenge! revenge! Timotheus cries.
      See the furies arise;
        See the snakes that they rear,
        How they hiss in their hair,
And the sparkles that flash from their eyes!
      Behold a ghastly band,
      Each a torch in his hand!
These are Grecian ghosts that in battle were slain,
      And unburied remain,
      Inglorious on the plain:
      Give the vengeance due
      To the valiant crew.
Behold how they toss their torches on high,
      How they point to the Persian abodes,
And glittering temples of their hostile gods!
    The princes applaud with a furious joy,
And the king seized a flambeau, with zeal to destroy:
      Thais led the way,
      To light him to his prey,
And, like another Helen, fired another Troy.

>   Thus, long ago,
> Ere heaving bellows learned to blow,
>   While organs yet were mute,
>   Timotheus, to his breathing flute
>   And sounding lyre,
> Could swell the soul to rage, or kindle soft desire.
>   At last divine Cecilia came,
>   Inventress of the vocal frame:
> The sweet enthusiast, from her sacred store,
>   Enlarged the former narrow bounds,
>   And added length to solemn sounds,
> With nature's mother-wit, and arts unknown before.
>   Let old Timotheus yield the prize,
>   Or both divide the crown:
>   He raised a mortal to the skies;
>   She drew an angel down.

[*From "A Song for St. Cecilia's Day, 1687."*]

[Music of the Organ.]

> But, oh! what art can teach,
> What human voice can reach,
> The sacred organ's praise?
>   Notes inspiring holy love,
> Notes that wing their heavenly ways
>   To mend the choirs above.
>
> Orpheus could lead the savage race;
> And trees uprooted left their place,
>   Sequacious of the lyre;
> But bright Cecilia raised the wonder higher.
> When to her organ vocal breath was given,

An angel heard, and straight appeared,
    Mistaking earth for heaven.

[*From* " *Threnodia Augustalis*," *to the Memory of King Charles II.*]

Thus long my grief has kept me dumb.
    Sure there's a lethargy in mighty woe,
    Tears stand congealed, and cannot flow,
And the sad soul retires into her inmost room.
Tears, for a stroke foreseen, afford relief;
    But, unprovided for a sudden blow,
    Like Niobe we marble grow;
And petrify with grief.

[*Joy caused by a report of his partial recovery.*]

The joyful, short-lived news soon spread around;
The drooping town in smiles again was dressed,
Gladness, in every face expressed,
Their eyes before their tongues confessed.
Men met each other with erected look,
The steps were higher that they took,
Friends to congratulate their friends made haste,
And long inveterate foes saluted as they past.

[*Charles described.*]

His conversation, wit, and parts,
His knowledge in the noblest useful arts,
Were such dead authors could not give,
But habitudes of those who live;
Who, lighting him, did greater lights receive.
He drained from all, and all they knew;
His apprehension quick, his judgment true;
That the most learned, with shame, confess
His knowledge more, his reading only less.

[*From Verses to the Duchess of York, on a Victory gained by the Duke,* etc.*]

While all the brave did his command obey,
The fair and pious under you did pray.
How powerful are chaste vows! the wind and tide
You bribed to combat on the English side.
Thus, to your much loved lord you did convey
An unknown succour, sent the nearest way.
For absent friends we were ashamed to fear,
When we considered what you ventured there.
Ships, men, and arms our country might restore,
But such a leader could supply no more.
Fortune and victory he did pursue,
To bring them as his slaves to wait on you.
Thus beauty ravished the rewards of fame,
And the fair triumphed when the brave o'ercame.
Then, as you meant to spread, another way,
By land your conquests, far as his by sea,
Leaving our southern clime, you marched along
The stubborn North, ten thousand Cupids strong.
Like commons, the nobility resort
In crowding heaps, to fill your moving court:
So, when the new-born phœnix first is seen,
Her feathered subjects all adore their queen,
And, while she makes her progress through the East,
From every grove her numerous train's increast,
Each *poet of the air* her glory sings,
And round him the pleased audience clap their wings.

* Afterwards King James II. This Duchess, like the Duke, was a Catholic convert.

[*From "Epistle to Sir Godfrey Kneller," the Court Painter.*]

Once I beheld the fairest of her kind,
And still the sweet idea charms my mind.
True she was dumb; for Nature gazed so long
Pleased with her work, that she forgot her tongue;
But smiling said, she still shall gain the prize,
I only have transferred it to her eyes.
Such are thy pictures, Kneller, such thy skill,
That Nature seems obedient to thy will;
Comes out and meets thy pencil in the draught;
Lives there, and wants but words to speak her thought
At least thy pictures look a voice, and we
Imagine sounds, deceived to that degree,
We think 'tis somewhat more than just to see.
 Shadows are but privations of the light:
Yet, when we walk, they shoot before the sight;
With us approach, retire, arise and fall;
Nothing themselves, and yet expressing all.
Such are thy pieces, imitating life
So near, they almost conquer in the strife;
And from their animated canvass came,
Demanding souls and loosened from the frame.
 Prometheus, were he here, would cast away
His Adam, and refuse a soul to clay;
And either would thy noble work inspire,
Or think it warm enough, without his fire.
 Long time the sister arts, in iron sleep,
A heavy sabbath did supinely keep;
At length, in Raphael's age, at once they rise,
Stretch all their limbs and open all their eyes.

Thence rose the Roman and the Lombard line ;
One colored best and one did best design.
Raphael's, like Homer's, was the nobler part,
But Titian's painting looked like Virgil's art.

   Thy genius gives thee both ; where true design,
Postures unforced and lively colours join :
Likeness is ever there, but still the best,
Like proper thoughts in lofty language drest ;
Where light, to shades descending, plays, not strives,
Dies by degrees, and by degrees revives.
Of various parts a perfect whole is wrought ;
Thy pictures think, and we divine their thought.

   A graceful truth thy pencil can command ;
The fair themselves go mended from thy hand.
Likeness appears in every lineament,
But likeness in thy work is eloquent.
Though Nature there her true resemblance bears,
A nobler beauty in thy piece appears.
So warm thy work, so glows the generous frame,
Flesh looks less living in the lovely dame.

   But we, who life bestow, ourselves must live ;
Kings cannot reign, unless their subjects give ;
And they, who pay the taxes, bear the rule :
Thus thou, sometimes, art forced to draw a fool ;
But so his follies in thy posture sink,
The senseless idiot seems at last to think.

   More cannot be by mortal art exprest,
But venerable age shall add the rest ;
For Time shall with his ready pencil stand,
Retouch your figures with his ripening hand ;
To future ages shall your fame convey,
And give more beauties than he takes away.

[*From " Epistle to the Duchess of York, on her return from Scotland."*]

When factious rage to cruel exile drove
The queen of beauty, and the court of love,
The Muses drooped, with their forsaken arts,
And the sad Cupids broke their useless darts:
Love could no longer after beauty stay,
But wandered northward to the verge of day.
But now the illustrious nymph, returned again,
Brings every grace triumphant in her train.
The wondering Nereids, though they raised no storm,
Foreshowed her passage, to behold her form:
Some cried a Venus, some, a Thetis passed;
But this was not so fair, nor that so chaste.
Far from her sight flew faction, strife and pride,
And envy did but look on her and died.

The muse resumes her long-forgotten lays,
And Love restored his ancient realm surveys;
His waste dominions peoples once again,
And from her presence dates his second reign.
But awful charms on her fair forehead sit,
Dispensing what she never will admit:
Pleasing, yet cold, like Cynthia's silver beam,
The people's wonder, and the poet's theme.
Distempered zeal, sedition, cankered hate,
No more shall vex the Church, and tear the state;
No more shall faction civil discords move,
Or only discords of too tender love;
Discord, like that of music's various parts,
Discord, that makes the harmony of hearts;
Discord, that only this dispute shall bring,
Who best shall love the Duke, and serve the King.

[*From " Epistle to Mr. Congreve."*]

Already I am worn with cares and age,
And just abandoning the ungrateful stage :
Unprofitably kept at Heaven's expense,
I live a rent-charge on His providence.
But you, whom every muse and grace adorn,
Whom I foresee to better fortune born,
Be kind to my remains ; and O defend,
Against your judgment, your departed friend !
Let not the insulting foe my fame pursue,
But shade those laurels which descend to you.

[*From a paraphrase of Chaucer's character of a good priest.*]

A parish priest was of the pilgrim train,
An awful, reverend and religious man.
His eyes diffused a venerable grace,
And charity itself was in his face.
Rich was his soul, though his attire was poor,
For such on earth his blessed Redeemer bore.
Of sixty years he seemed, and well might last
To sixty more, but that he lived too fast,
Refined himself to soul to curb the sense,
And made almost a sin of abstinence.
Yet had his aspect nothing of severe,
But such a face as promised him sincere.
Nothing reserved or sullen was to see ;
But sweet regards and pleasing sanctity.
With eloquence innate his tongue was armed ;
Though harsh the precept, yet the preacher charmed :
He preached the joys of heaven and pains of hell,

And warned the sinner with becoming zeal,
But on eternal mercy loved to dwell.
He taught the gospel rather than the law,
And forced himself to drive, but loved to draw.
To threats the stubborn sinner oft is hard,
Wrapped in his crimes, against the storm prepared,
But, when the milder beams of mercy play,
He melts and throws his cumbrous cloak away.
Lightning and thunder, heaven's artillery,
As harbingers before the Almighty fly:
Those but proclaim His style and disappear;
The stiller sound succeeds, and God is there.

 The tithes, his parish freely paid, he took;
But never sued, or cursed with bell and book;
With patience bearing wrong; but offering none;
Since every man is free to lose his own.
Yet of his little he had some to spare,
To feed the famished and to clothe the bare:
For mortified he was to that degree,
A poorer than himself he would not see.
True priests, he said, and preachers of the word,
Were only stewards of their sovereign Lord;
Nothing was theirs, but all the public store;
Intrusted riches to relieve the poor;
Who, should they steal for want of his relief,
He judged himself accomplice with the thief.

 Wide was his parish, not contracted close
In streets, but here and there a straggling house;
Yet still he was at hand, without request,
To serve the sick, to succor the distressed.

 The proud he tamed, the penitent he cheered,
Nor to rebuke the rich offender feared.
His preaching much, but more his practice wrought;

A living sermon of the truths he taught;
For priests, said he, are patterns for the rest,
The gold of Heaven, who bear the God impressed;
But when the precious coin is kept unclean,
The Sovereign's image is no longer seen.
  The prelate for his holy life he prized;
The worldly pomp of prelacy despised:
His Saviour came not with a gaudy show,
Nor was His kingdom of the world below;
Patience in want, and poverty of mind,
These marks of church and churchmen he designed.
The crown He wore was of the pointed thorn;
In purple He was crucified, not born.
They who contend for place and high degree,
Are not His sons, but those of Zebedee.
  Such was the saint; who shone with every grace,
Reflecting, Moses-like, his Maker's face.
God saw His image lively was expressed;
And His own work, as in creation, blessed.

Translation of the " Te Deum."

Thee, Sovereign God, our grateful accents praise;
We own Thee Lord, and bless Thy wondrous ways;
To·Thee, Eternal Father, earth's whole frame,
With loudest trumpets sounds immortal fame.
Lord God of Hosts! for Thee the heavenly powers
With sounding anthems fill the vaulted towers.
Thy cherubims thrice Holy, Holy, Holy, cry;
Thrice Holy, all the seraphims reply,
And thrice returning echoes endless songs supply.
Both heaven and earth Thy majesty display;
They owe their beauty to Thy glorious ray.
Thy praises fill the loud apostles' choir:

Dryden.

The train of prophets in the song conspire.
Legions of martyrs in the chorus shine,
And vocal blood with vocal music join.
By these Thy Church, inspired by heavenly art,
Around the world maintains a second part;
And tunes her sweetest notes, O God, to Thee,
The Father of unbounded majesty;
The Son, adored co-partner of Thy seat,
And equal, everlasting Paraclete.
Thou King of Glory, Christ of the Most High,
Thou co-eternal, filial Deity;
Thou, who, to save the world's impending doom,
Vouchsaf'st to dwell within a virgin's womb;
Old tyrant Death disarmed, before thee flew
The bolts of heaven, and back the foldings drew,
To give access and make Thy faithful way.
From God's right hand Thy filial beams display.
Thou art to judge the living and the dead;
Then spare those souls for whom Thy veins have bled.
O take us up amongst Thy blessed above,
To share with them Thy everlasting love.
Preserve, O Lord! Thy people and enhance
Thy blessing on Thine own inheritance.
Forever raise their hearts and rule their ways.
Each day we bless Thee and proclaim Thy praise:
No age shall fail to celebrate Thy name,
No hour neglect Thy everlasting fame.
Preserve our souls, O Lord! this day from ill;
Have mercy on us, Lord, have mercy still:
As we have hoped, do Thou reward our pain;
We've hoped in Thee, let not our hope be vain.

"*Veni Creator Spiritus,*" *paraphrased.*

Creator Spirit, by whose aid,
The world's foundations first were laid,
Come, visit every pious mind;
Come, pour Thy joys on human kind;
From sin and sorrow set us free,
And make Thy temples worthy Thee.

   O source of uncreated light,
The Father's promised Paraclete!
Thrice holy fount, thrice holy fire,
Our hearts with heavenly love inspire;
Come, and thy sacred unction bring
To sanctify us while we sing.

   Plenteous of grace, descend from high,
Rich in Thy sevenfold energy,
Thou strength of His Almighty hand
Whose power does heaven and earth command;
Proceeding Spirit, our defence,
Who dost the gift of tongues dispense,
And crown'st Thy gift with eloquence.

   Refine and purge our earthly parts;
But, oh, inflame and fire our hearts!
Our frailties help, our vice controul,
Submit the senses to the soul;
And, when rebellious they have grown,
Then lay Thy hand and hold them down.

   Chase from our minds the infernal foe,
And peace, the fruit of love, bestow;
And, lest our feet should step astray,
Protect and guide us in the way.

   Make us eternal truths receive;

And practice all that we believe;
Give us Thyself, that we may see
The Father and the Son by Thee.
  Immortal honor, endless fame
Attend the Almighty Father's name;
The Saviour Son be glorified,
Who for lost man's redemption died;
And equal adoration be,
Eternal Paraclete, to Thee!

*Hymn for St. John's Eve, a translation of the original,
    supposed to have been composed by Lactantius.*

O sylvan prophet! whose eternal fame
Echoes from Judah's hills and Jordan's stream,
The music of our numbers raise
And time our voices to thy praise.

A messenger from high Olympus came
To bear the tidings of thy life and name;
And told thy sire each prodigy
That Heaven designed to work in thee.

Hearing the news, and doubting in surprise,
His faltering speech in fettered accents dies;
But Providence, with happy choice,
In thee restored thy father's voice.

In the recess of nature's dark abode,
Though still inclosed, yet knewest thou thy God,
Whilst each glad parent told and blest
The secrets of each other's breast.

[FROM "ALL FOR LOVE," A TRAGEDY.*]
[*Cleopatra's Voyage down the Cydnus.*]
The tackling silk, the streamers waved with gold,
The gentle winds were lodged in purple sails:
Her nymphs, like Nereids, round her couch were placed;
Where she, another sea-born Venus, lay.
    Dolabella. No more: I would not hear it.
    Anthony. O, you must!
She lay, and leant her cheek upon her hand,
And cast a look so languishingly sweet,
As if, secure of all beholders' hearts,
Neglecting she could take them. Boys, like Cupids,
Stood fanning, with their painted wings, the winds
That played about her face. But, if she smiled,
A darting glory seemed to blaze abroad;
That men's desiring eyes were never wearied,
But hung upon the object. To soft flutes
The silver oars kept time; and, while they played,
The hearing gave new pleasure to the sight,
And both to thought. 'Twas heaven, or somewhat more:
For she so charmed all hearts, that gazing crowds
Stood panting on the shore, and wanted breath
To give their welcome voice.
        [*Attachment to life.*]
O, that I less could fear to lose this being,
Which, like a snow-ball, in my coward hand
The more 'tis grasped, the faster melts away.
    [*Omens presaging the downfall of Egypt.*]
Last night, between the hours of twelve and one,
In a lone aisle of the temple while I walked,
A whirlwind rose, that, with a violent blast,

---

* His, perhaps, principal drama.

Shook all the dome. The doors around me clapt;
The iron wicket, that defends the vault
Where the long race of Ptolemies is laid,
Burst open, and disclosed the mighty dead.
From out each monument in order placed,
An armed ghost starts up. The boy-king last
Reared his inglorious head. A peal of groans
Then followed, and a lamentable voice
Cried, " Egypt is no more!" My blood ran back;
My shaking knees against each other knocked;
On the cold pavement down I fell entranced,
And so, unfinished left the horrid scene.

DETACHED PASSAGES.*

Resistless force and immortality
Make but a lame, imperfect deity;
But justice is Heaven's self, so strictly He,
That, could it fail, the Godhead could not be.

For ill men, conscious of their inward guilt,
Think the best actions on by-ends are built.

Prizes would be for legs of slowest pace,
Were cripples made the judges of the race.

For not to wish is not to be deceived.

E'en victors are by victories undone.

For when we more than human homage pay,
The charming cause is justly snatched away.

---

* Not contained in the preceding " Selections."

Time was when none could preach without degrees,
And seven years' toil at universities.
But when the canting saints* came once in play,
The spirit did their business in a day:
A zealous cobbler with the gift of tongue,
If he could pray six hours, might preach as long.

But kings too tame are despicably good.

No force the free-born spirit can constrain,
But charity and great example gain.

Prompt to revenge, not daring to forgive,
Our lives unteach the doctrines we believe.

A prince's favors on but few can fall,
But justice is a virtue shared by all.

For few would love their God unless they feared.

The saint who walked on waves securely trod,
While he believed the beckoning of his God,
But, when his faith no longer bore him out,
Began to sink as he began to doubt.

Envy, that does with misery reside,
The joy and the revenge of ruined pride.

Beware the fury of a patient man.

[*Renegades.*]
Still violent, whatever cause he took,
But most against the party he forsook:

---

* The sectarian fanatics.

Dryden.

For renegadoes, who ne'er turn by halves,
Are bound in conscience to be double knaves.

For what can power give more than food and drink,
To live at ease, and not be bound to think?

Successful crimes alone are justified.

For in some soils republics will not grow.

War seldom enters but where wealth allures.

For alms are but the vehicles of prayer.

Two magnets, heaven and earth, allure to bliss;
The larger loadstone that, the nearer this:
The weak attraction of the greater fails;
We nod awhile, but neighborhood prevails.

Immortal powers the term of Conscience know,
But Interest is her name with men below.

For little souls on little shifts rely.

'Tis hard to find such wit as ne'er has been.

They judge but half who only faults will see.

Poets, like lovers, should be bold and dare,
They spoil their business with an over care;
And he, who servilely creeps after sense,
Is safe, but ne'er will reach an excellence.

Peace, the loathed manna which hot brains despise.

Love is no more a violent desire,
'Tis a mere metaphor, a painted fire.

What praise soe'er the poetry deserve,
Yet every fool can bid the poet starve.

The friends of Job, who railed at him before,
Came cap in hand, when he had three times more.

Some lazy ages, lost in sleep and ease,
No action leave to busy chronicles:
Such, whose supine felicity but makes
In story chasms, in épochas mistakes;
O'er whom Time gently shakes his wings of down,
Till with his silent sickle they are mown.

But life can never be sincerely blest;
Heaven punishes the bad, and proves the best.

For politicans neither love nor hate.

Nor is the people's judgment always true,
The most may err as grossly as the few.

The tampering world is subject to this curse,
To physic their disease into a worse.

[*Exercise.*]
The first physicians by debauch were made,
Excess began and sloth sustains the trade.
Better to hunt in fields for health unbought
Than fee the doctor for a nauseous draught:
The wise for cure on exercise depend;
God never made his work for man to mend.

A poet is not born in every race.

Like woman's anger, impotent and loud.

An honest man may take a fool's advice.

E'en wit's a burden when it talks too long.

[*The predestinarians confuted.*]
For how can that Eternal Power be just
To punish man who sins because he must?
Or how can He reward a virtuous deed
Which is not done by us, but first decreed?

Truth, which itself is light, does darkness shun,
And the true eaglet safely dares the sun.

For opposition makes a hero great.

Good actions still must be maintained with good,
As bodies nourished with resembling food.

[*The Sectarian fanatics.*]
'Gainst form and order they their power employ,
Nothing to build and all things to destroy.

[*Shakspeare's supernatural characters.*]
But Shakspeare's magic could not copied be,
Within that circle none durst walk but he.

For friendship, of itself a holy tie,
Is made more sacred by adversity.

But how can finite grasp infinity?

[*Dispensing with good works ridiculed.*]
The way to win the restive world to God,
Was to lay by the disciplining rod,
Unnatural fasts and foreign forms of prayer.
Religion frights us with a mien severe:
'Tis prudence to reform her into ease,
And put her in undress to make her please;
A lively faith will bear aloft the mind,
And leave the luggage of good works behind.

DRYDEN'S SONS.

CHARLES, the eldest of Dryden's sons, was born in 1666, and educated at Westminster School and Cambridge. About 1692, he went to Italy, and was made Chamberlain to the household of Pope Innocent, XII. He translated the *Seventh Satire in his father's Juvenal*, and was the author of a poem *On the Happiness of a Retired Life*, and of several *Latin poems*. He was drowned in the Thames, in 1704.*

JOHN, the second son, born in 1667 or 1668, was educated at Westminster School and Oxford. It is supposed that he went to Rome, about the end of 1692, where he officiated in the Pope's household, as his brother's deputy. He translated the *Fourteenth Satire in his father's Juvenal* and wrote a *Comedy*, which was acted in London. In 1700-1, he made a tour through Sicily and Malta, his account of which was published. He died at Rome in 1701.†

---

* This son is said to have been a Catholic previous to his father's change, and to have contributed to it.

† ERASMUS HENRY, the third son, born in 1669, was a captain in the Pope's guards. He died in 1710.

WILLIAM WYCHERLEY.

WILLIAM WYCHERLEY, was born about 1640. He was educated in France, where he abjured Protestantism. A short time before the Restoration in 1660, he returned and became a student in the Middle Temple. He was also, temporarily, a fellow-commoner at Oxford, where he resumed his former communion, in which, however, he failed to continue till the time of his death. Before going thither, and, at the age of nineteen, he wrote, *Love in a Wood*, a comedy, which and its successors, *The Gentleman Dancing-master*, *The Plaindealer*, and *The Country Wife*, became very popular, and introduced him into the first circles. Charles II admitted him to his private parties, and he seems to have been a special favorite with the Duchess of Cleveland. At length he gave offence * by marrying the Countess of Drogheda, and, though, at her death, she left him her fortune, his title was disputed, and he lay for several years in prison, probably for debt. At last he was released by James II, who settled on him a pension of 200*l*. a year. He died in 1715, a few days after his second marriage. Towards the close of his life, he again professed the Catholic faith.

Besides his comedies, he published in 1704, a *Volume of Poems*. His posthumous works appeared in 1728. As a poet, he is not distinguished, but among the comic dramatists of his country, perhaps, in some respects, he has no superior. Dryden, an excellent judge, has the following line;

"The satire, wit and strength of manly Wycherley."

* Probably to the Duchess.

We are told of his "amiableness" and "sincerity." His worst enemy appears to have been himself.

THOMAS WARD.

THOMAS WARD was born in 1652. For his having renounced Protestantism he was disinherited by his father, but subsequently converted his mother and all his family. He resided some years at Rome, and held a commission in the Pope's guards, but, in the reign of James II, returned, and became a noted writer against the established church. After the Revolution he went to France, where he died, in 1708. His two principal works are, the well-known *Errata of the Protestant Bible*, and *England's Reformation*, a Hudibrastic poem, of which the following is a specimen.

[*Defacement and spoliation of the churches.*]
There might you see an impious clown
Breaking our Saviour's image down;
And there you might behold another
Tearing the picture of Christ's Mother.
The peaceful tombs in which were laid
The sacred ashes of the dead,
Might now be seen in pieces broke,
And thence the holy bodies took.
Blest martyrs now you might behold,
Who died for Christ in days of old,
Torn from their tombs, and made to come
T'endure a second martyrdom.
Some steal away the crucifix
And some the silver candlesticks.
And what they thought not fit to steal,
They burn, as an effect of Zeal.

SIR SAMUEL GARTH.

SIR SAMUEL GARTH was of a good family in Yorkshire. The year and place of his birth are not certainly known. From some school not mentioned he proceeded to Cambridge, where he resided till he became a Doctor of Physic, in 1691. He now repaired to London, and was soon so much distinguished as to obtain an extensive practice. His personal character seems to have been social and liberal. He was the early encourager of Pope, an intimate friend of Addison, and, when Dryden died, he pronounced a Latin oration over his remains.

"And Garth, the best good christian he,
   Although he knows it not."
                        . *Pope.*

At the accession of the House of Hanover, he was knighted and made Physician in Ordinary to the King and Physician General to the Army. He died on the 18th of January, 1717-18.

His principal poem is *The Dispensary*, a mock-heroic production in six cantos, published in 1696. Though, as to its subject, of a local and temporary character, such was its popularity, that, in 1706, appeared a sixth edition. "Scarcely a line," says Johnson, "is left unfinished, nor is it easy to find an expression used by constraint or a thought imperfectly expressed." His last literary work was preparing an edition of a translation of *Ovid's Metamorphoses*, partly executed by himself. His death, which his conversion to the Catholic faith perhaps did not long precede,* is thus noticed by Pope:

"The best-natured of men, Sir Samuel Garth, has left me in the truest concern for his loss. His death was very heroical, and yet unaffected enough to have made a saint or a philosopher famous." In wit, good-sense, and verbal elegance, he reminds us of his eulogist, nor does he fail in poetical invention.

From " The Dispensary."

Speak, goddess! since 'tis thou that best canst tell,
How ancient leagues to modern discord fell;
And why physicians were so cautious grown
Of others' lives, and lavish of their own.
    Not far from that most celebrated place †
Where angry Justice shows her awful face;
Where little villains must submit to fate,
That great ones may enjoy the world in state;
There stands a dome,‡ majestic to the sight,
And sumptuous arches bear its oval height:
A golden globe, placed high with artful skill,
Seems to the distant sight a gilded pill.
This pile was, by the pious patron's aim,
Raised for a use as noble as its frame;
Nor did the learned society decline
The propagation of that great design.
    But now no grand inquiries are descried;
Mean faction reigns where knowledge should preside.
This place, so fit for undisturbed repose,

---

* See notices of him in Spence's Anecdotes.
† Old Bailey.   ‡ College of Physicians.

The god of sloth for his asylum chose.
Upon a couch of down, in these abodes,
Supine, with folded arms, he thoughtless nods;
The poppy and each numbing plant dispense
Their drowsy virtue and dull indolence;
No passions interrupt his easy reign,
No problems puzzle his lethárgic brain;
But dark oblivion guards his peaceful bed,
And lazy fogs hang lingering o'er his head.

[*From the Speech of Colocynthus, an apothecary.*]

Couldst thou propose that we, the friends of fate,
Who fill churchyards, and who unpeople states,
Who baffle nature, and dispose of lives,
Whilst Russel,* as we please, or starves, or thrives,
Should e'er submit to their despotic will,
Who out of consultation scarce can kill?
Our properties must on our arms depend;
'Tis next to conquer, bravely to defend.
'Tis to the vulgar death too harsh appears;
The ill we feel is only in our fears.
To die is landing on some foreign shore;
Ere well we feel the friendly stroke, 'tis o'er.
The wise through thought the insults of death defy,
The fools, through blest insensibility.
'Tis what the guilty fear, the pious crave,
Sought by the wretch, and vanquished by the brave.
It eases lovers, sets the captive free,
And, though a tyrant, offers liberty.

* An Undertaker.

[*From " Epilogue to Addison's Cato."*]

Oh, may once more the happy age appear
When words were artless, and the thoughts sincere;
When gold and grandeur were unenvied things,
And courts less coveted than groves and springs;
Love then shall only mourn when truth complains,
And constancy feel transport in its chains;
Virtue again to its bright station climb,
And beauty fear no enemy but time;
The fair shall listen to desert alone,
And every Lucia find a Cato's son.

[*From " Claremont."*]

[Ancient and modern manners.]

In times of old, when British nymphs were known
To love no foreign fashions like their own;
Of Spanish red unheard was then the name,
For cheeks were only taught to blush by shame.
No beauty, to increase her crowd of slaves,
Rose out of wash, as Venus out of waves;
Not yet lead-comb was on the toilet placed;
Not yet broad eye-brows were reduced by paste;
No shape-smith set up shop, and drove a trade,
To mend the work wise Providence had made.
Honor was placed in probity alone,
For villains had no titles but their own.
None traveled to return politely mad.
But still what fancy wanted, reason had.
No cook with art increased physicians' fees,
Nor served up death in soup and fricasees.

Garth.

[*Choice of a wife.*]

When coming time shall bless you with a bride,
Let passion not persuade, but reason guide ;
Instead of gold, let gentle truth endear ;
She has most charms who is the most sincere.
The nymph must fear to be inquisitive ;
'Tis for the sex's quiet to believe.
Her air an easy confidence must show,
And shun to find what she would dread to know.

[*To the Poetaster at Saddler's Hall.*]

Unwieldy pedant, let thy awkward muse
With censures praise, with flatteries abuse.
To lash, and not be felt, in thee's an art ;
Thou ne'er mad'st any, but thy school-boys, smart.
Then be advised, and scribble not again ;
Thou'rt fashioned for a flail, and not a pen.
If B—l's immortal wit thou would'st decry,
Pretend 'tis he that writ thy poetry :
Thy feeble satire ne'er can do him wrong ;
Thy poems and thy patients live not long.

[*Detached Passages.*]

You'll ne'er convince a fool himself is so.

———

Though projects please, projectors are undone.

———

None please the fancy who offend the ear.

———

Children at toys, as men at titles, aim ;
And, in effect, both covet but the same :
This Philip's son proved in revolving years,
And first for rattles, then for worlds shed tears.

Ingratitude's a weed of every clime.

But virtue is a crime when placed on high,
Though all the fault's in the beholder's eye.

ALEXANDER POPE.

"Such a 'Poet of a thousand years' was Pope. A thousand years will roll away before such another can be hoped for in our literature. But it can *want* them—he is himself a literature."

Lord Byron.

ALEXANDER POPE was born in London, on the 21st or, according to some authorities, 22d of May, 1688. His father was a linen-draper, who having acquired a sum of about £20,000,[1] retired to Binfield in Windsor Forest. His son received his first lessons in reading from an aunt, and taught himself to write by copying the printed characters in books. At the age of eight, he was, for some time, placed under the care of the family priest, and afterwards sent to a Catholic school at Twyford, and to another in London. While at the latter he composed a drama founded on certain parts of the Iliad, which was played by the upper boys and the master's gardener. Having returned to his parents soon after he had reached his twelfth year, he was put under the tuition of another priest, but, at the end of a few months, formed the resolution of educating himself,

---

[1] So some of Pope's biographers state. According to a passage in "Spence's Anecdotes," the sum might have been but £10,000. His father is said to have spent a portion of his fortune by living on the principal.

and from THAT TIME, IS SAID TO HAVE ATTENDED NO SCHOOL. His *Ode to Solitude* was written before his twelfth year, and, before his fifteenth, he composed a comedy, a tragedy, and four books of an epic poem, all which, except the ode, he destroyed. Among the productions of his early youth, may, also, be noticed the translations of the *First book of Statius's Thebais*, of *Ovid's Epistle from Sappho to Phaon*, and of about a fourth part of the *Metamorphoses; Imitations of English Poets;* rifacimenti of two of *Chaucer's* pieces; and a version of *Cicero's treatise de Senectute*. His *Pastorals* were composed at the age of sixteen. In 1711 appeared his *Essay on Criticism*, apparently written when he was but twenty-one, or, perhaps, even eighteen.[2] The ripeness of judgment which it displays is truly marvellous. In that year, also, was published *The Rape of the Lock*, in two cantos, and again, in 1714, amplified with the machinery of the Sylphs, a mock-heroic poem, as such, of unequaled excellence. In ridicule of the popular propensity to suspect a political meaning in the most innocent productions, he wrote an amusing prose piece, called *A Key to the Lock*. *Messiah*, that splendid imitation of *Virgil's Pollio*, *The Dying Christian to his Soul*, and *The Temple of Fame*, were first printed in 1712. The last piece was written in 1710. About 1712, we may date the production of the *Elegy to the Memory of an Unfortunate Lady*, whose story is still involved in mystery. *Windsor Forest*, mostly written in 1704, was published in 1713. In the same year he attacked his old enemy, John Dennis, the critic, in a highly humorous piece, entitled, *The Narrative of Dr.*

---

[2] See his remarks on it in Spence's Anecdotes.

Robert Norris of the Frenzy of J. D. Writing to Mr. Addison, in 1713, he says, "I generally employ the mornings in painting with Mr. Jervas."* About this time he composed his beautiful *Epistle* to that artist. He now commenced his translation of the *Iliad*, the last volume of which was published in 1720. The success of this translation, by which he obtained a clear sum of about £5,320, induced him to undertake that of the *Odyssey*, assisted by his friends Broome and Fenton, who translated twelve books. The last volume appeared in 1726. In 1715 he removed to Twickenham. The villa there, of which he had purchased a lease, continued to be his residence during the rest of his life. His most impassioned poem, the *Epistle from Eloisa to Abelard*, appears to have been composed in 1716. An edition of Shakspeare, on which he had been for several years employed, was completed in 1725. In 1727 was published a part, if not the whole, of Pope's and Swift's *Miscellanies*. The first perfect edition of his elaborate and splendid satire, *The Dunciad*, the last book excepted, was that of London, in 1728-9. In 1732, appeared the first, and, in 1734, the last part of the most celebrated, perhaps, of all his writings, the *Essay on Man*. Between 1730 and 1739, were published his inimitable *Moral Epistles* or *Essays*, and *Satires*, and, in 1738, his *Universal Prayer*. In 1742, he added a fourth book to *The Dunciad*.

A short time before his death, he complained of his inability to think, yet said, "I am so certain of the soul's being immortal, that I seem to feel it within me as it were by intuition." Such was the fervor of his

---

* He is said to have painted a portrait of Betterton.

devotion, that he exerted all his strength to throw himself out of bed, that he might receive the last sacrament kneeling on the floor. He died on the 30th of May, 1744.

[*From his Life by Dr. Johnson.*]

" After the priest had given him the last sacraments, he said, 'There is nothing that is meritorious but virtue and friendship, and, indeed, friendship itself is only a part of virtue.' He died so placidly that the attendants did not discover the exact time of his expiration."

"The virtues which seem to have had most of his affection, were liberality and fidelity of friendship. He was accused of loving money; but his love was eagerness to gain, not solicitude to keep it. The filial piety of Pope was, in the highest degree, amiable and exemplary. His parents had the happiness of living till he was at the summit of poetical reputation, at ease in his fortune, and without a rival in his fame, and found no diminution of his respect or tenderness."

"He is said to have been beautiful in his infancy. His deformity was probably in part the effect of his application. One side was contracted. His stature was so low, that, to bring him to a level with common tables, it was necessary to raise his seat. But his face was not displeasing, and his eyes were animated and vivid. His life was one long disease."

Though, according to the same authority, it does not appear that he excelled in familiar or convivial conversation, the deformity and diminutiveness of his figure are said to have been soon forgotten in the ease and elegance of his manners.

[*From " Windsor Forest."*]

The groves of Eden, vanished now so long,
Live in description, and look green in song;
These, were my breast inspired with equal flame,
Like them in beauty, should be like in fame.
Here hills and vales, the woodland and the plain,
Here earth and water, seem to strive again;
Not, chaos-like, together crushed and bruised,
But, as the world, harmoniously confused;
Where order in variety we see,
And where, though all things differ, all agree.
  Not thus the land appeared in ages past,
A dreary desert and a gloomy waste,
To savage beasts and savage laws a prey,
And kings more furious and severe than they;
Who claimed the skies, dispeopled air and floods,
The lonely lords of empty wilds and woods.
Cities laid waste, they stormed the dens and caves;
For wiser brutes were backward to be slaves.
What could be free, when lawless beasts obeyed
And even the elements a tyrant swayed?
What wonder then, a beast or subject slain
Were equal crimes in a despotic reign?
Both doomed alike, for sportive tyrants bled;
But while the subject starved, the beast was fed.
The leveled towns with weeds lie covered o'er,
The hollow winds through naked temples roar;
Round broken columns clasping ivy twined;
O'er heaps of ruin stalked the stately hind.

[*Field-sports.*]

  Ye vigorous swains! while youth ferments your blood,
And purer spirits swell the sprightly flood,

Pope.

Now range the hills, the gameful woods beset,
Wind the shrill horn, or spread the waving net.
　See, from the brake the whirring pheasant springs,
And mounts exulting on triumphant wings:
Short is his joy; he feels the fiery wound,
Flutters in blood, and panting beats the ground.
Ah! what avail his glossy, varying dyes,
His purple crest and scarlet-circled eyes,
The vivid green his shining plumes unfold,
His painted wings, and breast that flames with gold?
　With slaughtering guns the unwearied fowler roves,
When frosts have whitened all the naked groves;
Where doves in flocks the leafless trees o'ershade,
And lonely woodcocks haunt the watery glade.
He lifts the tube, and levels with his eye;
Straight a short thunder breaks the frozen sky.
Oft, as in airy rings they skim the heath,
The clamourous lapwings feel the leaden death;
Oft, as the mounting larks their notes prepare,
They fall, and leave their little lives in air.
　The patient fisher takes his silent stand,
Intent, his angle trembling in his hand:
With looks unmoved, he hopes the scaly breed,
And eyes the dancing cork and bending reed.
Our plenteous streams a various race supply,
The bright-eyed perch with fins of Tyrian dye,
The silver eel, in shining volumes rolled,
The yellow carp, in scales bedropped with gold,
Swift trouts, diversified with crimson stains,
And pikes the tyrants of the watery plains.
　Now Cancer glows with Phœbus' fiery car:
The youth rush eager to the sylvan war,
Swarm o'er the lawns, the forest-walks surround,

Rouse the fleet hart, and cheer the opening hound.
The impatient courser pants in every vein,
And pawing, seems to beat the distant plain;
Hills, vales, and floods, appear already crossed,
And, ere he starts, a thousand steps are lost.
See the bold youth strain up the threatening steep,
Rush through the thickets, down the valleys sweep,
Hang o'er their coursers' heads with eager speed,
And earth rolls back beneath the flying steed.

Happy the man whom this bright court approves,
His sovereign favors, and his country loves:
Happy next him, who to these shades retires,
Whom Nature charms, and whom the Muse inspires.
Whom humbler joys of home-felt quiet please,
Successive study, exercise, and ease.
He gathers health from herbs the forest yields,
And of their fragrant physic spoils the fields;
With chemic art exalts the mineral powers,
And draws the aromatic souls of flowers;
Now marks the course of rolling orbs on high;
O'er figured worlds now travels with his eye;
Of ancient writ unlocks the learned store,
Consults the dead, and lives past ages o'er:
Or, wandering thoughtful in the silent wood,
Attends the duties of the wise and good;
Or looks on heaven with more than mortal eyes,
Bids his free soul expatiate in the skies,
Amid her kindred stars familiar roam,
Survey the region, and confess her home.

Pope.

[*From " The Temple of Fame."*]

[The hint of this piece was taken from Chaucer's *House of Fame.*]

I stood, methought, betwixt earth, seas, and skies,
The whole creation open to my eyes;
In air self-balanced hung the globe below,
Where mountains rise, and circling oceans flow.
  O'er the wide prospect, as I gazed around,
Sudden I heard a wild, promiscuous sound,
Then, gazing up, a glorious pile beheld,
Whose towering summit ambient clouds concealed.
High on a rock of ice, the structure lay,
Steep its ascent, and slippery was the way;
The wondrous rock like Parian marble shone,
And seemed, to distant sight, of solid stone.
Inscriptions here of various names I viewed,
The greater part by hostile time subdued;
Yet wide was spread their fame in ages past,
And poets once had promised they should last.
Some fresh engraved appeared of wits renowned;
I looked again, nor could their trace be found.
Critics I saw, that other names deface,
And fix their own, with labor, in their place:
Their own, like others, soon their place resigned,
Or disappeared, and left the first behind.
Nor was the work impaired by storms alone,
But felt the approaches of too warm a sun;
For fame, impatient of extremes, decays
Not more by envy than excess of praise.
Yet part no injuries of heaven could feel,
Like crystal faithful to the graving steel:
The rock's high summit, in the temple's shade,

Nor heat could melt, nor beating storms invade :
Their names, inscribed unnumbered ages past
From time's first birth, with time itself shall last.

    So Zembla's rocks, the beauteous work of frost,
Rise white in air, and glitter o'er the coast;
Pale suns, unfelt, at distance roll away,
And on the impassive ice the lightnings play;
Eternal snows the growing mass supply,
Till the bright mountains prop the incumbent sky;
As Atlas fixed, each hoary pile appears,
The gathered winter of a thousand years.

    On this foundation Fame's high temple stands;
Stupendous pile ! not reared by mortal hands.
Four brazen gates, on columns lifted high,
Salute the different quarters of the sky.
Here fabled chiefs, in darker ages born,
Or worthies old, whom arms or arts adorn,
Who cities raised, or tamed a monstrous race,
The walls in venerable order grace :
Heroes in animated marble frown,
And legislators seem to think in stone.

    Around these wonders as I cast a look,
The trumpet sounded, and the temple shook,
And all the nations, summoned, at the call,
From different quarters, fill the crowded hall ;
The poor, the rich, the valiant, and the sage,
And boasting youth, and narrative old age.
Their pleas were different, their request the same ;
For good and bad alike are fond of fame.

    First at the shrine the learned world appear,
And to the Goddess thus prefer their prayer.
Long have we sought to instruct and please mankind,
With studies pale, with midnight vigils blind ;

But thanked by few, rewarded yet by none,
We here appeal to thy superior throne :
On wit and learning the just prize bestow,
For fame is all we must expect below.

  The Goddess heard, and bade the Muses raise
The golden trumpet of eternal praise :
From pole to pole the winds diffuse the sound,
That fills the circuit of the world around ;
Not all at once, as thunder breaks the cloud ;
The notes at first were rather sweet than loud ;
By just degrees they every moment rise,
Fill the wide earth, and gain upon the skies.

  Next these, the good and just, an awful train,
Thus, on their knees, address the sacred fane.
Since living virtue is with envy cursed,
And the best men are treated like the worst,
Do thou, just Goddess, call our merits forth,
And give each deed the exact intrinsic worth.
Not with bare justice, shall your acts be crowned,
Said Fame, but high above desert renowned :
Let fuller notes the applauding world amaze,
And the loud clarion labor in your praise. * *

  A troop came next, who crowns and armor wore,
And proud defiance in their looks they bore :
For thee, they cried, amidst alarms and strife,
We sailed in tempests down the stream of life ;
For thee whole nations filled with flames and blood,
And swam to empire through the purple flood.
Those ills we dared thy inspiration own,
What virtue seemed, was done for thee alone.
Ambitious fools ! the queen replied, and frowned,
Be all your acts in dark oblivion drowned ;
There sleep forgot, with mighty tyrants gone,

Your statues mouldered, and your names unknown!
A sudden cloud straight snatched them from my sight,
And each majestic phantom sunk in night.

    Then came the smallest tribe I yet had seen;
Plain was their dress, and modest was their mien.
Great idol of mankind! we neither claim
The praise of merit, nor aspire to fame:
But safe, in deserts, from the applause of men,
Would die unheard of, as we live unseen.
'Tis all we beg thee, to conceal from sight
Those acts of goodness which themselves requite.
O let us still the secret joy partake,
To follow virtue e'en for virtue's sake.

    And live there men who slight immortal fame?
Who then with incense shall adore our name?
But mortals! know, 'tis still our secret pride
To blaze those virtues which the good would hide.
Rise! Muses, rise! add all your tuneful breath!
These must not sleep in darkness and in death.
She said: in air the trembling music floats,
And on the winds triumphant swell the notes:
So soft, though high, so loud, and yet so clear,
Even listening angels leaned from heaven to hear.

    This having heard and seen, some power unknown
Straight changed the scene, and snatched me from the
        throne.
Before my view appeared a structure fair,
Its site uncertain, if in earth, or air.
Not less in number were the spacious doors
Than leaves on trees, or sands upon the shores.
Above, below, without, within, around,
Confused, unnumbered multitudes are found.
Each talked aloud, or in some secret place,

And wild impatience stared in every face.
The flying rumors gathered, as they rolled;
Scarce any tale was sooner heard than told,
And all who told it added something new,
And all who heard it made enlargements too.
There, at one passage, oft you might survey
A lie and truth contending for the way;
And long 'twas doubtful, both so closely pent,
Which first should issue through the narrow vent:
At last agreed, together out they fly,
Inseparable now, the truth and lie.
   While thus I stood, intent to see and hear,
One came, methought, and whispered in my ear:
What could thus high thy rash ambition raise?
Art thou, fond youth, a candidate for praise?
   'Tis true, said I, not void of hopes I came,
For who so fond as youthful bards of Fame?
But few, alas! the casual blessing boast,
So hard to gain, so easy to be lost.
How vain that second life in others' breath,
The estate which wits inherit after death!
Ease, health, and life for this they must resign;
(Unsure the tenure, but how vast the fine!)
The great man's curse, without the gains endure,
Be envied, wretched, and be flattered, poor;
All luckless wits their enemies professed,
And all successful, jealous friends at best.
Nor Fame I slight, nor for her favors call;
She comes unlooked for, if she comes at all.
But if the purchase costs so dear a price,
As soothing folly, or exalting vice;
Oh! if the Muse must flatter lawless sway,
And follow still where fortune leads the way;

Or if no basis bear my rising name,
But the fallen ruins of another's fame;
Then teach me, Heaven! to scorn the guilty bays;
Drive from my breast that wretched lust of praise;
Unblemished let me live, or die unknown;
Oh! grant an honest fame, or grant me none!

The Messiah.

Ye nymphs of Solyma! begin the song;
To heavenly themes sublimer strains belong.
The mossy fountains and the sylvan shades,
The dreams of Pindus and the Aonian maids,
Delight no more. O Thou my voice inspire,
Who touched Isaiah's hallowed lips with fire!
  Rapt into future times the bard begun:
A Virgin shall conceive, a Virgin bear a son!
From Jesse's root behold a branch arise,
Whose sacred flower with fragrance fills the skies:
The Ethereal Spirit o'er its leaves shall move,
And on its top descends the Mystic Dove.
Ye heavens! from high the dewy nectar pour,
And in soft silence shed the kindly shower.
The sick and weak the healing plant shall aid,
From storms a shelter, and from heat a shade.
All crimes shall cease, and ancient fraud shall fail;
Returning Justice lift aloft her scale;
Peace o'er the world her olive wand extend,
And white-robed Innocence from heaven descend.
Swift fly the years, and rise the expected morn!
Oh, spring to light, auspicious Babe, be born!
See, Nature hastes her earliest wreaths to bring,
With all the incense of the breathing spring!

See lofty Lebanon his head advance!
See nodding forests on the mountains dance!
See spicy clouds from lowly Sharon rise,
And Carmel's flowery top perfumes the skies!
Hark! a glad voice the lonely desert cheers;
Prepare the way! a God, a God, appears.
A God! a God! the vocal hills reply;
The rocks proclaim the approaching Deity.
Lo! earth receives Him from the bending skies;
Sink down, ye mountains, and, ye valleys, rise;
With heads declined, ye cedars, homage pay;
Be smooth, ye rocks: ye rapid floods, give way!
The Saviour comes, by ancient bards foretold;
Hear Him, ye deaf! and, all ye blind, behold!
He from thick films shall purge the visual ray,
And on the sightless eyeball pour the day:
'Tis He the obstructed paths of sound shall clear,
And bid new music charm the unfolding ear.
The dumb shall sing, the lame his crutch forego,
And leap exulting, like the bounding roe.
No sigh, no murmur the wide world shall hear;
From every face He wipes off every tear.
In adamantine chains shall Death be bound,
And hell's grim tyrant feel the eternal wound.
As the good shepherd tends his fleecy care,
Seeks freshest pasture and the purest air;
Explores the lost, the wandering sheep directs,
By day o'ersees them and by night protects;
The tender lambs he raises in his arms,
Feeds from his hand, and in his bosom warms;
Thus shall mankind His guardian care engage,
The promised Father of the future age.
No more shall nation against nation rise,

Nor ardent warriors meet with hateful eyes;
Nor fields with gleaming steel be covered o'er;
The brazen trumpets kindle rage no more:
But useless lances into scythes shall bend,
And the broad falchion in a ploughshare end.
Then palaces shall rise; the joyful son
Shall finish what his short-lived sire begun;
Their vines a shadow to their race shall yield,
And the same hand that sowed, shall reap the field;
The swain, in barren deserts, with surprise
See lilies spring and sudden verdure rise;
And start, amid the thirsty wilds, to hear
New falls of water murmuring in his ear.
On rifted rocks, the dragons' late abodes,
The green reed trembles and the bulrush nods.
Waste, sandy valleys, once perplexed with thorn,
The spiry fir and shapely box adorn:
To leafless shrubs the flowery palms succeed,
And odorous myrtle to the noisome weed.
The lambs with wolves shall graze the verdant mead.
And boys in flowery bands the tyger lead:
The steer and lion at one crib shall meet,
And harmless serpents lick the pilgrim's feet.
The smiling infant in his hand shall take
The crested basilisk and speckled snake;
Pleased the green lusture of the scales survey,
And with their forky tongue shall innocently play.
Rise, crowned with light, imperial Salem, rise!
Exalt thy towery head and lift thy eyes!
See a long race thy spacious courts adorn!
See future sons and daughters, yet unborn,
In crowding ranks on every side arise,
Demanding life, impatient for the skies!

See barbarous nations at thy gates attend,
Walk in thy light and in thy temple bend!
See thy bright altars thronged with prostrate kings,
And heaped with products of Sabean springs!
For thee Idume's spicy forests blow,
And seeds of gold in Ophir's mountains glow.
See heaven its sparkling portals wide display
And break upon thee in a flood of day!
No more the rising sun shall gild the morn,
Nor evening Cynthia fill her silver horn,
But lost, dissolved in thy superior rays,
One tide of glory, one unclouded blaze
O'erflow thy courts: the Light Himself shall shine
Revealed, and God's eternal day be thine.
The seas shall waste, the skies in smoke decay,
Rocks fall to dust, and mountains melt away;
But fixed His word, His saving power remains;
Thy realm forever lasts, thy own MESSIAH reigns.

[*From the " Essay on Criticism."*]

'Tis hard to say if greater want of skill
Appear in writing or in judging ill;
But of the two less dangerous is the offence
To tire our patience than mislead our sense.

'Tis with our judgments as our watches; none
Go just alike, yet each believes his own.

All fools have still an itching to deride
And fain would be upon the laughing side.

Thus in the soul while memory prevails,
The solid power of understanding fails;
Where beams of warm imagination play,
The memory's soft figures melt away.
One science only will one genius fit;
So vast is art, so narrow human wit.
Like kings we lose the conquests gained before,
By vain ambition still to make them more:
Each might his several province well command,
Would all but stoop to what they understand.
Some to whom Heaven in wit has been profuse,
Want as much more to turn it to its use;
For wit and judgment often are at strife,
Though meant each other's aid, like man and wife.
'Tis more to guide than spur the Muses' steed,
Restrain his fury, than provoke his speed;
The wingéd courser, like a generous horse,
Shows most true mettle when you check his course.

Some beauties yet no precepts can declare,
For there's a happiness, as well as care.
Music resembles poetry; in each
Are nameless graces which no methods teach:
Great wits, sometimes may gloriously offend,
And rise to faults true critics dare not mend;
From vulgar bounds with brave disorder part,
And snatch a grace beyond the reach of art.

Those oft are stratagems which errors seem,
Nor is it Homer nods, but we that dream.

Of all the causes which conspire to blind
Man's erring judgment, and misguide the mind,

What the weak head with strongest bias rules,
Is pride, the never-failing vice of fools.

Trust not yourself: but, your defects to know,
Make use of every friend, and every foe.

A little learning is a dangerous thing;
Drink deep, or taste not the Pierian spring:
There shallow draughts intoxicate the brain,
And drinking largely sobers us again.

Fired at first sight with what the Muse imparts,
In fearless youth we tempt the heights of arts,
While, from the bounded level of our mind,
Short views we take, nor see the lengths behind;
But more advanced, behold, with strange surprise,
New distant scenes of endless science rise.
So pleased at first the towering Alps we try,
Mount o'er the vales, and seem to tread the sky,
The eternal snows appear already passed,
And the first clouds and mountains seem the last:
But, those attained, we tremble to survey
The growing labors of the lengthened way,
The increasing prospect tires our wandering eyes,
Hills peep o'er hills, and Alps on Alps arise.

Whoever thinks a faultless piece to see,
Thinks what ne'er was, nor is, nor e'er shall be.

A perfect judge will read each work of wit
With the same spirit that its author writ.

True wit is nature to advantage dressed,
What oft was thought, but ne'er so well expressed.

Words are like leaves ; and, where they most abound,
Much fruit of sense beneath is rarely found.

In words, as fashions, the same rule will hold ;
Alike fantastic, if too new, or old :
Be not the first by whom the new are tried,
Nor yet the last to lay the old aside.
   But most by numbers judge a poet's song,
And smooth or rough, with them, is right or wrong :
Who haunt Parnassus but to please their ear,
Not mend their minds ; as some to church repair,
Not for the doctrine, but the music there.
These equal syllables alone require,
Though oft the ear the open vowels tire,
While expletives their feeble aid do join,
And ten low words oft creep in one dull line.
A needless Alexandrine ends the song,
That, like a wounded snake, drags its slow length along.

True ease in writing comes from art, not chance,
As those move easiest who have learned to dance.
'Tis not enough no harshness gives offence,
The sound must seem an echo to the sense.
Soft is the strain when Zephyr gently blows,
And the smooth stream in smoother numbers flows ;
But when loud surges lash the sounding shore,
The hoarse rough verse should like the torrent roar :
When Ajax strives some rock's vast weight to throw,

The line too labors and the words move slow;
Not so when swift Camilla scours the plain,
Flies o'er the unbending corn and skims along the main.

Envy will merit as its shade pursue,
But like a shadow proves the substance true:
For envied wit, like Sol eclipsed, makes known
The opposing body's grossness, not its own.

Some foreign writers, some our own despise;
The ancient only, or the moderns prize.* *
Others for language all their care express,
And value books, as women men, for dress.

Good-nature and good sense must ever join;
To err is human, to forgive divine.

'Tis not enough your counsel still be true;
Blunt truths more mischiefs than nice falsehoods do:
Men must be taught as if you taught them not,
And things unknown proposed as things forgot.
Without good breeding truth is disapproved;
That only makes superior sense beloved.
    Be niggards of advice on no pretence;
For the worst avarice is that of sense.
With mean complacence ne'er betray your trust,
Nor be so civil as to prove unjust.
Fear not the anger of the wise to raise:
Those best can bear reproof, who merit praise.

'Tis best sometimes your censure to restrain,
And charitably let the dull be vain:

Your silence there is better than your spite,
For who can rail so long as they can write?
Still, humming on, their drowsy course they keep,
And, lashed so long, like tops, are lashed asleep.

The bookful blockhead, ignorantly read,
With loads of learnéd lumber in his head,
With his own tongue still edifies his ears,
And always listening to himself appears.

But see! each Muse, in Leo's* golden days,
Starts from her trance, and trims her withered bays;
Rome's ancient Genius, o'er its ruins spread,
Shakes off the dust, and rears his reverend head.
Then sculpture and her sister-arts revive;
Stones leaped to form, and rocks began to live;
With sweeter notes each rising temple rung:
A Raphael painted, and a Vida sung.

[*The ancient poets.*]
Still green with bays each ancient altar stands
Above the reach of sacrilegious hands;
Secure from flames, from envy's fiercer rage,
Destructive war, and all-involving age.
See from each clime the learned their incense bring!
Hear in all tongues consenting pæans ring!
In praise so just let every voice be joined,
And fill the general chorus of mankind.

    Hail, bards triumphant! born in happier days,
Immortal heirs of universal praise!

* Pope Leo X.

Whose honors with increase of ages grow,
As streams roll down, enlarging as they flow;
Nations unborn your mighty names shall sound,
And worlds applaud that must not yet be found.

[*From " The Rape of the Lock."*]

[The subject of this piece, which Dr. Johnson terms 'the most airy, ingenious and delightful' of all Pope's compositions, is the stealing of a lock of Miss Arabella Fermour's hair by her lover, Lord Petre; which it seems, was taken seriously and caused an estrangement between the families. Pope wrote his poem to make a jest of the affair and "laugh them together again."]

[*The Toilet.*]

And now unveiled the toilet stands displayed,
Each silver vase in mystic order laid.
First, robed in white, the nymph intent adores,
With head uncovered, the cosmetic powers.
A heavenly image in the glass appears,
To that she bends, to that her eyes she rears:
The inferior priestess, at her altar's side,
Trembling begins the sacred rites of pride.
Unnumbered treasures ope at once, and here
The various offerings of the world appear;
From each she nicely culls with curious toil,
And decks the goddess with the glittering spoil.
This casket India's glowing gems unlocks,
And all Arabia breathes from yonder box.
The tortoise here and elephant unite,
Transformed to combs, the speckled and the white.
Here files of pins extend their shining rows,
Puffs, powders, patches, bibles, billets-doux.
Now awful beauty puts on all its arms,

The fair each moment rises in her charms,
Repairs her smiles, awakens every grace,
And calls forth all the wonders of her face;
Sees by degrees a purer blush arise,
And keener lightnings quicken in her eyes.
The busy Sylphs surround their darling care,
These set the head, and those divide the hair,
Some fold the sleeve, whilst others plait the gown;
And Betty's praised for labors not her own.

[*Belinda and the Sylphs.*]

Not with more glories in the ethereal plain,
The sun first rises o'er the purpled main,
Than, issuing forth, the rival* of his beams
Launched on the bosom of the silver Thames.
Fair nymphs and well-dressed youths around her shone,
But every eye was fixed on her alone.
On her white breast a sparkling cross she wore,
Which Jews might kiss and Infidels adore.
Her lively looks a sprightly mind disclose,
Quick as her eyes, and as unfixed as those.
Favors to none, to all she smiles extends;
Oft she rejects, but never once offends.
Bright as the sun, her eyes the gazers strike,
And like the sun, they shine on all alike.
Yet graceful ease, and sweetness void of pride,
Might hide her faults, if belles had faults to hide:
If to her share some female errors fall,
Look on her face, and you'll forget them all.

 This nymph, to the destruction of mankind,
Nourished two locks, which graceful hung behind
In equal curls, and well conspired to deck

---

* Belinda or Miss Fermour.

With shining ringlets the smooth, ivory neck.
Love in these labyrinths his slaves detains,
And mighty hearts are held in slender chains.
Fair tresses man's imperial race insnare,
And beauty draws us with a single hair.
    The adventurous Baron the bright locks admired;
He saw, he wished, and to the prize aspired.
    But now secure the painted vessel glides,
The sun-beams trembling on the floating tides:
Smooth flow the waves, the zephyrs gently play,
BELINDA smiled, and all the world was gay,
All but the Sylph; with careful thoughts opprest,
The impending woe sat heavy on his breast.
He summons straight his denizens of air;
The lucid squadrons round the sails repair;
Soft o'er the shrouds aërial whispers breathe,
That seemed but zephyrs to the train beneath.
Some to the sun their insect-wings unfold,
Waft on the breeze, or sink in clouds of gold;
Transparent forms, too fine for mortal sight,
Their fluid bodies half dissolved in light;
Loose to the wind their airy garments flew,
Thin, glittering textures of the filmy dew,
Dipt in the richest tincture of the skies,
Where light disports in ever-mingling eyes;
While every beam new, transient colors flings,
Colors that change whene'er they wave their wings.
Amid the circle, on the gilded mast,
Superior by the head, was Ariel placed;
His purple pinions opening to the sun,
He raised his azure wand, and thus begun.
    Ye Sylphs and Sylphids, to your chief give ear,
Fays, fairies, genii, elves, and demons, hear!

Ye know the spheres and various tasks assigned
By laws eternal to the aerial kind.
Some in the fields of purest ether play,
And bask and whiten in the blaze of day.
Some guide the course of wandering orbs on high,
Or roll the planets through the boundless sky;
Some, less refined, beneath the moon's pale light,
Pursue the stars that shoot athwart the night,
Or suck the mists in grosser air below,
Or dip their pinions in the painted bow,
Or brew fierce tempests on the wintry main,
Or o'er the globe distil the kindly rain.
Others on earth o'er human race preside,
Watch all their ways, and all their actions guide.

   Our humbler province is to tend the fair,
Not a less pleasing, though less glorious care;
To save the powder from too rude a gale,
Nor let the imprisoned essences exhale;
To draw fresh colors from the vernal flowers;
To steal from rainbows, ere they drop in showers,
A brighter wash; to curl their waving hairs,
Assist their blushes, and inspire their airs;
Nay, oft, in dreams, invention we bestow,
To change a flounce, or add a furbelow.

   This day black omens threat the brightest fair
That e'er deserved a watchful spirit's care;
Some dire disaster, or by force, or sleight,
But what, or where, the fates have left in night.
Whatever spirit, careless of his charge,
His post neglects, or leaves the fair at large,
Shall feel sharp vengeance soon o'ertake his sins,
Be stopped in vials, or transfixed with pins;
Or plunged in lakes of bitter washes lie,

Or wedged whole ages in a bodkin's eye ;
Gums and pomatums shall his flight restrain,
While clogged he beats his silken wings in vain ;
Or alum styptics, with contracting power,
Shrink his thin essence, like a riveled flower.
Or, as Ixion fixed, the wretch shall feel
The giddy motion of the whirling mill,
In fumes of burning chocolate shall glow,
And tremble at the sea that froths below.

 He spoke ; the spirits from the sails descend ;
Some, orb in orb, around the nymph extend ;
Some thrid the mazy ringlets of her hair ;
Some hang upon the pendants of her ear ;
With beating hearts the dire events they wait,
Anxious, and trembling for the events of fate.

[*A tea-party at Hampton-Court.*]
Hither the heroes and the nymphs resort
To taste awhile the pleasures of a court ;
In various talk the instructive hours they passed,
Who gave the ball, or paid the visit last.
One speaks the glory of the British queen,
And one describes a charming Indian screen ;
A third interprets motions, looks, and eyes ;
At every word a reputation dies.
Snuff, or the fan, supplies each pause of chat,
With singing, laughing, ogling, *and all that.*

 Meanwhile, declining from the noon of day,
The sun obliquely shoots his burning ray ;
The hungry judges soon the sentence sign,
And wretches hang that jurymen may dine.

    * * *

 Oh thoughtless mortals ! ever blind to fate,
Too soon dejected, and too soon elate.

Sudden these honors shall be snatched away,
And cursed forever this victorious day.

    For lo! the board with cups and spoons is crowned,
The berries crackle, and the mill turns round;
From silver spouts the grateful liquors glide,
While China's earth receives the smoking tide.
Coffee, which makes the politican wise
And see through all things with his half-shut eyes,
Sent up in vapors to the Baron's brain
New stratagems the radiant lock to gain.
Ah! cease, rash youth, desist ere 'tis too late,
Fear the just gods, and think of Scylla's fate!*

    But when to mischief mortals bend their will,
How soon they find fit instruments of ill!
Just then Clarissa drew, with tempting grace,
A two-edged weapon from her shining case;
So ladies in romance assist their knight,
Present the spear and arm him for the fight.
He takes the gift with reverence, and extends
The little engine on his fingers' ends;
Swift to the lock a thousand sprites repair,
A thousand wings by turns blow back the hair.
And thrice they twitched the diamond in her ear;
Thrice she looked back, and thrice the foe drew near.

    The peer now spreads the glittering forceps wide,
To inclose the lock; now joins it, to divide.
Even then, before the fatal engine closed,
A wretched Sylph too fondly interposed;
Fate urged the shears and cut the Sylph in twain,
(But airy substance soon unites again,)
The meeting points the sacred hair dissever
From the fair head, for ever, and forever!

          * See Ovid. Met. [8]

Then flashed the living lightning from her eyes,
And screams of horror rend the affrighted skies:
Not louder shrieks to pitying Heaven are cast,
When husbands, or when lap-dogs, breathe their last.
Not youthful kings in battle seized alive,
Not scornful virgins who their charms survive,
Not tyrants fierce that unrepenting die,
Not Cynthia when her manteau's pinned awry,
E'er felt such rage, resentment and despair,
As thou, sad virgin! for thy ravished hair.

[*Belinda's lament.*]

Forever cursed be this detested day,
Which snatched my best, my favorite curl away!
Yet am I not the first mistaken maid
By love of courts to numerous ills betrayed.
Oh, had I rather unadmired remained,
In some lone isle, or distant northern land!
Where the gilt chariot never marks the way,
Where none learn ombre, none e'er taste Bohea.
What moved my mind with youthful lords to roam?
Oh, had I staid, and said my prayers at home!
'Twas this the morning omens seemed to tell;
Thrice from my trembling hand the patch-box fell,
The tottering china shook without a wind,
Nay, Poll sat mute, and Shock * was most unkind.
See the poor remnants of these slighted hairs!
My hands shall rend what even thy rapine spares.
These, in two sable ringlets taught to break,
Once gave new beauties to the snowy neck;
The sister lock now sits uncouth, alone,
And in its fellow's fate foresees its own;

* Lap-dog.

Uncurled it hangs, the fatal shears demands,
And tempts, once more, thy sacrilegious hands.
    She said, the pitying audience melt in tears,
But Fate and Jove had stopped the Baron's ears.
Then grave Clarissa graceful waved her fan;
Silence ensued, and thus the nymph began.
    Say, why are beauties praised and honored most,
The wise man's passion, and the vain man's toast?
Why decked with all that land and sea afford,
Why angels called, and angel-like adored?
Why round our coaches crowd the white-gloved beaux,
Why bows the side-box from its inmost rows?
How vain are all these glories, all our pains,
Unless good sense preserve what beauty gains?
That men may say, when we the front-box grace,
Behold the first in virtue as in face.
Oh! if to dance all night, and dress all day,
Charmed the small-pox, or chased old-age away,
Who would not scorn what housewife's cares produce,
Or who would learn one earthly thing of use?
To patch, nay, ogle, might become a saint,
Nor could it sure be such a sin to paint.
But since, alas! frail beauty must decay,
Curled, or uncurled, since locks will turn to grey;
What then remains but well our power to use,
And keep good humor still, whate'er we lose?
And trust me, dear, good humor can prevail,
When airs, and flights, and screams, and scolding fail.
Beauties in vain their pretty eyes may roll;
Charms strike the sight, but merit wins the soul.
    So spake the dame, but no applause ensued;
Belinda frowned, Thalestris called her prude.

Pope.

[*From the battle scene.*]

See, fierce Belinda on the Baron flies,
With more than usual lightning in her eyes.* *
But this bold lord, with manly strength endued,
She, with one finger and a thumb subdued.
Just where the breath of life his nostrils drew
A charge of snuff the wily virgin threw;
The gnomes direct, to every atom just,
The pungent grains of titillating dust.
Sudden with starting tears each eye o'erflows,
And the high dome re-echoes to his nose.

Restore the lock! she cries; and, all around,
Restore the lock! the vaulted roofs rebound.
Not fierce Othello, in so loud a strain,
Roared for the handkerchief that caused his pain.
But see how oft ambitious aims are crossed,
And chiefs contend till all the prize is lost!
The lock, obtained with guilt and kept with pain,
In every place is sought, but sought in vain.
Some thought it mounted to the lunar sphere,
Since all things lost on earth are treasured there.
There heroes' wits are kept in ponderous vases,
And beaux', in snuff-boxes and tweezer-cases.
There broken vows, and death-bed alms are found,
And lovers' hearts, with ends of riband bound;
Cages for gnats, and chains to yoke a flea,
Dried butterflies, and tomes of casuistry.

But trust the Muse! she saw it upward rise,
Though marked by none but quick, poetic eyes;
A sudden star, it shot through liquid air,
And drew behind a radiant trail of hair.
The Sylphs behold it, kindling as it flies,

And pleased pursue its progress through the skies.
This the beau monde shall from the Mall survey
And hail with music its propitious ray ;
This the blest lover shall for Venus take,
And send up vows from Rosamonda's lake.
    Then cease, bright nymph! to mourn thy ravished hair,
Which adds new glory to the shining sphere.
Not all the tresses that fair head can boast,
Shall draw such envy as the lock you lost.
For after all the murders of your eye,
When, after millions slain, yourself shall die ;
When those fair suns shall set, as set they must,
And all those tresses shall be laid in dust ;
This lock the Muse shall consecrate to fame,
And 'midst the stars inscribe Belinda's name.

[*From Eloisa to Abelard.*]

In these deep solitudes and awful cells,
Where heavenly-pensive Contemplation dwells,
And ever-musing Melancholy reigns,
What means this tumult in a vestal's veins?
Why rove my thoughts beyond this last retreat?
Why feels my heart its long forgotten heat?
Yet, yet I love : from Abelard it came,
And Eloisa yet must kiss the name.
    Dear fatal name! rest ever unrevealed,
Nor pass these lips in holy silence sealed :
Hide it, my heart, within that close disguise,
Where, mixed with God's, his loved idea lies :
O write it not, my hand! the name appears
Already written ; wash it out my tears!

Pope.

In vain lost Eloisa weeps and prays,
Her heart still dictates, and her hand obeys.
   Relentless walls! whose darksome round contains
Repentant sighs, and voluntary pains:
Ye rugged rocks, which holy knees have worn;
Ye grots and caverns, shagged with horrid thorn;
Shrines, where their vigils pale-eyed virgins keep,
And pitying saints, whose statues learn to weep!
Though cold like you, unmoved and silent grown,
I have not yet forgot myself to stone.
All is not Heaven's while Abelard has part,
Still rebel nature holds out half my heart;
Nor prayers nor fasts its stubborn pulse restrain,
Nor tears for ages taught to flow in vain.
   Soon as thy letters trembling I unclose,
That well-known name awakens all my woes.
O, name forever sad! forever dear!
Still breathed in sighs, still ushered with a tear.
I tremble, too, where'er my own I find,
Some dire misfortune follows close behind.
Line after line my gushing eyes o'erflow,
Led through a sad variety of wo;
Now warm in love, now withering in my bloom,
Lost in a convent's solitary gloom.
There stern religion quenched the unwilling flame,
There died the best of passions, love and fame.
   Yet write, Oh! write me all, that I may join
Griefs to thy griefs, and echo sighs to thine.
Nor foes nor fortune take this power away;
And is my Abelard less kind than they?
Tears still are mine, and those I need not spare;
Love but demands what else were shed in prayer:
No happier task these faded eyes pursue;
To read and weep is all they now can do.

Then share thy pain, allow that sad relief;
Ah, more than share it! give me all thy grief.
Heaven first taught letters for some wretch's aid,
Some banished lover, or some captive maid;
They live, they speak, they breathe what love inspires,
Warm from the soul, and faithful to its fires;
The virgin's wish without her fears impart,
Excuse the blush, and pour out all the heart,
Speed the soft intercourse from soul to soul
And waft a sigh from Indus to the pole.

Ah, think at least thy flock deserves thy care,
Plants of thy hand and children of thy prayer;
From the false world in early youth they fled,
By thee to mountains, wilds, and deserts led.
You raised these hallowed walls; the desert smiled,
And Paradise was opened in the wild.
No weeping orphan saw his father's stores
Our shrines irradiate, or emblaze the floors;
No silver saints, by dying misers given,
Here bribed the rage of ill-requited Heaven:
But such plain roofs as piety could raise,
And only vocal with the Maker's praise.
In these lone walls (their days' eternal bound),
These moss-grown domes with spiry turrets crowned,
Where awful arches make a noonday night,
And the dim windows shed a solemn light;
Thy eyes diffused a reconciling ray,
And gleams of glory brightened all the day.
But now no face divine contentment wears,
'Tis all blank sadness, or continual tears.
See how the force of others' prayers I try;
O pious fraud of amorous charity!
But why should I on others' prayers depend?

Come thou, my father, brother, husband, friend!
Ah, let thy handmaid, sister, daughter move,
And all those tender names in one, thy love!
The darksome pines that, o'er yon rocks reclined,
Wave high, and murmur to the hollow wind;
The wandering streams that shine between the hills,
The grots that echo to the tinkling rills,
The dying gales that pant upon the trees,
The lakes that quiver to the curling breeze;
No more these scenes my meditation aid,
Or lull to rest the visionary maid:
But, o'er the twilight groves and dusky caves,
Long-sounding aisles and intermingled graves,
Black Melancholy sits, and round her throws
A death-like silence and a dread repose:
Her gloomy presence shadows all the scene,
Shades every flower and darkens every green,
Deepens the murmur of the falling floods
And breathes a browner horror on the woods.

How happy is the blameless vestal's lot!
The world forgetting, by the world forgot;
Eternal sunshine of the spotless mind,
Each prayer accepted, and each wish resigned,
Labor and rest, that equal periods keep,
"Obedient slumbers that can wake and weep,"*
Desires composed, affections ever even,
Tears that delight, and sighs that waft to heaven.
Grace shines around her with serenest beams,
And whispering angels prompt her golden dreams.
For her the unfading rose of Eden blooms,

---

* This beautiful line was taken from what appears to be a version, by Crashaw, of a passage in Barclay.

And wings of seraphs shed divine perfumes ;
For her the Spouse prepares the bridal ring,
For her white virgins hymeneals sing,
To sounds of heavenly harps she dies away,
And melts in visions of eternal day.

What scenes appear where'er I turn my view!
The dear ideas, where I fly, pursue.
I waste the matin lamp in sighs for thee,
Thy image steals between my God and me.
Thy voice I seem in every hymn to hear,
With every bead I drop too soft a tear.
When from the censer clouds of fragrance roll,
And swelling organs lift the rising soul,
One thought of thee puts all the pomp to flight,
Priests, tapers, temples, swim before my sight;
In seas of flame my plunging soul is drowned,
While altars blaze, and angels tremble round.
　While prostrate here in humble grief I lie,
Kind virtuous drops just gathering in my eye ;
While praying, trembling in the dust I roll,
And dawning grace is opening on my soul ;
Come, if thou darest, all charming as thou art,
Oppose thyself to Heaven; dispute my heart :
Come, with one glance of those deluding eyes,
Blot out each bright idea of the skies ;
Take back that grace, those sorrows, and those tears ;
Take back my fruitless penitence and prayers ;
Snatch me, just mounting, from the blest abode ;
Assist the fiends, and tear me from my God!
　No, fly me, fly me! far as pole from pole ;
Rise alps between us, and whole oceans roll !

Pope.

Ah, come not, write not, think not once of me,
Nor share one pang of all I felt for thee.
Thy oaths I quit, thy memory I resign;
Forget, renounce me, hate whate'er was mine.
Fair eyes, and tempting looks, which yet I view,
Long loved, adored ideas, all adieu!
Oh grace serene! O heavenly virtue fair!
Divine oblivion of low-thoughted care!
Fresh-blooming hope, gay daughter of the sky!
And faith, our early immortality!
Enter, each mild, each amicable guest;
Receive and wrap me in eternal rest!
 See in her cell sad Eloisa spread,
Propt on some tomb, a neighbour of the dead.
In each low wind methinks a spirit calls,
And more than echoes talk along the walls.
Here, as I watched the dying lamps around,
From yonder shrine I heard a solemn sound.
"Come, sister, come! (it said or seemed to say)
Thy place is here, sad sister, come away;
Once, like thyself, I trembled, wept and prayed,
Love's victim then, though now a sainted maid."
 I come, I come, prepare your roseate bowers:
Celestial palms and ever-blooming flowers:
Thither, where sinners may have rest, I go,
Where flames refined in breasts seraphic glow.
Thou, Abelard! the last sad office pay,
And smooth my passage to the realms of day:
See my lips tremble and my eyeballs roll,
Suck my last breath, and catch my flying soul!
Ah, no! in sacred vestments may'st thou stand,
The hallowed taper trembling in thy hand,
Present the cross before my lifted eye,

Teach me, at once, and learn of me, to die.
Ah, then, thy once-loved Eloisa see!
It will be then no crime to gaze on me.
See from my cheek the transient roses fly!
See the last sparkle languish in my eye!
Till every motion, pulse, and breath be o'er,
And even my Aberlard be loved no more.
O death, all-eloquent! you only prove
What dust we dote on when 'tis man we love.

 May one kind grave unite each hapless name,
And graft my love immortal on thy fame!
Then, ages hence, when all my woes are o'er,
When this rebellious heart shall beat no more,
If ever chance two wandering lovers brings
To Paraclete's* white walls and silver springs,
O'er the pale marble shall they join their heads,
And drink the falling tears each other sheds;
Then sadly say, with mutual pity moved,
"O, may we never love as these have loved!"

[*From "Epistle to Robert, Earl of Oxford."*]

In vain to deserts thy retreat is made,
The Muse attends thee to thy silent shade;
'Tis hers the brave man's latest steps to trace,
Rejudge his acts, and dignify disgrace.
When Interest calls off all her sneaking train,
When all the obliged desert, and all the vain,
She waits, or to the scaffold, or the cell,
When the last lingering friend has bid farewell.

---

 * Abelard and Eloisa were interred in the same grave, or in monuments adjoining, in the Monastery of the Paraclete. He died in 1142, she in 1163.

Pope.

[*From " Epistle to Mr. Jervas, the Painter."*]

Smit with the love of sister arts we came,
And met congenial, mingling flame with flame.
What flattering scenes our wandering fancy wrought,
Rome's pompous glories rising to our thought!
With thee on Raphael's monument I mourn,
Or wait inspiring dreams at Maro's urn;
With thee repose where Tully once was laid,
Or seek some ruin's formidable shade:
While fancy brings the vanished piles to view,
And builds imaginary Rome anew.
Here thy well studied marbles fix our eye;
A fading fresco here demands a sigh;
Each heavenly piece unwearied we compare,
Match Raphael's grace with thy loved Guido's air,
Caracci's strength, Corregio's softer line,
Paulo's free stroke, and Titian's warmth divine.

 Beauty, frail flower, that every season fears,
Blooms in thy colours for a thousand years;
Thus Churchill's race shall other hearts surprise
And other beauties envy Worsley's eyes,
Each pleasing Blount shall other smiles bestow,
And soft Belinda's blush forever glow.

 Oh, lasting as those colours may they shine,
Free as thy stroke, yet faultless as thy line;
New graces yearly, like thy works, display,
Soft without weakness, without glaring, gay;
Led by some rule that guides, but not constrains,
And finished more through happiness than pains.

 Yet should the Graces all thy figures place,
And breathe an air divine on every face;

Yet, should the Muses bid my numbers roll,
Strong as their charms, and gentle as their soul;
Alas! how little from the grave we claim!
Thou but preserv'st a face, and I a name.

[*From " Epistle to Miss Blount."*]

Too much your sex is by their forms confined,
Severe to all, but most to womankind:
Marriage may all those petty tyrants chase,
But sets up one, a greater in its place:
Well might you wish for change, by those accurst,
But the last tyrant ever proves the worst:
Whole years neglected for some months adored,
The fawning servant turns a haughty lord.

   The gods, to curse Pamela with her prayers,
Gave the gilt coach and dappled Flanders mares,
The shining robes, rich jewels, beds of state,
And, to complete her bliss, a fool for mate.
She glares in balls, front boxes, and the ring,
A vain, unquiet, glittering, wretched thing.
Pride, pomp, and state, but reach her outward part;
She sighs, and is no Duchess at her heart.

   But, Madam, if the fates withstand, and you
Are destined Hymen's willing victim too;
Trust not too much your now resistless charms,
Those age, or sickness, soon or late, disarms.
Good-humor only teaches charms to last,
Still makes new conquests, and maintains the past;
Love, raised on beauty, will, like that, decay,
Our hearts may bear its slender chains a day,
As flowery bands in wantonness are worn,
A morning's pleasure, and at evening torn;

This binds in ties more easy, yet more strong,
The willing heart and only holds it long.

To Mr. John Moore, author of the celebrated worm-powder.

    How much, egregious Moore! are we
        Deceived by shows and forms!
    Whate'er we think, whate'er we see,
        All humankind are worms.

    Man is a very worm by birth,
        Vile reptile, weak and vain:
    Awhile he crawls upon the earth,
        Then shrinks to earth again.

    The fops are painted butterflies,
        That flutter for a day;
    First from a worm they take their rise,
        And in a worm decay.

    The flatterer an earwig grows:
        Thus worms suit all conditions;
    Misers are muck-worms, silk-worms beaux,
        And death-watches physicians.

    That statesmen have the worm, is seen
        By all their winding play;
    Their conscience is a worm within,
        That gnaws them night and day.

    Ah Moore! thy skill were well employed,
        And greater gain would rise,
    If thou couldst make the courtier void
        The worm that never dies.

[*From "Elegy on an unfortunate Lady."*]

Who this suicidal lady was, appears to be still a mystery. "The verses," says Dyce, "seem unintelligible, unless they allude to some connection to which her highest hope, though nobly connected herself, could not aspire."

What beckoning ghost, along the moonlight shade,
Invites my steps and points to yonder glade?
'Tis she! but why that bleeding bosom gored?
Why dimly gleams the visionary sword?
O ever beauteous, ever friendly! tell,
Is it a crime in heaven to love too well? †
To bear too tender, or too firm a heart,
To act a lover's or a Roman's part?
Is there no bright reversion in the sky
For those who greatly think, or bravely die?

Most souls, 'tis true, but peep out once an age,
Dull, sullen prisoners in the body's cage,
Dim lights of life, that burn a length of years,
Useless, unseen, as lamps in sepulchres,
Like eastern kings, a lazy state they keep,
And, close confined to their own palace, sleep.

From these, perhaps, ere nature bade her die,
Fate snatched her early to the pitying sky;
As into air the purer spirits flow,
And separate from their kindred dregs below,
So flew the soul to its congenial place,
Nor left one virtue to redeem her race.

† This passage, though merely interrogatory, is scarcely less objectionable than if not so qualified. The author must really have believed that, in the sight of Heaven, suicide is always criminal. The poem was not the production of his maturer years, and the interest which he took in the unfortunate subject of it, was perhaps the result of a warmer affection than mere friendship.

But thou, false guardian of a charge too good,
Thou mean deserter of thy brother's blood!
See on these ruby lips the trembling breath,
These cheeks now fading at the blast of death:
Cold is that breast which warmed the world before,
And those love-darting eyes must roll no more.
Thus, if eternal justice rule the ball,
Thus shall your wives, and thus your children fall:
On all the line a sudden vengeance waits,
And frequent hearses shall besiege your gates:
There passengers shall stand, and, pointing, say,
(While the long funerals blacken all the way,)
Lo! these were they, whose souls the furies steeled
And cursed with hearts unknowing how to yield.
Thus, unlamented, pass the proud away,
The gaze of fools and pageants of a day;
So perish all, whose breasts ne'er learned to glow
For others' good, or melt at others' wo.

What can atone, O ever injured shade!
Thy fate unpitied, and thy rites unpaid?
No friend's complaint, no kind domestic tear
Pleased thy pale ghost, or graced thy mournful bier:
By foreign hands thy dying eyes were closed,
By foreign hands thy decent limbs composed,
By foreign hands thy humble grave adorned,
By strangers honoured and by strangers mourned.
What though no friends in sable weeds appear,
Grieve for an hour, perhaps, then mourn a year,
And bear about the mockery of woe
To midnight dances and the public show;
What though no weeping loves thy ashes grace,
Nor polished marble emulate thy face;
What though no sacred earth allow thee room,

Nor hallowed dirge be muttered o'er thy tomb:
Yet shall thy grave with rising flowers be dressed,
And the green turf lie lightly on thy breast.
There shall the morn her earliest tears bestow;
There the first roses of the year shall blow;
While angels with their silver wings o'ershade
The ground, now sacred by thy relics made.
   So, peaceful rests, without a stone, a name,
That once had beauty, titles, wealth and fame.
A heap of dust alone remains of thee;
'Tis all thou art, and all the proud shall be.

Epitaph on Mrs. Corbet.

Here rests a woman, good without pretence,
Blest with plain reason and with sober sense;
No conquest she, but o'er herself desired,
No arts essayed, but not to be admired.
Passion and pride were to her soul unknown,
Convinced that virtue only is our own.
So unaffected, so composed a mind,
So firm yet soft, so strong yet so refined,
Heaven, as its purer gold, by tortures tried;
The saint sustained it, but the woman died.

[From "On two Lovers killed by lightning."]

When eastern lovers feed the funeral fire,
On the same pile the faithful pair expire:
Here pitying Heaven that virtue mutual found,
And blasted both that It might neither wound.
Hearts so sincere th' Almighty saw well pleased,
Sent His own lightning, and the victims seized.

Epitaph on Fenton, the poet.

This modest stone, what few vain marbles can,
May truly say, Here lies an honest man:
A poet, blest beyond the poet's fate,
Whom Heaven kept sacred from the proud and great:
Foe to loud praise, and friend to learned ease,
Content with science in the vale of peace.
Calmly he looked on either life, and here
Saw nothing to regret, or there to fear;
From nature's temperate feast rose satisfied,
Thanked Heaven that he had lived, and that he died.

Epitaph on Gay, the poet.

Of gentle manners, of affection mild,
In wit a man, simplicity a child;
With native humor tempering virtuous rage,
Formed to delight at once and lash the age;
Above temptation in a low estate,
And uncorrupted even among the great;
A safe companion, and an easy friend;
Unblamed through life, lamented in thy end:
These are thy honors! not that here thy bust
Is mixed with heroes, or with kings thy dust;
But that the worthy and the good shall say,
Striking their pensive bosoms, "Here lies Gay."

[FROM "MORAL ESSAYS." EPISTLE I.]

On the knowledge and characters of men.

That each from others differs first confess,
Next, that he varies from himself no less.
On human actions reason though you can,

It may be reason, but it is not man:
His principle of action once explore,
That instant 'tis his principle no more.
Like following life through creatures you dissect,
You lose it in the moment you detect.

    Yet more; the difference is as great between
The optics seeing, as the objects seen.
All manners take a tincture from our own,
Or come discolored through our passions shown.

    Nor will life's stream for observation stay,
It hurries all too fast to mark their way.
In vain sedate reflections we would make,
When half our knowledge we must snatch, not take.

    True, some are open and to all men known,
Others so very close they're hid from none.
But these plain characters we seldom find;
Though strong the bent, yet quick the turns of mind:
The dull flat falsehood serves for policy,
And in the cunning truth itself's a lie;
Unthought of frailties cheat us in the wise,
The fool lies hid in inconsistencies.
Know God and nature only are the same;
In man the judgment shoots at flying game.

II. In vain the sage with retrospective eye
Would from the apparent What conclude the Why,
Infer the motive from the deed, and show
That what we chanced was what we meant to do.
Behold! if fortune or a mistress frowns,
Some plunge in business, others shave their crowns:
To ease the soul of one oppressive weight,
This quits an empire, that embroils a state:
The same adust complexion has impelled
Charles to the convent, Philip to the field.

Pope.

    Not always actions show the man : we find
Who does a kindness is not therefore kind ;
Perhaps prosperity becalmed his breast,
Perhaps the wind just shifted from the east :
Not therefore humble he who seeks retreat,
Pride guides his steps, and bids him shun the great.
Who combats bravely is not therefore brave,
He dreads a death-bed, like the meanest slave ;
Who reasons wisely is not therefore wise,
His pride in reasoning, not in acting lies.
    'Tis from high life high characters are drawn ;
A saint in crape is twice a saint in lawn.
A judge is just, a chancellor juster still ;
A gown-man learned ; a bishop, what you will :
Wise, if a minister ; but, if a king,
More wise, more learned, more just, more everything.
Court-virtues bear, like gems, the highest rate,
Born where Heaven's influence scarce can penetrate ;
In life's low vale, the soil the virtues like,
They please as beauties, here* as wonders strike.
Though the same sun, with all diffusive rays,
Blush in the rose, and in the diamond blaze,
We praise the stronger effort of his power,
And justly set the gem before the flower.
    'Tis education forms the common mind,
Just as the twig is bent the tree's inclined.
Boastful and rough, your first son is a squire ;
The next a tradesman, meek and much a liar ;
Tom struts a soldier, open, bold, and brave ;
Will sneaks a scrivener, an exceeding knave.
Is he a churchman ? † then he's fond of power ;

    * At Court.
    † A member of the English established church ?

A quaker? sly; a presbyterian? sour;
A smart freethinker? all things in an hour.
  Judge we by nature? habit can efface,
Interest o'ercome, or policy take place;
By actions? those uncertainty divides;
By passions? these dissimulation hides;
Opinions? they still take a wider range;
Find, if you can, in what you cannot change.
Manners with fortunes, humors turn with climes,
Tenets with books, and principles with times.*
III. Search then the RULING PASSION; there alone
The wild are constant, and the cunning known;
This clue once found unravels all the rest,
The prospect clears, and Wharton stands confest:
Wharton, the scorn and wonder of our days,
Whose ruling passion was the lust of praise.
Though wondering senates hung on all he spoke,
The club must hail him master of the joke.
Shall parts so various aim at nothing new?
He'll shine a Tully and a Wilmot too.
Thus with each gift of nature and of art,
And wanting nothing but an honest heart;
Grown all to all, from no one vice exempt,
And most contemptible to shun contempt;
His passion, still to covet general praise,
His life, to forfeit it a thousand ways;
A constant bounty, which no friend has made;
An angel tongue, which no man can persuade;
A fool, with more of wit than half mankind;
Too rash for thought, for action too refined;
A tyrant to the wife his heart approves;

---

  * Not true religious tenets, not rational principles.

A rebel to the very king he loves;
He dies, sad outcast of each church and state,
And, harder still! flagitious, yet not great.
Ask you why Wharton broke through every rule?
'Twas all for fear the knaves would call him fool.

In this one passion* man can strength enjoy,
As fits give vigor just when they destroy.
Time that on all things lays his lenient hand,
Yet tames not this; it sticks to our last sand.
Consistent in our follies and our sins,
Here honest Nature ends as she begins.
Old politicians chew on wisdom past,
And totter on in business to the last;
The frugal crone, whom praying priests attend,
Still strives to save the hallowed taper's end,
Collects her breath, as ebbing life retires,
For one puff more, and in that puff expires.

"Odious! in woollen! 'twould a saint provoke,"
Were the last words that poor Narcissa spoke;
"No! let a charming chintz and Brussels lace
Wrap my cold limbs and shade my lifeless face;
One would not, sure, be frightful when one's dead;
And, Betty, give these cheeks a little red."

The courtier smooth, who forty years had shined
An humble servant to all human kind,
Just brought out this, when scarce his tongue could stir,
"If where I'm going I could serve you, Sir?"

"I give and I devise," old Euclio said,
And sighed, "my lands and tenements to Ned."
"Your money, Sir!" "My money, Sir! what all?
Why, if I must, (then wept,) I give it Paul."

* The ruling passion.

"The manor, Sir?" "The manor? hold!" he cried,
"Not that, I cannot part with that," and died.

[FROM "MORAL ESSAYS." EPISTLE II.]
To a Lady.
Of the characters of women.

For his ludicrous exhibition of some of the sex in this piece, the author perhaps amply compensates by the admired passage near the close, commencing with "Ah! friend," and ending with "Though China fall."

Nothing so true as what you once let fall,
"Most women have no characters at all:"*
Matter too soft a lasting mark to bear,
And best distinguished by black, brown, or fair.
How many pictures of one nymph we view,
All how unlike each other, all how true.
  How soft is Silia, fearful to offend,
The frail one's advocate, the weak one's friend.
To her Calista proved her conduct nice,
And good Simplicius asks of her advice.
Sudden she storms! she raves! you tip the wink,
But spare your censure, Silia does not drink,
All eyes may see from what the change arose;
All eyes may see a pimple on her nose.
  Papilia, wedded to her amorous spark,
Sighs for the shades; "How charming is a park!"
A park is purchased, but the fair he sees
All bathed in tears; "Oh odious, odious trees!"
  Ladies like variegated tulips show;
'Tis to their changes half their charms we owe;

---
* No fixed characters.

Fine by defect, and delicately weak,
Their happy spots the nice admirer take.
'Twas thus Calypso once each heart alarmed,
Awed without virtue, without beauty charmed;
Her tongue bewitched as oddly as her eyes;
Less wit than mimic, more a wit than wise.
Strange graces still, and stranger flights she had,
Was just not ugly, and was just not mad;
Yet ne'er so sure our passion to create,
As when she touched the brink of all we hate.
　Narcissa's nature, tolerably mild,
To make a wash, would hardly stew a child;
Has even been proved to grant a lover's prayer,
And paid a tradesman once, to make him stare:
Gave alms at Easter, in a Christian trim,
And made a widow happy, for a whim.
Why then declare good-nature is her scorn,
When 'tis by that alone she can be borne?
Why pique all mortals, yet affect a name?
A fool to pleasure, yet a slave to fame;
Now deep in Taylor, and the Book of martyrs,
Now drinking citron with his grace and Chartres;
Now conscience chills her, and now passion burns,
And atheism and religion take their turns.
　Flavia's a wit, has too much sense to pray;
To toast our wants and wishes, is her way;
Nor ask of God, but of her stars, to give
The mighty blessing, "While we live to live."
Then all for death, that opiate of the soul!
Lucretia's dagger, Rosamonda's bowl.
Wise wretch! with pleasures too refined to please;
With too much spirit to be e'er at ease;
With too much quickness ever to be taught;

With too much thinking to have common thought;
You purchase pain with all that joy can give,
And die of nothing but a rage to live.

    Turn then from wits, and look on Simo's mate,
No ass so meek, no ass so obstinate:
Or her, that owns her faults, but never mends,
Because she's honest, and the best of friends:
Or her, whose life the church and scandal share,
For ever in a passion, or a prayer.
Or her, who laughs at hell, but, like her Grace,
Cries, "Ah! how charming if there's no such place!"
Or who in sweet vicissitude appears,
Of mirth and opium, ratifie and tears,
The daily anodyne, and nightly draught,
To kill those foes to fair ones, time and thought.

    But what are these to great Atossa's mind?
Scarce once herself, by turns all womankind.
Who with herself, or others, from her birth
Finds all her life one warfare upon earth:
Shines in exposing knaves, and painting fools,
Yet is whate'er she hates and ridicules.
Full sixty years the world has been her trade,
The wisest fool much time has ever made:
Her every turn with violence pursued,
No more a storm her hate than gratitude.
Offend her, and she knows not to forgive;
Oblige her, and she'll hate you while you live;
But die and she'll adore you; then the bust
And temple rise—then fall again to dust.
Last night her lord was all that's good and great;
A knave this morning, and his will a cheat.
Strange! by the means defeated of the ends,
By spirit robbed of power, by warmth of friends,

By wealth of followers, without one distress,
Sick of herself through very selfishness!
  "Yet Chloe sure was formed without a spot."
Nature in her then erred not, but forgot.
"With every pleasing, every prudent part,
Say, what can Chloe want?" She wants a heart.
She speaks, behaves, and acts just as she ought;
But never, never, reached one generous thought.
Virtue she finds too painful an endeavour,
Content to dwell in decencies forever.
So very reasonable, so unmoved,
As never yet to love, or to be loved.
Of all her dears she never slandered one,
But cares not if a thousand are undone.
Would Chloe know if you're alive or dead?
She bids her footman put it in her head.
  Yet mark the fate of a whole sex of queens!
Power all their end, but beauty all the means.
In youth they conquer with so wild a rage,
As leaves them scarce a subject in their age.
For foreign glory, foreign joy they roam,
No thought of peace or happiness at home.
But wisdom's triumph is well-timed retreat,
As hard a science to the fair as great.
Beauties, like tyrants, old and friendless grown,
Yet hate repose, and dread to be alone,
Worn out in public, weary every eye,
Nor leave one sigh behind them when they die.
  See how the world its veterans rewards!
A youth of pleasure, an old age of cards;
Fair to no purpose, artful to no end,
Young without lovers, old without a friend;
A fop their passion, but their prize a sot;
Alive ridiculous, and dead forgot.

Ah! friend! to dazzle let the vain design;
To raise the thought, and touch the heart be thine!
That charm shall grow, while what fatigues the ring,
Flaunts and goes down, an unregarded thing.
So when the sun's broad beam has tired the sight,
All mild ascends the moon's more sober light;
Serene in virgin modesty she shines,
And unobserved the glaring orb declines.

Oh! blest with temper, whose unclouded ray
Can make to-morrow cheerful as to-day;
She, who can love a sister's charms, or hear
Sighs for a daughter with unwounded ear;
She, who ne'er answers till a husband cools,
Or, if she rules him, never shows she rules;
Charms by accepting, by submitting sways,
Yet has her humor most when she obeys;
Let fops or fortune fly which way they will,
Disdains all loss of tickets, or codille;
Spleen, vapours, or small-pox, above them all,
And mistress of herself though China fall.

And yet, believe me, good as well as ill,
Woman's at best a contradiction still.
Heaven, when it strives to polish all it can
Its last, best work, but forms a softer man;
Picks from each sex, to make the favorite blest,
Your love of pleasure, our desire of rest;
Blends in exception to all general rules,
Your taste of follies, with our scorn of fools;
Reserve with frankness, art with truth allied,
Courage with softness, modesty with pride;
Fixed principles, with fancy ever new;
Shakes all together, and produces—you.

[From "Moral Essays." Epistle III.]

[*Of the use of riches.*]

In vain may heroes fight, and patriots rave,
If secret gold sap on from knave to knave.
Blest paper-credit! last and best supply!
That lends corruption lighter wings to fly.
Gold imped by thee, can compass hardest things,
Can pocket states, can fetch or carry kings;
A single leaf shall waft an army o'er,
Or ship off senates to a distant shore;
A leaf, like Sibyl's, scatter to and fro
Our fates and fortunes, as the winds shall blow:
Pregnant with thousands flits the scrap unseen,
And silent sells a king, or buys a queen.

Riches, like insects, when concealed they lie,
Wait but for wings, and in their season fly.
Old Cotta shamed his fortune and his birth,
Yet was not Cotta void of wit or worth:
What though, the use of barbarous spits forgot,
His kitchen vied in coolness with his grot?
His court with nettles, moats with cresses stored,
With soups unbought, and salads blessed his board?
If Cotta lived on pulse, it was no more
Than Bramins, saints, and sages did before;
To cram the rich was prodigal expense,
And who would take the poor from Providence?
Like some lone chartreux stands the good old hall,
Silence without, and fasts within the wall;
No raftered roofs with dance and tabor sound,
No noon-tide bell invites the country round:
Tenants with sighs the smokeless towers survey,

And turn the unwilling steeds another way;
Benighted wanderers, the forest o'er,
Curse the saved candle and unopening door;
While the gaunt mastiff, growling at the gate,
Affrights the beggar whom he longs to to eat.

  Not so his son, he marked this oversight,
And then mistook reverse of wrong for right.
For what to shun will no great knowledge need,
But what to follow, is a task indeed.
Yet sure, of qualities deserving praise,
More go to ruin fortunes, than to raise.

  But all our praises why should lords engross?
Rise honest Muse! and sing the MAN OF ROSS.*
Who hung with woods yon mountain's sultry brow?
From the dry rock who made the waters flow?
Not to the skies in useless columns tossed,
Or in proud falls magnificently lost;
But clear and artless, pouring, through the plain,
Health to the sick, and solace to the swain.
Whose causeway parts the vale with shady rows;
Whose seats the weary traveller repose?
Who taught that heaven-directed spire to rise?
"The MAN OF ROSS," each lisping babe replies.
Behold the market-place with poor o'erspread!
The MAN OF ROSS divides the weekly bread:
He feeds yon alms-house, neat, but void of state,
Where age and want sit smiling at the gate:
Him portioned maids, apprenticed orphans blest,
The young who labour, and the old who rest.
Is any sick? the MAN OF ROSS relieves,
Prescribes, attends, the medicine makes and gives.

    * Said to be Mr. John Kyrle.

Is there a variance? enter but his door,
Baulked are the courts, and contest is no more:
Despairing quacks with curses fled the place,
And vile attorneys, now a useless race.
O say, what sums that generous hand supply,
What mines, to swell that boundless charity?
Of debts, and taxes, wife, and children clear,
This man possessed five hundred pounds a-year.
Blush, grandeur, blush! proud courts withdraw your
    blaze!
Ye little stars! hide your diminished rays.
    And what? no monument, inscription, stone?
His race, his form, his name almost unknown?
    Who builds a church to God, and not to fame,
Will never mark the marble with his name:
Go, search it there, where to be born and die,
Of rich and poor, makes all the history;
Enough, that virtue filled the space between;
Proved by the ends of being, to have been.
When Hopkins dies, a thousand lights attend
The wretch, who living saved a candle's end;
Shouldering God's altar a vile image stands,
Belies his features, nay, extends his hands;
That live-long wig which Gorgon's self might own,
Eternal buckle takes in Parian stone.
Behold what blessings wealth to life can lend!
And see what comfort it affords our end!
    In the worst inn's worst room, with mat half-hung,
The floors of plaster and the walls of dung,
On once a flock-bed, but repaired with straw,
With tape-tied curtains never meant to draw,
The George and Garter dangling from that bed,
Where tawdry yellow strove with dirty red,

Great Villiers* lies; alas! how changed from him,
That life of pleasure, and that soul of whim!
Gallant and gay, in Clieveden's proud alcove,
The bower of wanton Shrewsbury† and love;
Or just as gay at council, in a ring
Of mimic statesmen and their merry king.
No wit to flatter, left of all his store;
No fool to laugh at, which he valued more.
There, victor of his health, of fortune, friends,
And fame, this lord of useless thousands ends.

   His Grace's fate sage Cutler could foresee,
And well (he thought) advised him, "Live like me."
As well his Grace replied, "Like you, Sir John?
That I can do, when all I have is gone."
Resolve me, reason, which of these is worse,
Want with a full, or with an empty purse?
Thy life more wretched, Cutler, was confessed,
Arise, and tell me, was thy death more blessed?
Cutler saw tenants break, and houses fall,
For very want; he could not build a wall:
His only daughter in a stranger's power,
For very want; he could not pay a dower.
A few gray hairs his reverend temples crowned,
'Twas very want that sold them for two pound.
What even denied a cordial at his end,
Banished the doctor, and expelled the friend?
What but a want, which you, perhaps, think mad,
Yet numbers feel—the want of what he had!

   * Duke of Buckingham, the "Zimri" of Dryden's "Absalom and Achitophel."

   † The Countess of Shrewsbury, whose husband this Duke killed in a duel, on her account. She is said to have held the Duke's horses, disguised as a page, during the combat.

Cutler and Brutus, dying, both exclaim,
"Virtue! and wealth! what are ye but a name!"
   Where London's column* pointing to the skies,
Like a tall bully, lifts the head, and lies;
There dwelt a citizen, of sober fame,
A plain, good man, and Balaam was his name;
Religious, punctual, frugal, and so forth;
His word would pass for more than he was worth.
Constant at church and 'Change; his gains were sure,
His givings rare, save farthings to the poor.
   The devil was piqued such saintship to behold,
And longed to tempt him, like good Job of old;
But Satan now is wiser than of yore,
And tempts by making rich, not making poor.
   Roused by the prince of air, the whirlwinds sweep
The surge, and plunge his father in the deep;
Then full against his Cornish lands they roar,
And two rich shipwrecks bless the lucky shore.
   Sir Balaam now, he lives like other folks,
He takes his chirping pint, and cracks his jokes.
"Live like yourself," was soon my lady's word;
And lo! two puddings smoked upon the board.
   Asleep and naked as an Indian lay,
An honest factor stole a gem away:
He pledged it to the knight; the knight had wit;
So kept the diamond, and the rogue was bit.
Some scruple rose, but thus he eased his thought,
"I'll now give sixpence where I gave a groat;
Where once I went to church, I'll now go twice,
And am so clear, too, of all other vice."
   Behold Sir Balaam, now a man of spirit,

* The monument, with an inscription importing that London was burnt by the Catholics.

Ascribes his gettings to his parts and merit.
Things change their titles as our manners turn;
His counting-house employed the Sunday-morn;
Seldom at church, ('twas such a busy life,)
But duly sent his family and wife.
    In Britain's senate he a seat obtains,
And one more pensioner St. Stephen gains.
My lady falls to play; so bad her chance
He must repair it; takes a bribe from France;
The House impeach him; Coningsby harangues;
The Court forsake him, and Sir Balaam hangs.

[FROM "MORAL ESSAYS." EPISTLE IV.]

Of the use of riches.

'Tis strange, the miser should his cares employ
To gain those riches he can ne'er enjoy:
Is it less strange the prodigal should waste
His wealth to purchase what he ne'er can taste?
    At Timon's villa, let us pass a day;
Where all cry out, "What sums are thrown away!"
Greatness with Timon dwells in such a draught,
As brings all Brobdignag before your thought.
To compass this, his building is a town,
His pond an ocean, his parterre a down.
Who but must laugh, the master when he sees,
A puny insect, shivering in the breeze!
Lo, what huge heaps of littleness around!
The whole a labored quarry above ground.
Two Cupids squirt before; a lake behind
Improves the keenness of the northern wind.
His gardens next your admiration call;

On every side you look, behold the wall!
No pleasing intricacies intervene,
No artful wilderness to perplex the scene;
Grove nods at grove, each alley has a brother,
And half the platform just reflects the other.
The suffering eye inverted nature sees,
Trees cut to statues, statues thick as trees;
With here a fountain never to be played,
And there a summer-house that knows no shade;
Here Amphitritè sails through myrtle bowers,
There gladiators fight, or die in flowers;
Unwatered see the drooping sea-horse mourn,
And swallows roost in Nilus' dusty urn.

    His study! with what authors is it stored?
In books, not authors, curious is my lord.
To all their dated backs he turns you round;
These Aldus printed, those Du Suëil has bound:
Lo, some are vellum, and the rest as good
For all his lordship knows, but they are wood.
For Locke or Milton 'tis in vain to look;
These shelves admit not any modern book.

    And now the chapel's silver bell you hear,
That summons you to all the pride of prayer.
Light quirks of music, broken and uneven,
Make the soul dance upon a jig to heaven.
To rest the cushion and soft dean invite,
Who never mentions hell to ears polite.

    But hark! the chiming clocks to dinner call;
A hundred footsteps scrape the marble hall:
Is this a dinner, this a genial room?
No, 'tis a temple, and a hecatomb,
A solemn sacrifice performed in state:
You drink by measure, and to minutes eat.

So quick retires each flying course, you'd swear
Sancho's dread doctor and his wand were there.
In plenty starving, tantalized in state,
And complaisantly helped to all I hate,
Treated, caressed, and tired, I take my leave,
Sick of his civil pride from morn to eve;
I curse such lavish cost, and little skill,
And swear no day was ever passed so ill.

[FROM "EPISTLE V. TO MR. ADDISON.]

Occasioned by his dialogues on medals.

See the wild waste of all-devouring years!
How Rome her own sad sepulchre appears!
With nodding arches, broken temples spread,
The very tombs now vanished like their dead;
Huge theatres, that now unpeopled woods,
Now drained a distant country of her floods;
Fanes, which admiring gods with pride survey,
Statues of men, scarce less alive than they.
Perhaps, by its own ruins saved from flame,
Some buried marble half preserves a name;
That name the learned with fierce disputes pursue,
And give to Titus old Vespasian's due.
 Ambition sighed: she found it vain to trust
The faithless column, and the crumbling bust;
Huge moles, whose shadows stretched from shore to shore,
Their ruins perished, and their place no more.
Convinced, she now contracts her vast design,
And all her triumphs shrink into a coin.
A narrow orb each crowded conquest keeps;

Beneath her palm here sad Judæa weeps;
Now scantier limits the proud arch confine;
And scarce are seen the prostrate Nile or Rhine;
A small Euphrates through the piece is rolled,
And little eagles wave their wings in gold.

  The medal, faithful to its charge of fame,
Through climes and ages bears each form and name;
In one short view subjected to our eye,
Gods, emperors, heroes, sages, beauties lie.
With sharpened sight pale antiquaries pore,
Th' inscription value, but the rust adore.
This the blue varnish, that the green endears,
The sacred rust of twice ten hundred years.
To gain Pescennius one employs his schemes,
One grasps a Cecrops in extatic dreams.
Poor Vadius, long with learnèd spleen devoured,
Can taste no pleasure since his shield was scoured;
And Curio, restless by the fair one's side,
Sighs for an Otho and neglects his bride.

  Theirs is the vanity, the learning thine;
Touched by thy hand again Rome's glories shine;
Her gods and godlike heroes rise to view,
And all her faded garlands bloom anew.

[*From the Essay on Man.*]

I.

Awake, my St. John! leave all meaner things
To low ambition, and the pride of kings.
Let us, since life can little more supply
Than just to look about us and to die,
Expatiate free o'er all this scene of man;

A mighty maze! but not without a plan;
A wild, where weeds and flowers promiscuous shoot;
Or garden, tempting with forbidden fruit.
Together let us beat this ample field,
Try what the open, what the covert yield,
The latent tracts, the giddy heights explore
Of all who blindly creep, or sightless soar;
Eye Nature's walks, shoot folly as it flies,
And catch the manners living as they rise;
Laugh where we must, be candid where we can;
But vindicate the ways of God to man.

 I. Say first, of God above, or man below,
What can we reason, but from what we know? * *
Through worlds unnumber'd though the God be known,
'Tis ours to trace Him only in our own.
He who through vast immensity can pierce,
See worlds on worlds compose one universe,
Observe how system into system runs,
What other planets circle other suns,
What varied beings people every star,
May tell why Heaven has made us as we are.
But of this frame the bearings, and the ties,
The strong connections, nice dependencies,
Gradations just, has thy pervading soul
Looked through? or can a part contain the whole?
 Is the great chain, that draws all to agree,
And drawn supports, upheld by God, or thee?

 II. Presumptuous man! the reason would'st thou find
Why formed so weak, so little, and so blind?
First, if thou canst, the harder reason guess,
Why formed no weaker, blinder, and no less?
Ask of thy mother earth, why oaks are made
Taller or stronger than the weeds they shade?

Or ask of yonder argent fields above,
Why Jove's satellités are less than Jove? * *
  In human works, though labored on with pain,
A thousand movements scarce one purpose gain;
In God's, one single can its end produce,
Yet serves to second too some other use.
So man, who here seems principal alone,
Perhaps acts second to some sphere unknown,
Touches some wheel, or verges to some goal;
'Tis but a part we see, and not a whole. * *
  If to be perfect in another sphere,
What matters soon or late, or here or there?
The blest to-day is as completely so
As who began a thousand years ago.
  III. Heaven from all creatures hides the book of fate,
All but the page prescribed, their present state:
From brutes what men, from men what spirits know;
Or who could suffer being here below? * *
Oh, blindness to the future! kindly given,
That each may fill the circle marked by Heaven;
Who sees with equal eye, as God of all,
A hero perish, or a sparrow fall,
Atoms or systems into ruin hurled,
And now a bubble burst, and now a world.
  Hope humbly, then: with trembling pinions soar;
Wait the great teacher death; and God adore.
What future bliss He gives not thee to know,
But gives that hope to be thy blessing now.
Hope springs eternal in the human breast;
Man never is, but always to be, blest.
The soul, uneasy and confined from home,
Rests and expatiates in a life to come.
  Lo! the poor Indian! whose untutored mind

Sees God in clouds, or hears Him in the wind;
His soul proud science never taught to stray
Far as the solar walk, or milky way;
Yet simple nature to his hope has given,
Behind the cloud-topped hill, an humbler heaven;
Some safer world in depth of woods embraced,
Some happier island in the watery waste,
Where slaves once more their native land behold,
No fiends torment, no Christians thirst for gold.
To be contents his natural desire,
He asks no angel's wing, no seraph's fire,
But thinks, admitted to that equal sky,
His faithful dog shall bear him company.

    IV. Go, wiser thou! and, in thy scale of sense,
Weigh thy opinion against Providence;
Call imperfection what thou fanciest such,
Say, here He gives too little, there too much;
Destroy all creatures for thy sport, or gust,
Yet cry, if man's unhappy, God's unjust.
If man alone engross not Heaven's high care,
Alone made perfect here, immortal there,
Snatch from His hand the balance and the rod,
Rejudge His justice, be the god of God.
In pride, in reasoning pride, our error lies;
All quit their sphere, and rush into the skies.
Pride still is aiming at the blest abodes,
Men would be angels, angels would be gods.
Aspiring to be gods, if angels fell,
Aspiring to be angels, men rebel:
And who but wishes to invert the laws
Of order, sins against the Eternal Cause.

    V. Ask for what end the heavenly bodies shine,
Earth for whose use? Pride answers, "Tis for mine:

For me kind Nature wakes her genial power,
Suckles each herb, and spreads out every flower; * *
Seas roll to waft me, suns to light me rise,
My footstool earth, my canopy the skies." * *

    Better for us, perhaps, it might appear,
Were there all harmony, all virtue here;
That never air, or ocean felt the wind,
That never passion discomposed the mind;
But all subsists by elemental strife,
And passions are the elements of life. * *

    VI. What would this man? Now upward will he soar,
And, little less than angel, would be more;
Now looking downwards, just as grieved appears,
To want the strength of bulls, the fur of bears. * *
Shall he alone whom rational we call,
Be pleased with nothing, if not blest with all? * *

    Why has not man a microscopic eye?
For this plain reason, man is not a fly.
Say what the use, were finer optics given,
To inspect a mite, not comprehend the heaven?
Or touch, if tremblingly alive all o'er,
To smart and agonize at every pore?
Or quick effluvia darting through the brain,
Die of a rose in aromatic pain?
If nature thundered in his opening ears,
And stunned him with the music of the spheres,
How could he wish that Heaven had left him still
The whispering zephyr, and the purling rill?
Who finds not Providence all good and wise,
Alike in what it gives, and what denies? * *

    VIII. See, through this air, this ocean, and this earth,
All matter quick and bursting into birth! * *

Vast chain of being! which from God began,
Natures ethereal, human, angel, man,
Beast, bird, fish, insect, what no eye can see,
No glass can reach; from infinite to thee,
From thee to nothing. On superior powers
Were we to press, inferior might on ours,
Or in the full creation leave a void,
Where, one step broken, the great scale's destroyed:
From nature's chain whatever link you strike,
Tenth or tenthousandth, breaks the chain alike. * *

    Let earth unbalanced from her orbit fly,
Planets and stars run lawless through the sky;
Let ruling angels from their spheres be hurled,
Being on being wrecked, and world on world;
Heaven's whole foundations to their centre nod,
And nature tremble to the throne of God.
All this dread order break, for whom? for thee?
Vile worm! O madness, pride, impiety!

    IX. What if the foot, ordained the dust to tread,
Or hand, to toil, aspired to be the head?
What if the head, the eye, or ear repined
To serve mere engines to the ruling mind?
Just as absurd for any part to claim
To be another, in this general frame:
Just as absurd, to mourn the tasks or pains
The great directing Mind of all ordains.

    All are but parts of one stupendous whole,
Whose body nature is, and God the soul;*

---

    * God can be no part of a whole. By '*All*,' however, (what immediately precedes this sublime description of the Deity considered,) the author perhaps may mean all *created* existences only, and them, collectedly taken, as constituting what he terms 'nature.'

That, changed through all, and yet in all the same,
Great in the earth, as in th' ethereal frame,
Warms in the sun, refreshes in the breeze,
Glows in the stars, and blossoms in the trees,
Lives through all life, extends through all extent,
Spreads undivided, operates unspent;
Breathes in our soul, informs our mortal part,
As full, as perfect, in a hair as heart;
As full, as perfect, in vile man that mourns,
As the rapt seraph that adores and burns.
To Him no high, no low, no great, no small;
He fills, He bounds, connects, and equals all.
x. Cease then, nor order imperfection name;
Our proper bliss depends on what we blame.* *
All nature is but art unknown to thee;
All chance direction which thou canst not see;
All discord, harmony not understood;
All partial evil, universal good.
And spite of pride, in erring reason's spite,
One truth is clear, whatever is right.*

II.

1. Know then thyself, presume not God to scan,
The proper study of mankind is man.
Placed on this isthmus of a middle state,
A being darkly wise, and rudely great,
With too much knowledge for the sceptic side,
With too much weakness for the stoic's pride,
He hangs between, in doubt to act, or rest,
In doubt to deem himself a god, or beast,
In doubt his mind, or body to prefer,

---

* All is right, sin excepted.

Born but to die, and reasoning but to err;*
Alike in ignorance, his reason such,
Whether he thinks too little, or too much;
Chaos of thought and passion, all confused;
Still by himself abused, or disabused;
Created half to rise, and half to fall;
Great lord of all things, yet a prey to all;
Sole judge of truth, in endless error hurled;
The glory, jest and riddle of the world!

   Go, wondrous creature! mount where science guides,
Go, measure earth, weigh air, and state the tides;
Instruct the planets in what orbs to run,
Correct old time, and regulate the sun;* *
Go, teach Eternal Wisdom how to rule;
Then drop into thyself and be a fool! * *

II. Two principles in human nature reign,
Self-love to urge, and reason to restrain.* *
Self-love, the spring of motion, acts the soul;
Reason's comparing balance rules the whole.
Man, but for that, no action could attend,
And, but for this, were active to no end.* *

   Self-love and reason to one end aspire,
Pain their aversion, pleasure their desire;
But greedy that its object would devour,
This taste the honey, and not wound the flower;
Pleasure, or wrong or rightly understood,
Our greatest evil, or our greatest good.* *

III. Passions, though selfish, if their means be fair,
List under Reason and deserve her care.* *

   In lazy apathy let Stoics boast
Their virtue fixed; 'tis fixed as in a frost.* *

---

   * Exaggeration of the weakness of man's reason. He does not always reason but to err.

Pope.

On life's vast ocean diversely we sail,
Reason the card, but passion is the gale.* *
   Pleasures are ever in our hands or eyes,
And when, in act, they cease, in prospect, rise ;* *
All spread their charms, but charm not all alike ;
On different senses different objects strike :
Hence different passions more or less inflame,
As strong or weak, the organs of the frame ;
And hence one master-passion in the breast,
Like Aaron's serpent, swallows up the rest.* *
Reason itself but gives it edge and power,
As heaven's blest beams turn vinegar more sour.* *
VI. Whate'er the passion, knowledge, fame, or pelf,
Not one will change his neighbor with himself.
The learned is happy nature to explore,
The fool is happy that he knows no more ;
The rich is happy in the plenty given,
The poor contents him with the care of Heaven.
See the blind beggar dance, the cripple sing,
The sot a hero, lunatic a king ;
The starving chemist in his golden views
Supremely blest, the poet in his muse.
See some strange comfort every state attend,
And pride bestowed on all, a common friend :
See some fit passion every age supply,
Hope travels through, nor quits us when we die.
Behold the child, by nature's kindly law
Pleased with a rattle, tickled with a straw ;
Some livelier play-thing gives his youth delight,
A little louder, but as empty quite.* *
   Meanwhile opinion gilds with varying rays
Those painted clouds that beautify our days ;
Each want of happiness by hope supplied,

And each vacuity of sense by pride.
These build as fast as knowledge can destroy,
In folly's cup still laughs the bubble, joy;
One prospect lost, another still we gain;
And not a vanity is given in vain.
Even mean self-love becomes, by force divine,
The scale to measure others' wants by thine.
See, and confess one comfort still must rise;
'Tis this, though man's a fool, yet God is wise.

III.

Here then we rest: "The Universal Cause
Acts to one end, but acts by various laws." * *
    Look round our world; behold the chain of love
Combining all below and all above.
See plastic nature working to this end,
The single atoms each to other tend,
Attract, attracted to, the next in place
Formed and impelled its neighbour to embrace.
See matter next, with various life endued,
Press to one centre still, the general good.
See dying vegetables life sustain,
See life dissolving vegetate again;
All forms that perish other forms supply,
By turns we catch the vital breath, and die;
Like bubbles on the sea of matter borne,
They rise, they break, and to that sea return.* *
    Has God, thou fool, worked solely for thy good,
Thy joy, thy pastime, thy attire, thy food? * *
    Know Nature's children all divide her care;
The fur that warms a monarch, warms a bear,
While man exclaims, "See all things for my use!"
"See man for mine!" replies a pampered goose:

And just as short of reason he must fall,
Who thinks all made for one, not one for all.* *

   To each unthinking being Heaven a friend,
Gives not the useless knowledge of its end:
To man imparts it, but with such a view,
As, while he dreads it, makes him hope it too;
The hour concealed, and so remote the fear,
Death still draws nearer, never seeming near.
Great standing miracle! that Heaven assigned
Its only thinking thing this turn of mind.* *
II. Reason, however able, cool at best,
Cares not for service, or but serves when prest,
Stays till we call, and then not often near;
But honest instinct comes a volunteer.* *
This too serves always, reason never long,
One must go right, the other may go wrong.* *
And reason raise o'er instinct as you can,
In this 'tis God directs, in that 'tis man.

   Who taught the nations of the field and wood
To shun their poison, and to choose their food?
Prescient, the tides or tempests to withstand,
Build on the wave, or arch beneath the sand?
Who made the spider parallels design,
Sure as De Moivre, without rule or line?
Who bid the stork, Columbus-like, explore
Heavens not his own, and worlds unknown before?
Who calls the council, states the certain day,
Who forms the phalanx, and who points the way?

   III. God in the nature of each being founds
Its proper bliss, and sets its proper bounds;
But as He framed a whole, the whole to bless,
On mutual wants builds mutual happiness:
So from the first eternal order ran,
And creature linked to creature, man to man.* *

IV. See him from nature rising slow to art:
To copy instinct then was reason's part;
Thus then to man the voice of Nature spake:
" Go, from the creatures thy instructions take;
Learn from the birds what food the thickets yield;
Learn from the beasts the physic of the field;
Thy arts of building from the bee receive;
Learn of the mole to plough, the worm to weave;
Learn of the little nautilus to sail,
Spread the thin oar, and catch the driving gale.* *
Here subterranean works and cities see;
There towns aërial on the waving tree.
Learn each small people's genius, policies,
The ants' republic and the realm of bees;
How those in common all their wealth bestow,
And anarchy without confusion know;
And these forever, though a monarch reign,
Their separate cells and properties maintain." * *

IV.

1. Oh happiness! our being's end and aim!
Good, pleasure, ease, content! whate'er thy name,
That something still which prompts the eternal sigh,
For which we bear to live, or dare to die,
Which still so near us, yet beyond us lies,
O'erlooked, seen double, by the fool, and wise:
Plant of celestial seed! if dropt below,
Say, in what mortal soil thou deign'st to grow. * *
Where grows? where grows it not? If vain our toil,
We ought to blame the culture, not the soil:
Fixed to no spot is happiness sincere,
'Tis nowhere to be found, or everywhere.* *

Take nature's path and mad opinion's leave;
All states can reach it, and all heads conceive;
Obvious her goods, in no extreme they dwell;
There needs but thinking right, and meaning well.* *
II. Remember, man, the Universal Cause
Acts not by partial, but by general laws;
And makes what happiness we justly call
Subsist not in the good of one, but all.* *
Who most to shun or hate mankind pretend,
Seek an admirer, or would fix a friend.
Abstract what others feel, what others think,
All pleasures sicken, and all glories sink:
Each has his share; and who would more obtain,
Shall find the pleasure pays not half the pain.
 Order is Heaven's first law; and this confest,
Some are, and must be greater than the rest,
More rich, more wise; but who infers from hence
That such are happier, shocks all common sense.
Heaven to mankind impartial we confess,
If all are equal in their happiness:
But mutual wants this happiness increase;
All nature's difference keeps all nature's peace.
Condition, circumstance, is not the thing;
Bliss is the same in subject or in king.* *
 Not present good or ill, the joy or curse,
But future views of better, or of worse.
 Oh sons of earth! attempt ye still to rise,
By mountains piled on mountains to the skies?
Heaven still with laughter the vain toil surveys,
And buries madmen in the heaps they raise.
III. Know, all the good that individuals find,
Or God and nature meant to mere mankind,
Reason's whole pleasure, all the joys of sense,

Lie in three words, health, peace and competence.
But health consists with temperance alone,
And peace, Oh virtue! peace is all thy own.
The good or bad the gifts of fortune gain;
But these less taste them, as they worse obtain.* *
Count all th' advantage prosperous vice attains,
'Tis but what virtue flies from and disdains:
And grant the bad what happiness they would,
One they must want, which is, to pass for good.
O blind to truth, and God's whole scheme below,
Who fancy bliss to vice, to virtue woe!* *

    What makes all physical, or moral ill?
There deviates nature, and here wanders will.
God sends not ill, if rightly understood,
Or partial ill is universal good. * *
IV. Think we, like some weak prince, th' Eternal Cause
Prone for His favorites to reverse His laws? * *
When the loose mountain trembles from on high,
Shall gravitation cease if you go by? * *
V. Whatever is is right.* This world, 'tis true,
Was made for Cæsar, but for Titus too:
And which more blest, who chained his country, say,
Or he whose virtue sighed to lose a day?

    But sometimes virtue starves while vice is fed.
What then? is the reward of virtue bread? * *
VI. What nothing earthly gives, or can destroy,
The soul's calm sunshine, and the heart-felt joy,
Is virtue's prize: a better would you fix?
Then give humility a coach and six,
Justice a conqueror's sword, or truth a gown,
Or public spirit its great cure, a crown. * *

    Honor and shame from no condition rise;

---

* All is right, sin excepted.

Pope.

Act well your part, there all the honor lies.
Fortune in men has some small difference made,
One flaunts in rags, one flutters in brocade.   *   *
"What differ more," you cry, "than crown and cowl?"
I'll tell you, friend! a wise man and a fool.   *   *
Worth makes the man, and want of it the fellow;
The rest is all but leather, or prunella.   *   *

   Go! if your ancient but ignoble blood
Has crept through scoundrels, ever since the flood,
Go! and pretend your family is young,
Nor own your fathers have been fools so long.
What can ennoble sots, or slaves, or cowards?
Alas! not all the blood of all the Howards.
Look next on greatness; say where greatness lies:
"Where, but among the heroes and the wise?"
Heroes are much the same, the point's agreed,
From Macedonia's madman to the Swede;
The whole strange purpose of their lives, to find
Or make an enemy of all mankind.
Not one looks backward, onward still he goes,
Yet ne'er looks forward further than his nose.
No less alike the politic and wise;
All sly, slow things, with circumspective eyes:
Men in their loose, unguarded hours they take,
Not that themselves are wise, but others weak.
But grant that those can conquer, these can cheat;
'Tis phrase absurd to call a villain great.
Who wickedly is wise, or madly brave,
Is but the more a fool, the more a knave.
Who noble ends by noble means obtains,
Or failing, smiles in exile or in chains,
Like good Aurelius let him reign, or bleed
Like Socrates; that man is great indeed.

What's fame? a fancied life in other's breath,
A thing beyond us, even before our death.   * *
All that we feel of it begins and ends
In the small circle of our foes or friends.   * *
A wit's a feather, and a chief a rod,
An honest man's the noblest work of God.
Fame but from death a villain's name can save,
As justice tears his body from the grave;
When what to oblivion better were resigned,
Is hung on high, to poison half mankind.
All fame is foreign, but of true desert,
Plays round the head, but comes not to the heart:
One self-approving hour whole years outweighs
Of stupid starers, and of loud huzzas;
And more true joy Marcellus exiled feels,
Than Cæsar, with a senate at his heels.

   In parts superior what advantage lies?
Tell (for you can) what is it to be wise?
'Tis but to know how little can be known;
To see all others' faults, and feel our own:
Condemned in business or in arts to drudge,
Without a second, or without a judge.
Truths would you teach, or save a sinking land?
All fear, none aid you, and few understand.
Painful pre-eminence! yourself to view
Above life's weakness, and its comforts too.   * *

   Is yellow dirt the passion of thy life?
Look but on Gripus, or on Gripus' wife.
If parts allure thee, think how Bacon shined,
The wisest, brightest, meanest of mankind:
Or ravished with the whistling of a name,
See Cromwell, damned to everlasting fame.
If all, united, thy ambition call,

From ancient story learn to scorn them all.
There, in the rich, the honored, famed, and great,
See the false scale of happiness complete ! * *
Mark by what wretched steps their glory grows,
From dirt and sea-weed as proud Venice rose ;
In each how guilt and greatness equal ran,
And all that raised the hero, sunk the man.
VII. Know then this truth, enough for man to know,
Virtue alone is happiness below :
The only point where human bliss stands still,
And tastes the good without the fall to ill.
Where only merit constant pay receives,
Is blest in what it takes and what it gives ;
The joy unequaled, if its end it gain,
And, if it lose, attended with no pain :
Without satiety though e'er so blessed,
And but more relished as the more distressed :
The broadest mirth unfeeling folly wears,
Less pleasing far than virtue's very tears ;
Good, from each object, from each place acquired,
Forever exercised, yet never tired ;
Never elated while one man's oppressed,
Never dejected, while another's blessed,
And where no wants, no wishes can remain,
Since but to wish more virtue, is to gain. * *

God loves from whole to parts ; but human soul
Must rise from individual to the whole.
Self-love but serves the virtuous mind to wake,
As the small pebble stirs the peaceful lake ;
The centre moved, a circle straight succeeds,
Another still, and still another spreads ;
Friend, parent, neighbor, first it will embrace,
His country next, and next all human race :

Wide and more wide, the o'erflowings of the mind
Take every creature in, of every kind;
Earth smiles around, with boundless bounty blest,
And Heaven beholds Its image in his breast.

[*From " Prologue to the Satires," a humorous Epistle to
Dr. Arbuthnot, on the impertinence of scribblers, etc.*]

P. Shut, shut the door good, John! fatigued I said,
Tie up the knocker, say I'm sick, I'm dead.
The dog-star rages! nay, 'tis past a doubt
All Bedlam or Parnassus is let out:
Fire in each eye, and papers in each hand,
They rave, recite and madden round the land.
What walls can guard me, or what shades can hide?
They pierce my thickets, through my grot they glide,
By land, by water, they renew the charge,
They stop the chariot and they board the barge.
No place is sacred, not the church is free,
E'en Sunday shines no Sabbath-day to me;
Then from the mint walks forth the man of rhyme,
Happy to catch me just at dinner-time.
Is there a parson much bemused in beer,
A maudlin poetess, a rhyming peer,
A clerk, foredoomed his father's soul to cross,
Who pens a stanza when he should engross?
Is there who, locked from ink and paper, scrawls
With desperate charcoal round his darkened walls?
All fly to *Twit'nam*, and, in humble strain,
Apply to me, to keep them mad or vain. * *
Poor Cornus sees his frantic wife elope,
And curses wit, and poetry, and Pope.
Friend to my life, which did not you prolong,

The world had wanted many an idle song,
What drop or nostrum can this plague remove?
Or which must end me, a fool's wrath, or love?
A dire dilemma! either way I'm sped;
If foes, they write, if friends, they read me dead.
Seized and tied down to judge, how wretched I!
Who can't be silent, and who will not lie:
To laugh, were want of goodness and of grace,
And to be grave, exceeds all power of face.
I sit with sad civility, I read
With honest anguish, and an aching head;
And drop at last, but in unwilling ears,
This saving counsel, "Keep your piece nine years."

"Nine years!" cries he, who, high in Drury Lane,
Lulled by soft zephyrs through the broken pane,
Rhymes ere he wakes, and prints before term ends,
Obliged by hunger, and request of friends;
"The piece, you think, is incorrect? why, take it,
I'm all submission, what you'd have it make it."

Three things another's modest wishes bound,
My friendship, and a prologue, and ten pound.

Pitholeon sends to me: "You know his Grace,
I want a patron; ask him for a place."
Pitholeon libeled me—"But here's a letter
Informs you, sir, 'twas when he knew no better."

Bless me! a packet. "'Tis a stranger sues,
A virgin tragedy, an orphan muse."
If I dislike it, "Furies, death and rage!"
If I approve, "Commend it to the stage."
There (thank my stars) my whole commission ends,
The players and I are, luckily, no friends.
Fired that the house reject him, "'Sdeath! I'll print it

And shame the fools.   Your interest, Sir, with Lintot." *
Lintot, dull rogue ! will think your price too much :
" Not, Sir, if you revise it and retouch."
All my demurs but double his attacks :
At last he whispers, " Do, and we go snacks."
Glad of a quarrel, straight I clap the door,
Sir, let me see your works and you no more.
 You think this cruel ?   Take it for a rule,
No creature smarts so little as a fool.
Let peals of laughter, Codrus ! round thee break,
Thou unconcerned canst hear the mighty crack :
Pit, box, and gallery in convulsions hurled,
Thou stand'st unshook amid a bursting world.
Who shames a scribbler?   Break one cobweb through,
He spins the slight, self-pleasing thread anew :
Destroy his fib, or sophistry, in vain,
The creature's at his dirty work again ;
Throned in the centre of his new designs,
Proud of a vast extent of flimsy lines.
Whom have I hurt ! has poet yet, or peer,
Lost the arched eye-brow, or Parnassian sneer?
Does not one table Bavius still admit ?
Still to one bishop Philips seem a wit ?
Still Sappho—*A.*   Hold ! for God's sake you'll offend.
No names, be calm, learn prudence of a friend :
I, too could write, and I am twice as tall ;
But foes like these—*P.*   One flatterer's worse than all.
 Of all mad creatures, if the learned are right,
It is the slaver kills, and not the bite.
A fool quite angry is quite innocent,
Alas ! 'tis ten times worse when they repent.

* A publisher.

One dedicates in high heroic prose,
And ridicules beyond a hundred foes :
One from all Grub-street will my fame defend,
And, more abusive, calls himself my friend.
This prints my letters, that expects a bribe,
And others roar aloud, " Subscribe ! subscribe ! "
   There are who to my person pay their court :
I cough like Horace, and, though lean, am short.
Ammon's great son one shoulder had too high,
Such Ovid's nose, and, " Sir ! you have an eye."
Go on, obliging creatures, make me see
All that disgraced my betters met in me.
Say for my comfort, languishing in bed,
" Just so immortal Maro held his head ; "
And, when I die, be sure you let me know
Great Homer died three thousand years ago.
   Why did I write ? what sin to me unknown
Dipped me in ink, my parents,' or my own ?
As yet a child, nor yet a fool to fame,
I lisped in numbers, for the numbers came.
I left no calling for this idle trade,
No duty broke, no father disobeyed :
The muse but served to ease some friend, not wife ;
To help me through this long disease, my life ;
To second, Arbuthnot ! thy art and care,
And teach the being you preserved to bear.
   Soft were my numbers ; who could take offence
While pure description held the place of sense ?
Yet then did Gildon draw his venal quill ;
I wished the man a dinner and sat still.
Yet then did Dennis rave in furious fret ;
I never answered, I was not in debt.
If want provoked, or madness made them print,
I waged no war with bedlam or the mint.

Did some more sober critic come abroad,
If wrong, I smiled; if right, I kissed the rod.
Pains, reading, study, are their just pretence,
And all they want is spirit, taste and sense.
Commas and points, they set exactly right,
And 'twere a sin to rob them of their mite:
Yet ne'er one sprig of laurel graced these ribalds,
From slashing Bentley down to piddling Tibbalds.
Each wight who reads not, and but scans and spells,
Each word-catcher that lives on syllables,
Even such small critics some regard may claim,
Preserved in Milton's or in Shakspeare's name. * *

Were others angry? I excused them too;
Well might they rage, I gave them but their due.
A man's true spirit 'tis not hard to find;
But each man's secret standard in his mind,
That casting-weight pride adds to emptiness,
This who can gratify, for who can guess?
The bard whom pilfered pastorals renown,
Who turns a Persian tale for half a crown,
Just writes to make his barreness appear
And strains from hard-bound brains eight lines a year;
He who, still wanting, though he lives on theft,
Steals much, spends little, yet has nothing left;
And he, who now to sense, now nonsense leaning,
Means not, but blunders round about a meaning;
And he, whose fustian's so sublimely bad,
It is not poetry, but prose run mad:
All these my modest satire bade translate,
And owned that nine such poets made a Tate.

Peace to all such! but were there one whose fires
True genius kindles, and fair fame inspires;
Blest with each talent and each art to please,

And born to write, converse, and live with ease;
Should such a man, too fond to rule alone,
Bear, like the Turk, no brother near the throne,
View him with scornful, yet with jealous eyes,
And hate for arts that caused himself to rise;
Damn with faint praise, assent with civil leer,
And, without sneering, teach the rest to sneer;
Willing to wound, and yet afraid to strike,
Just hint a fault and hesitate dislike;
Alike reserved to blame, or to commend,
A timorous foe, and a suspicious friend;
Dreading even fools, by flatterers besieged,
And so obliging, that he ne'er obliged;
Like Cato, give his little senate laws,
And sit attentive to his own applause;
While wits and templars every sentence raise,
And wonder with a foolish face of praise:
Who must but laugh, if such a man there be?
Who would not weep if Atticus * were he?

 What though my name stood rubric on the walls,
Or plastered posts, with claps, in capitals,
Or smoking forth, a hundred hawkers' load,
On wings of wind came flying all abroad;
I sought no homage from the race that write;
I kept, like Asian monarchs, from their sight.
I ne'er with wits nor witlings passed my days,
To spread about the itch of verse and praise;
But sick of fops, and poetry, and prate,
To Bufo left the whole Castalian state.

 I was not born for courts or great affairs;
I pay my debts, believe, and say my prayers;

* Addison.

Can sleep without a poem in my head,
Nor know if Dennis be alive or dead.

    Cursed be the verse, how well soe'er it flow,
That tends to make one worthy man my foe,
Give virtue scandal, innocence a fear,
Or from the soft-eyed virgin steal a tear.
But he who hurts a harmless neighbor's peace,
Insults fallen worth, or beauty in distress;
Who loves a lie lame slander helps about,
Who writes a libel, or who copies out;
That fop, whose pride affects a patron's name,
Yet absent wounds an author's honest fame;
Who can your merit selfishly approve
And show the sense of it without the love;
Who has the vanity to call you friend,
Yet wants the honor, injured, to defend;
Who tells whate'er you think, whate'er you say,
And, if he lie not, must at least betray;
Who reads but with a lust to misapply,
Make satire a lampoon, and fiction lie;
A lash like mine no honest man shall dread,
But all such babbling blockheads in his stead.

    Let Sporus* tremble—*A.* What? that thing of silk,
Sporus, that mere white curd of ass's milk?
Satire or sense, alas! can Sporus feel?
Who breaks a butterfly upon a wheel?
P. Yet let me flap this bug with gilded wings,
Whose buzz the witty and the fair annoys,
Yet wit ne'er tastes, nor beauty e'er enjoys;
So well-bred spaniels civilly delight
In mumbling of the game they dare not bite.

    * Lord H——.

Eternal smiles his emptiness betray,
As shallow streams run dimpling all the way.
Whether in florid impotence he speaks,
And, as the prompter breathes, the puppet squeaks,
Or, at the ear of Eve, familiar toad,
Half froth, half venom, spits himself abroad,
Amphibious thing! that, acting either part,
The trifling head, or the corrupted heart,
Fop at the toilet, flatterer at the board,
Now trips a lady, and now struts a lord.
Eve's tempter thus the Rabbins have expressed,
A cherub's face, a reptile all the rest;
Beauty that shocks you, parts that none will trust,
Wit that can creep, and pride that licks the dust.
  Not fortune's worshipper, nor fashion's fool,
Not lucre's madman, nor ambition's tool,
Not proud nor servile, be one poet's praise,
That, if he pleased, he pleased by manly ways;
That flattery, even to kings, he held a shame,
And thought a lie in verse or prose the same;
That not in fancy's maze he wandered long,
But stooped to truth, and moralized his song;
That not for fame, but virtue's better end,
He stood the furious foe, the timid friend,
The damning critic, half-approving wit,
The coxcomb hit, or fearing to be hit;
Laughed at the loss of friends he never had,
The dull, the proud, the wicked, and the mad;
The distant threats of vengeance on his head;
The blow unfelt, the tear he never shed;
The tale revived, the lie so oft o'erthrown,
The imputed trash, and dulness not his own;
The morals blackened when the writings scape,

The libeled person, and the pictured shape;
Abuse on all he loved, or loved him, spread,
A friend in exile, or a father dead;
The whisper, that, to greatness still too near,
Perhaps yet vibrates on his sovereign's ear.
Welcome to thee, fair virtue, all the past;
For thee, fair virtue, welcome even the last!
 A. But why insult the poor, offend the great?
 P. A knave's a knave to me in every state.
Alike my scorn if he succeed or fail,
Sporus at court, or Japhet in a jail,
A hireling scribbler, or a hireling peer,
Knight of the post corrupt, or of the shire;
If on a pillory, or near a throne,
He gain a prince's ear, or lose his own.
    [*His father described.*]
 Born to no pride, inheriting no strife,
Nor marrying discord in a noble wife,
Stranger to civil and religious rage,
The good man walked innoxious through his age.
No courts he saw, no suits would ever try,
Nor dared an oath, nor hazarded a lie.
Unlearned, he knew no schoolman's subtle art,
No language, but the language of the heart;
By nature honest, by experience wise,
Healthy by temperance, and by exercise.
His life, though long, to sickness past unknown,
His death was instant, and without a groan.
 O friend! may each domestic bliss be thine!
Be no unpleasing melancholy mine:
Me let the tender office long engage
To rock the cradle of reposing age,
With lenient arms extend a mother's breath,

Make languor-smile, and smooth the bed of death,
Explore the thought, explain the asking eye,
And keep awhile one parent from the sky.

[FROM "EPILOGUE TO THE SATIRES."]

In two dialogues.

I.

Let humble Allen, with an awkward shame,
Do good by stealth, and blush to find it fame.
Vice is undone, if she forgets her birth,
And stoops from angels to the dregs of earth.
Lo! at the wheels of her triumphal car,
Old England's genius, rough with many a scar,
Dragged in the dust! his arms hang idly round,
His flag inverted trails along the ground;
Our youth, all liveried o'er with foreign gold,
Before her dance; behind her, crawl the old;
See thronging millions to the pagod run,
And offer country, parent, wife, or son!
Hear her black trumpet through the land proclaim
That not to be corrupted is the shame!
In soldier, churchman, patriot, man in power,
'Tis avarice all, ambition is no more.
See all our nobles begging to be slaves!
See all our fools aspiring to be knaves!
All, all look up, with reverential awe,
At crimes that 'scape, or triumph o'er the law;
While truth, worth, wisdom, daily they decry.
" Nothing is sacred now but villainy."

II.

Vice with such giant strides comes on amain,
Invention strives to be before in vain;
Feign what I will, and paint it e'er so strong,
Some rising genius sins up to my song.
    Yet think not friendship only prompts my lays;
I follow Virtue; where she shines I praise:
Point she to Priest, or Elder, Whig or Tory,
Or round a Quaker's beaver cast a glory.
Some in their choice of friends (nay, look not grave)
Have still a secret bias to a knave:
To find an honest man I beat about,
And love him, court him, praise him, in or out.
    F. Then why so few commended?
                                P. Not so fierce;
Find you the virtue, and I'll find the verse.
But random praise—the task can ne'er be done;
Each mother asks it for her booby son,
Each widow asks it for the best of men,
For him she weeps, for him she weds again.
Praise cannot stoop, like satire, to the ground;
The number may be hanged, but not be crowned.
Enough for half the greatest of these days
To 'scape my censure, not expect my praise.
Are they not rich? what more can they pretend?
Dare they to hope a poet for their friend?
What Richelieu wanted, Louis scarce could gain,
And what young Ammon wished, but wished in vain.
No power the muse's friendship can command;
No power, when virtue claims it, can withstand:
To Cato Virgil paid one honest line;
O let my country's friend illumine mine!

Ask you what provocation I have had?
The strong antipathy of good to bad.
When truth or virtue an affront endures,
The affront is mine, my friend, and should be yours.
  F. You're strangely proud.
           P. So proud, I am no slave:
So impudent, I own myself no knave.
Yes, I am proud; I must be proud to see
Men, not afraid of God, afraid of me:
Safe from the bar, the pulpit and the throne,
Yet touched and shamed by ridicule alone.
O sacred weapon! left for truth's defence,
Sole dread of folly, vice, and insolence!
To all but Heaven-directed hands denied,
The muse may give thee, but the gods must guide.
Reverent I touch thee, but with honest zeal;
To rouse the watchmen of the public weal,
To virtue's work provoke the tardy hall,
And goad the prelate slumbering in his stall.
Ye tinsel insects! whom a court maintains,
That counts your beauties only by your stains,
Spin all your cobwebs o'er the eye of day!
The muse's wing shall brush you all away.
All, all but truth, drops dead-born from the press,
Like the last gázette, or the last address.
Truth guards the poet, sanctifies the line,
And makes immortal verse as mean as mine.

"THE DUNCIAD."

[*The Triumph of Dulness.*]

In vain, in vain; the all composing hour
Resistless falls; the muse obeys the power.

She comes! she comes! the sable throne behold,
Of Night primeval, and of Chaos old.
Before her fancy's gilded clouds decay,
And all its varying rainbows die away.
Wit shoots in vain its momentary fires,
The meteor drops, and in a flash expires.
As one by one, at dread Medea's strain,
The sickening stars fade off the ethereal plain,
Thus, at her felt approach, and secret might,
Art after art goes out, and all is night.
Philosophy, that leaned on Heaven before,
Shrinks to her second cause, and is no more.
Religion blushing veils her sacred fires,
And unawares morality expires.
Nor public flame, nor private dares to shine;
Nor human spark is left, nor glimpse divine.
Lo! thy dread empire, Chaos! is restored;
Light dies before thy uncreating word:
Thy hand, great, anarch! lets the curtain fall,
And universal darkness buries all.

[*From " Imitations of Horace."*]

Peace is my dear delight, not Fleury's more;
But touch me, and no minister so sore.
Whoe'er offends, at some unlucky time
Slides into verse, and hitches in a rhyme,
Sacred to ridicule his whole life long,
And the sad burthen of some merry song.
   What? armed for virtue when I point the pen,
Brand the bold front of shameless, guilty men,
Dash the proud gamester in his gilded car,
Bare the mean heart that lurks beneath a star,

Can there be wanting, to defend her cause,
Lights of the Church, or guardians of the laws?
Yes, while I live, no rich or noble knave
Shall walk the world, in credit, to his grave.
To Virtue only and her friends a friend,
The world beside may murmur or commend.
Know, all the distant din that world can keep,
Rolls o'er my grotto, and but soothes my sleep.
There, my retreat the best companions grace,
Chiefs out of war, and statesmen out of place.
There St. John mingles with my friendly bowl
The feast of reason and the flow of soul.

Long as the year's dull circle seems to run,
When the brisk minor pants for twenty-one;
So slow the unprofitable moments roll
That lock up all the functions of my soul;
That keep me from myself, and still delay
Life's instant business to a future day:
That task, which as we follow, or despise,
The eldest is a fool, the youngest wise;
Which done, the poorest can no wants endure,
And which not done, the richest must be poor.

'Tis the first virtue, vices to abhor;
And the first wisdom, to be fool no more.
But, to the world no bugbear is so great,
As want of figure, and a small estate.
To either India see the merchant fly,
Scared at the spectre of pale poverty!
See him, with pains of body, pangs of soul,
Burn through the tropics, freeze beneath the pole!
Wilt thou do nothing for a nobler end,

Nothing to make philosophy thy friend?
To stop thy foolish views, thy long desires,
And ease thy heart of all that it admires?
Here wisdom calls, "Seek virtue first, be bold!
As gold to silver, virtue is to gold."
There London's voice, "Get money, money, still!
And then let virtue follow, if she will."
   True, conscious honor is to feel no sin;
He's armed without who's innocent within.

Let me for once presume to instruct the times,
To know the poet from the man of rhymes:
'Tis he, who gives my breast a thousand pains,
Can make me feel each passion that he feigns;
Enrage, compose, with more than magic art,
With pity and with terror, tear my heart;
And snatch me, o'er the earth, or through the air,
To Thebes, to Athens, when he will, and where.

A vile encomium doubly ridicules:
There's nothing blackens like the ink of fools.
If true, a woful likeness; and if lies,
"Praise undeserved is scandal in disguise."

In vain, bad rhymers all mankind reject,
They treat themselves with most profound respect.
'Tis to small purpose that you hold your tongue,
Each praised within, is happy all day long.
But how severely with themselves proceed
The men, who write such verse as we can read?
Their own strict judges, not a word they spare
That wants or force, or light, or weight, or care:

Such they'll degrade ; and sometimes, in its stead,
In downright charity revive the dead.

[*Catholic disabilities.*]

Besides, my father taught me from a lad,
The better art to know the good from bad ;
But knottier points we knew not half so well,
Deprived us soon of our paternal cell ;
And certain laws, by sufferers thought unjust,
Denied all posts of profit or of trust.
Hopes after hopes of pious papists failed,
While mighty William's thundering arm prevailed.
For right hereditary taxed and fined,
He * stuck to poverty with peace of mind ;
And me the Muses helped to undergo it ;
Convict a papist he, and I a poet.

[*Part of Ode* 9, *B.* 4, *imitated.*]

Sages and chiefs long since had birth,
    Ere Cæsar was, or Newton named ;
Those raised new empires o'er the earth,
    And these, new heavens and systems framed.

Vain was the chief's, the sage's pride !
They had no poet, and they died.
In vain they schemed, in vain they bled !
They had no poet, and are dead.

[*From Prologue to Addison's Cato.*]

To wake the soul by tender strokes of art,
To raise the genius and to mend the heart,
To make mankind, in conscious virtue, bold,

---
* His father.

Live o'er each scene, and be what they behold:
For this the Tragic Muse first trod the stage,
Commanding tears to stream through every age;
Tyrants no more their savage nature kept,
And foes to virtue wondered how they wept.
Our author shuns by vulgar springs to move
The hero's glory, or the virgin's love;
In pitying love we but our weakness show,
And wild ambition well deserves its woe.
Here tears shall flow from a more generous cause,
Such tears as patriots shed for dying laws:
He bids your breasts with ancient ardor rise,
And calls forth Roman drops from British eyes.
Virtue confessed in human shape he draws,
What Plato thought, and godlike Cato was:
No common object to your sight displays,
But what with pleasure Heaven Itself surveys,
A brave man struggling in the storms of fate,
And greatly falling with a falling state.
While Cato gives his little Senate laws,
What bosom beats not in his country's cause?
Who sees him act, but envies every deed?
Who hears him groan, and does not wish to bleed?
Even when proud Cæsar, midst triumphal cars,
The spoils of nations, and the pomp of wars,
Ignobly vain, and impotently great,
Showed Rome her Cato's figure, drawn in state,
As her dead father's reverend image passed,
The pomp was darkened, and the day o'ercast;
The triumph ceased, tears gush'd from every eye;
The world's great victor passed unheeded by;
Her last good man dejected Rome adored,
And honored Cæsar's less than Cato's sword.

[*Translation of the Emperor Adrian's address to his soul.*]

Ah! fleeting spirit, wandering fire,
  That long hast warmed my tender breast,
Must thou no more this frame inspire,
  No more a pleasing cheerful guest?
Whither, ah whither art thou flying,
  To what dark, undiscovered shore?
Thou seem'st all trembling, shivering, dying,
  And wit and humor are no more.

The Universal Prayer.

Deo Opt. Max.

Father of all! in every age,
  In every clime adored,
By saint, by savage, and by sage,
  Jehovah, Jove, or Lord!*

Thou great First Cause, least understood,
  Who all my sense confined,
To know but this, that Thou art good,
  And that myself am blind.

Yet gave me, in this dark estate,
  To see the good from ill,
And binding nature fast in fate,
  Left free the human will.

What conscience dictates to be done,
  Or warns me not to do,
This, teach me more than hell to shun,
  That, more than heaven pursue.

---

* God is really everywhere adored, though not always with freedom from error.

What blessings Thy free bounty gives,
    Let me not cast away;
For God is paid when man receives,
    To enjoy is to obey.

Yet not to earth's contracted span
    Thy goodness let me bound,
Or think Thee Lord alone of man,
    When thousand worlds are round.

Let not this weak unknowing hand,
    Presume Thy bolts to throw,
And deal damnation round the land
    On each I judge Thy foe.

If I am right, thy grace impart
    Still in the right to stray;
If I am wrong, oh teach my heart
    To find that better way!

Save me alike from foolish pride,
    Or impious discontent,
At aught Thy wisdom has denied,
    Or aught Thy goodness lent.

Teach me to feel another's woe,
    To hide the fault I see,
That mercy I to others show,
    That mercy show to me.

Mean though I am, not wholly so,
    Since quickened by Thy breath;
Oh lead me, wheresoe'er I go,
    Through this day's life or death!

This day, be bread and peace my lot,
    All else beneath the sun,
Thou know'st if best bestowed or not,
    And let Thy will be done.

To Thee, whose temple is all space,
    Whose altar, earth, sea, skies,
One chorus let all beings raise!
    All nature's incense rise!

[*From "Ode on St. Cecilia's day."*]
[Music.]
Music the fiercest grief can charm
And fate's severest rage disarm;
Music can soften pain to ease,
And make despair and madness please:
Our joys below it can improve,
And antedate the bliss above.
  This the divine Cecilia found,
And to her Maker's praise confined the sound.
When the full organ joins the tuneful quire,
  The immortal powers incline their ear;
Borne on the swelling notes our souls aspire,
  And angels lean from heaven to hear.
Of Orpheus now no more let poets tell:
  To bright Cecilia greater power is given;
His numbers raised a shade from hell,
  Hers lift the soul to heaven.

The dying Christian to his Soul.

Vital spark of heavenly flame,
Quit, oh quit this mortal frame!

Trembling, hoping, lingering, flying—
Oh the pain, the bliss of dying!
Cease, fond nature, cease thy strife,
And let me languish into life!

Hark! they whisper; angels say
Sister spirit, come away!
What is this absorbs me quite,
Steals my senses, shuts my sight,
Drowns my spirit, draws my breath?
Tells me, my soul, can this be death?

The world recedes, it disappears,
Heaven opens on my eyes, my ears
   With sounds seraphic ring:
Lend, lend your wings! I mount, I fly:
O grave! where is thy victory?
   O death! where is thy sting?

Ode on Solitude.

[Composed before his twelfth year.]

Happy the man, whose wish and care
   A few paternal acres bound,
Content to breathe his native air,
   In his own ground.

Whose herds with milk, whose fields with **bread,**
   Whose flocks supply him with attire;
Whose trees in summer yield him shade,
   In winter, fire.

Blest, who can unconcern'dly find
   Hours, days, and years, slide soft away,

In health of body, peace of mind,
    Quiet by day;

Sound sleep by night, study and ease,
   Together mixt, sweet recreation;
And innocence, which most does please
   With meditation.

Thus let me live, unseen, unknown,
   Thus unlamented let me die,
Steal from the world, and not a stone
   Tell where I lie.

On a Lady singing to her Lute.

Orpheus could charm the trees; but thus a tree,
Taught by your hand, can charm no less than he.
A poet made the silent wood pursue;
This vocal wood had drawn the poet too.

On a certain Lady at Court.

I know the thing that's most uncommon;
   Envy, be silent and attend!
I know a reasonable woman,
   Handsome and witty, yet a friend;

Not warped by passion, awed by rumor
   Not grave through pride, or gay through folly,
An equal mixture of good humor
   And sensible, soft melancholy.

"Has she no faults, then," envy says, "Sir?"
   Yes, she has one, I must aver;

When all the world conspires to praise her,
The woman's deaf and does not hear.

To Miss M. B. on her birth-day.*

Oh be thou blest with all that Heaven can send,
Long health, long youth, long leisure, and a friend :
Not with those toys the female world admire,
Riches that vex, and vanities that tire.
With added years, if life bring nothing new,
But, like a sieve, let every blessing through,
Some joy still lost, as each vain year runs o'er,
And all we gain, some sad reflection more ;
Is that a birth-day ? 'tis, alas ! too clear,
'Tis but the funeral of the former year.

Let joy or ease, let affluence or content,
And the gay conscience of a life well spent,
Calm every thought, inspirit every grace,
Glow in thy heart, and smile upon thy face.
Let day improve on day, and year on year,
Without a pain, a trouble, or a fear ;
Till death unfelt that tender frame destroy,
In some soft dream, or ecstasy of joy ;
Peaceful sleep out the sabbath of the tomb,
And wake to raptures in a life to come.

On his grotto at Twickenham.

Thou who shalt stop where Thames' translucent wave
Shines a broad mirror through the shadowy cave ;
Where lingering drops from mineral roofs distil,

---

* Probably Miss Martha Blount.

And pointed crystals break the sparkling rill;
Unpolished gems no ray on pride bestow,
And latent metals innocently glow:
Approach, but awful! Lo! the Ægerian grot,
Where, nobly pensive, St. John sate and thought;
Where British sighs from dying Wyndham stole,
And the bright flame was shot through Marchmont's soul.
Let such, such only, tread this sacred floor,
Who dare to love their country and be poor.

On a celebrated Opera Singer.

So bright is thy beauty, so charming thy song,
As had drawn both the beasts and their Orpheus along;
But such is thy avarice, and such is thy pride,
That the beasts must have starved, and the poet have died.

The Balance of Europe.

Now, Europe balanced, neither side prevails;
For nothing's left in either of the scales.

From the French.

Sir, I admit your general rule,
That every poet is a fool:
But you yourself may serve to show it,
That every fool is not a poet.

[FROM THE TRANSLATION OF THE ODYSSEY.]

[*The garden of Alcinous.*]

Close to the gates a spacious garden lies,
From storms defended, and inclement skies.

Four acres was the allotted space of ground,
Fenc'd with a green enclosure all around:
Tall, thriving trees confess'd the fruitful mould;
The reddening apple ripens here to gold,
Here the blue fig with luscious juice o'erflows,
With deeper red the full pomegranate glows,
The branch here bends beneath the weighty pear,
And verdant olives flourish round the year.
The balmy spirit of the western gale
Eternal breathes on fruits untaught to fail:
Each dropping pear a following pear supplies,
On apples apples, figs on figs arise:
The same mild season gives the blooms to blow,
The buds to harden and the fruits to glow.

[From the same.]

[*The companions of Ulysses transformed by Circè.*]
The palace in a woody vale they found,
High rais'd of stone; a shaded space around:
Where mountain-wolves and brindled lions roam,
By magic tam'd, familiar to the dome.
With gentle blandishment our men they meet,
And wag their tails, and fawning lick their feet.

Now on the threshold of the dome they stood,
And heard a voice resounding through the wood:
Plac'd at her loom within the goddess sung;
The vaulted roofs and solid pavement rung.
O'er the fair web the rising figures shine,
Immortal labor! worthy hands divine.* *

The goddess, rising, ask'd her guests to stay,
Who blindly follow where she leads the way.
On thrones around, with downy coverings grac'd,
With semblance fair the unhappy men are plac'd;

Milk newly press'd, the sacred flour of wheat,
And honey fresh, and Pramnian wines, the treat.
But venom'd was the bread, and mix'd the bowl,
With drugs of force to darken all the soul:
Soon in the luscious feast themselves they lost,
And drank oblivion of their native coast.
Instant her circling wand the goddess waves,
To hogs transforms them, and the sty receives.
No more was seen the human form divine;
Head, face, and members, bristled into swine:
Still curs'd with sense, their minds remain alone,
And their own voice affrights them when they groan.

[FROM THE TRANSLATION OF THE ILIAD.]

[The parting of Hector and Andromaché.]

Hector, this heard, returned without delay;
Swift through the town he trod his former way,
Through streets of palaces and walks of state,
And met the mourner at the Scæan gate.
With haste to meet him sprung the joyful fair,
His blameless wife, Aëtion's wealthy heir.
The nurse stood near, in whose embraces pressed,
His only hope hung smiling at her breast,
Whom each soft charm and early grace adorn,
Fair as the new-born star that gilds the morn.
Silent the warrior smiled, and pleased resigned
To tender passions all his mighty mind.
His beauteous princess cast a mournful look,
Hung on his hand, and then dejected spoke;
Her bosom labored with a boding sigh,
And the big tear stood trembling in her eye.

"Too daring prince! ah, whither dost thou run?
Ah, too forgetful of thy wife and son!
And think'st thou not how wretched we shall be,
A widow I, a helpless orphan he?
For sure such courage length of life denies,
And thou must fall, thy virtue's sacrifice.
Greece in her single heroes strove in vain;
Now hosts oppose thee and thou must be slain.
O grant me, gods, ere Hector meets his doom,
All I can ask of Heaven, an early tomb!
So shall my days in one sad tenor run,
And end with sorrows as they first begun.
No parent now remains my griefs to share,
No father's aid, no mother's tender care,
Yet, while my Hector still survives, I see
My father, mother, brethren, all in thee.
Alas! my parents, brothers, kindred, all
Once more will perish, if my Hector fall.
Thy wife, thy infant in thy danger share;
O, prove a husband's and a father's care!
Let others in the field their arms employ,
But stay my Hector here, and guard his Troy."

The chief replied; "That post shall be my care,
Nor that alone, but all the works of war.
How would the sons of Troy, in arms renowned,
And Troy's proud dames, whose garments sweep the ground,
Attaint the lusture of my former name,
Should Hector basely quit the field of fame?
My early youth was bred to martial pains;
My soul impels me to the embattled plains.
Let me be foremost to defend the throne,
And guard my father's glories and my own.

"Yet come it will, the day decreed by fates,
(How my heart trembles while my tongue relates!)
The day when thou, imperial Troy! must bend,
And see thy warriors fall, thy glories end.
And yet no dire presage so wounds my mind,
My mother's death, the ruin of my kind,
Not Priam's hoary hairs, defiled with gore,
Not all my brothers gasping on the shore,
As thine, Andromaché! Thy griefs I dread;
I see thee trembling, weeping, captive, led,
In Argive looms our battles to design,
And woes, of which so large a part was thine;
To bear the victor's hard commands, or bring
The weight of waters from Hyperia's spring.
There, while you groan beneath the load of life,
They cry, 'Behold the mighty Hector's wife!'
Some haughty Greek, who lives thy tears to see,
Imbitters all thy woes by naming me.
The thoughts of glory past, and present shame,
A thousand griefs shall waken at the name.
May I lie cold, before that dreadful day,
Pressed with a load of monumental clay!
Thy Hector, wrapt in everlasting sleep,
Shall neither hear thee sigh nor see thee weep."

Thus having spoke, the illustrious chief of Troy,
Stretched his fond arms to clasp the lovely boy.
The babe clung crying to his nurse's breast,
Scared at the dazzling helm, and nodding crest.
With secret pleasure each fond parent smiled,
And Hector hasted to relieve his child,
The glittering terrors from his brows unbound,
And placed the beaming helmet on the ground;

Then kissed the child, and, lifting high in air,
Thus to the gods preferred a parent's prayer :
  "O, thou ! whose glory fills the ethereal throne,
And all ye deathless powers ! protect my son !
Grant him, like me, to purchase just renown,
To guard the Trojans, to defend the crown,
Against his country's foes the war to wage,
And rise the Hector of the future age !
So, when triumphant from successful toils,
Of heroes slain he bears the reeking spoils,
Whole hosts may hail him with deserved acclaim,
And say, 'This chief transcends his father's fame !
While pleased amid the general shouts of Troy,
His mother's conscious heart o'erflows with joy."
  He spoke, and fondly gazing on her charms
Restored the pleasing burden to her arms ;
Soft on her fragrant breast the babe she laid,
Hushed to repose, and with a smile surveyed.
The troubled pleasure soon chastised by fear,
She mingled with a smile a tender tear.
The softened chief with kind compassion viewed,
And dried the falling drops, and thus pursued.
  "Andromaché ! my soul's far dearer part,
Why with untimely sorrows heaves thy heart?
No hostile hand can antedate my doom,
Till fate condemns me to the silent tomb.
Fixed is the term to all the race of earth ;
And such the hard condition of our birth ;
No force can then resist, no flight can save,
All sink alike, the fearful and the brave.
No more ; but hasten to thy tasks at home,
There guide the spindle, and direct the loom :
Me glory summons to the martial scene,

The field of combat is the sphere for men.
Where heroes war, the foremost place I claim,
The first in danger, as the first in fame."
Thus having said, the glorious chief resumes
His towery helmet, black with shading plumes.
His princess parts with a prophetic sigh,
Unwilling parts and oft reverts her eye,
That streamed at every look : then, moving slow,
Sought her own palace, and indulged her woe.
There, while her tears deplored the godlike man,
Through all her train the soft infection ran ;
The pious maids their mingled sorrows shed,
And mourn the living Hector as the dead.

[*The battle of the Gods, from Translation of The Iliad.*]

But when the powers descending swelled the fight,
Then tumult rose : fierce rage and pale affright
Varied each face ; then Discord sounds alarms,
Earth echoes, and the nations rush to arms.
Now through the trembling shores Minerva calls,
And now she thunders from the Grecian walls.
Mars, hovering o'er his Troy, his terror shrouds
In gloomy tempests and a night of clouds :
Now, through each Trojan heart he fury pours,
With voice divine, from Ilion's topmost towers ;
Now shouts to Simois, from her beauteous hill ;
The mountain shook, the rapid stream stood still.
Above, the sire of gods his thunder rolls,
And peals on peals redoubled rend the poles.
Beneath, stern Neptune shakes the solid ground ; .
The forests wave, the mountains nod around ;
Through all their summits tremble Ida's woods,
And from their sources boil her hundred floods.

Troy's turrets totter on the rocking plain,
And the tossed navies beat the heaving main.
Deep in the dismal regions of the dead,
The infernal monarch reared his horrid head,
Leaped from his throne, lest Neptune's arm should lay
His dark dominions open to the day,
And pour in light on Pluto's drear abodes,
Abhorred by men, and dreadful even to Gods.

[*Night-scene, from the Translation of The Iliad.*]

The troops exulting sat in order round,
And beaming fires illumined all the ground.
As, when the moon, refulgent lamp of night,
O'er heaven's pure azure spreads her sacred light,
When not a breath disturbs the deep serene,
And not a cloud o'ercasts the solemn scene;
Around her throne the vivid planets roll,
And stars unnumbered gild the glowing pole,
O'er the dark trees a yellower verdure shed,
And tip with silver every mountain's head.
Then shine the vales, the rocks in prospect rise,
A flood of glory bursts from all the skies;
The conscious swains rejoicing in the sight,
Eye the blue vault, and bless the useful light.

[*Ulysses recognized by his old dog, Argus.*]

Him when he saw he rose and crawled to meet,
('Twas all he could,*) and fawned and kissed his feet,
Seized with dumb joy; then, falling by his side,
Owned his returning lord, looked up, and died.

* In consequence of his age.

DETACHED PASSAGES.*

Critics in wit or life are hard to please,
Few write to those, and none can live to these,

For not to know some trifles is a praise.

At every trifle scorn to take offence ;
That always shows great pride, or little sense.

For fools rush in where angels fear to tread.

Who shall decide when doctors disagree?

The ruling passion, be it what it will,
The ruling passion conquers reason still.†

There swims no goose so gray, but, soon or late,
She finds some honest gander for her mate.

Wealth in the gross is death, but life diffused,
As poison heals, in just proportion used.

For fools admire, but men of sense approve.

Good sense, which only is the gift of Heaven,
And, though no science, fairly worth the seven,

All human virtue, to its latest breath,
Finds envy never conquer'd but by death.

For virtue's self may too much zeal be had,
The worst of madness is a saint run mad. ‡

---

* Not contained in the preceding "Selections."
† But not always. ‡ The madman ceases to be a saint.

Had ancient times conspired to disallow
What then was new, what had been ancient now?

For forms of government let fools contest;
Whate'er is best administered is best:*
For modes of faith let graceless zealots fight;
His can't be wrong whose life is in the right: †
In faith and hope the world will disagree,
But all mankind's concern is charity.

Who pants for glory finds but short repose,
A breath revives him, or a breath o'erthrows.

Kind self-conceit to some her glass applies,
Which no one looks in with another's eyes.

Blockheads with reason wicked wits abhor,
But fool with fool is barbarous civil war.

[*Scholiasts.*]
There, dim in clouds, the poring scholiasts mark,
Wits, who, like owls, see only in the dark,
A lumberhouse of books in every head,
Forever reading, never to be read.
[*Sciolists.*]
What though we let some better sort of fool
Thrid every science, run through every school?

---

* According to his friend and associate, Warburton, the poet means, not that one form of government is not, in itself, better than another, but that no one, however, in itself, excellent, can make a people happy, " unless it be administered with integrity."

† He may mean that a right life necessarily implies a right faith, and not that modes of faith are justly matters of indifference, an opinion which he could not entertain as a Catholic, nor consistently, even as a friend merely to the wellbeing of society.

Never by tumbler through the hoops was shown
Such skill in passing all, and touching none.
[*Scribblers.*]
These write to lords, some mean reward to get,
As needy beggars sing at doors for meat.
Those write because all write, and so have still
Excuse for writing, and for writing ill.
[*Solitude.*]
Bear me, some god! oh quickly bear me hence
To wholesome solitude, the nurse of sense;
Where Contemplation prunes her ruffled wings,
And the free soul looks down to pity kings.

And yet the fate of all extremes is such,
Men may be read, as well as books, too much.

[*Riches.*]
No grace of Heaven, or token of the elect.

[*Man's insignificance.*]
His knowledge measured to his state and place,
His time a moment, and a point his space.

To build, to plant, whatever you intend,
To rear the column, or the arch to bend,
To swell the terrace, or to sink the grot,
In all, let Nature never be forgot;
But treat the goddess like a modest fair,
Nor over-dress, nor leave her wholly bare:
Let not each beauty everywhere be spied,
Where half the skill is decently to hide.

Vice is a monster of so frightful mien,
As, to be hated, needs but to be seen;

Yet seen too oft, familiar with her face,
We first endure, then pity, then embrace.

The rogue and fool by fits are fair and wise.

The same ambition can destroy, or save,
And makes a patriot, as it makes a knave.

Man, like the generous vine, supported lives,
The strength he gains is from the embrace he gives.

Authors, like coins, grow dear as they grow old;
It is the rust we value, not the gold.*

WILLIAM HAMILTON.

WILLIAM HAMILTON of Bangour, was born in Scotand in 1704. In 1745 he joined the standard of the Pretender, Prince Charles. On the discomfiture of the party, he escaped to France, but was soon pardoned, and restored to his native country and his estates. He was the author of *Contemplation*, a serious poem; a national one on the *Thistle;* *The Braes of Yarrow*, an admired and popular Ballad; *Songs*, etc. His best are said to be his early lyrical poems. He died in 1754. He appears to have been much esteemed, both as a poet and as a man.

[FROM "CONTEMPLATION."]

[Self-love.]

And thou, Self-love! who tak'st from earth
With the vile, crawling worm, thy birth,

---

* Not always. They perhaps are generally "old" because they are good.

Untouch'd with others' joy or pain,
The social smile, the tear humane;
Thyself thy sole, intemperate guest,
Uncall'd thy neighbor to the feast;
As if—Heaven's universal heir—
'Twas thine to seize, and not to share.

[*Impiety.*]

Impiety! of harden'd mind,
Gross, dull, presuming, stubborn, blind,
Unmov'd, amid this mighty all,
Deaf to the universal call.
In vain above the systems glow,
In vain earth spreads her charms below,
Confiding in himself to rise,
He hurls defiance to the skies,
And, steel'd in dire and impious deeds,
Blasphemes his feeder while he feeds.

END.

www.ingramcontent.com/pod-product-compliance
Lightning Source LLC
Chambersburg PA
CBHW030018240426
43672CB00007B/998